ROBERT MACINTOSH

DONALD MACLEAN

# STRATEGIC

## MANAGEMENT

### STRATEGISTS AT WORK

 macmillan education · palgrave

First published 2015 by
PALGRAVE

Palgrave in the UK is an imprint of Macmillan Publishers Limited, registered in England, company number 785998, of 4 Crinan Street, London N1 9XW.

Palgrave Macmillan in the US is a division of St Martin's Press LLC, 175 Fifth Avenue, New York, NY 10010.

Palgrave is a global imprint of the above companies and is represented throughout the world.

Palgrave® and Macmillan® are registered trademarks in the United States, the United Kingdom, Europe and other countries.

ISBN: 978–1–137–03544–8 paperback

This book is printed on paper suitable for recycling and made from fully managed and sustained forest sources. Logging, pulping and manufacturing processes are expected to conform to the environmental regulations of the country of origin.

A catalogue record for this book is available from the British Library.

A catalog record for this book is available from the Library of Congress.

Printed in China

For my beautiful wife Anne and our children Euan, Eilidh and Eva. Thank you for the laughter and happiness your company brings and for your support, without which this book would never have been completed.

Robert

Donald would like to dedicate the book to everyone out there who's just trying to cut through the gobbledegook and make organisational life, paid and voluntary, a more positive and productive experience for themselves and others – keep going please!

# Contents

# List of Figures

# List of Tables

# Acknowledgements

This book would not have been possible without the efforts of many friends and colleagues. We owe a debt of gratitude to the members of classes, courses and management teams over the last two decades for helping us road-test The Strategy Cycle model which is presented in these pages. We have named several individuals in the book to acknowledge specific contributions and ideas but we are particularly grateful to Kate Buell-Armstrong, Harry Burns and Sandy Rowan for the privileged access they have offered us into their lives as strategists. We are also indebted to Martin Drewe (then of Palgrave) for his forbearance during what has been a slow writing process beset by new jobs and general busyness on our part. Rachel Bridgewater took over the project in its latter stages and we are grateful for her thoroughness in the process of submitting and preparing the final manuscript. Thanks to Neil Wallace from the design agency O Street for his help with creating some of the images in the book and to Val Turner for transcription of various interviews with strategists. The case studies were produced by Angeliki Papachroni and the detail and rigour with which she produced them was invaluable. Palgrave Macmillan were kind enough to source reviews of an early draft which were extremely helpful in shaping the final manuscript and we would like to thank David Mackay and Simon Haslam in particular for their feedback. Finally, thanks are due to John Sanders of Heriot-Watt University for helping pilot some of the materials and proof reading early drafts. Whilst we have had an abundance of support in preparing this manuscript, we would like to acknowledge that any remaining errors are our own.

# About the Authors

**Robert MacIntosh** is Professor of Strategic Management and Head of the School of Management and Languages at Heriot-Watt University. He holds a PhD in engineering and has worked at the Universities of Glasgow and Strathclyde. His research interests centre on strategy and organizational change and he has been published over 100 articles, book chapters and conference papers in these areas. He has consulted extensively with public and private sector organizations and currently sits on the board of the charity Turning Point Scotland. His status as a life-long fan of Aberdeen Football Club is a case study in unending optimism. He lives near Glasgow with his wife Anne and their children, Euan, Eilidh and Eva.

**Donald MacLean** received a BSc in Physics from the University of Strathclyde, a PhD in optoelectronics from the University of Cambridge and an MBA from Kingston University. He spent ten years working in the optoelectronics industry before joining the University of Glasgow in 1993 where he is now a part-time professorial research fellow. He has published extensively on strategy, transformation, complexity theory, action theory and research process in a range of journals including the *Strategic Management Journal, The Journal of Management Studies, Organization Studies and Human Relations*. He combines his part-time academic work with on-going commercial, public and third-sector consultancy engagements and directorships and lives with his family and an ensemble of assorted animals in Connel by Oban in Argyll.

# SECTION A

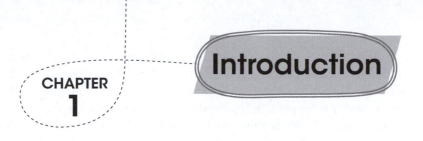

**CHAPTER 1**

## Introduction

The best laid schemes o' mice an' men
Gang aft agley

(**Robert Burns**)

The primary focus of this book is the study of strategists at work. Our purpose is to share with you what we have learnt through two decades of strategy work with a myriad of organizations of all shapes and sizes. In "you" we imagine someone who is keen to develop their business or organization – small or large, public or private; someone who senses that strategy is an important topic, a possible key to success, or at least something that you should know about. Whilst we take a little time to locate the subject of strategy in its historical contexts, and to give guidance to those seeking qualifications in strategy, our intention is to address those who are keen to get on with it. The book is therefore focussed on what matters in practice.

So what is **strategy**? Many things to many people it would seem since there are various definitions of strategy. As we progress, it will become clear that our definition of strategy relates to the coherence of the alignment of broad intentions, environmental circumstances and available resources but that the process of assessing alignment should be done in relation to a perceived challenge, opportunity or difficulty. Planning plays a key part in strategy. As Robert Burns reminds us, even the best laid and most carefully conceived of plans often bite the dust. And yet still we plan. Indeed, in our own experience we have witnessed countless abandoned plans but we nevertheless feel that planning plays a crucial and possibly decisive role.

> **Strategy** is the craft of collectively rising to a significant challenge and accomplishing more than might be reasonably expected as a result of self-knowledge, resolve, foresight, creativity and genuine capabilities cultivated over the medium to long term.

Scholars have debated the relationship between strategic planning and strategy as an emergent artful and creative response to a world that can only ever be partly anticipated known and understood. Our bold claim in this book is that we cast the relationship between strategic planning and emergent strategy into new light, and, importantly, we do so in a way that is both simple and helpful to practitioners.

Of course, strategy is not new. It has been studied in military and political contexts for centuries and in organizational contexts for decades. What's more, strategy matters. It has helped groups and individuals across the ages to build empires. In antiquity those empires were political and geographic in their nature. In today's modern and organizational context, our view of empires has shifted to include corporations whose expanse is gauged in terms like market share or profit levels. Yet, as the opening quote from Robert Burns tells us, plans, schemes and strategies often go wrong. Despite, or perhaps because of this, strategy itself has become something of an empire – a multibillion dollar industry. Academics may debate nuanced points relating to its nature and value, but its status as a significant social practice is largely taken for granted. One key observation remains true however, across political or organizational, modern or ancient settings. Empires eventually fall. George Orwell argued that "whoever is winning at the moment will always seem to be invincible", yet history tells us that no empire lasts in perpetuity. At some point, a new strategist arrives on the scene and a new order is established. In our view this applies to the field of strategy itself. We aim in this book to combine ideas from challenging new theories with real insights from strategists about what they actually do. The resulting combination is a simple but powerful way of practising strategy.

In the early years of computing it was difficult to imagine anyone threatening the dominance of computer manufacturers such as International Business Machines (IBM). Yet Microsoft led a shift from hardware and circuitry to software and operating systems. In so doing, Microsoft became dominant to the point where it controlled over 90% market share for operating systems. Manufacturers were left making commodity products at low margins. Whilst Microsoft is still a major player, it is clear that the ground is shifting again with firms such as Google and Apple pursuing new strategies, which are in danger of marginalizing Microsoft just as they marginalized IBM and other computer manufacturers. The inescapable fact is that strategies and strategic management practices themselves have a shelf-life. The ability to create, dismantle and recreate strategic order is the domain of the strategist. As individuals, strategists lead their organizations, sometimes directly, sometimes indirectly and as we move into progressively more global, more networked and more challenging times it appears that the role of the strategist is changing.

Our starting point therefore, is a simple one. Whilst strategy matters, strategists matter more. Some firms get lucky and happen upon a strategy, which allows them to compete effectively, or perhaps even dominate for a period. Yet even in these happy circumstances, the so-called **Icarus paradox** looms as an explanation of the eventual

---

In this context, the **Icarus Paradox** is a phrase coined by Canadian academic Danny Miller to explain how exceptional success can lead to the eventual downfall of a firm. Miller argues that success can lead to overconfidence and complacency. In Greek mythology, Icarus managed to fly using wings created from wax and feathers. However, he flew too close to the sun with catastrophic consequences when the heat melted the wax and his wings disintegrated.

failure of seemingly dominant players (Miller, 1991). As circumstances change, a once winning strategy can become a weakness not a strength. Where IBM's capabilities in design and manufacturing were the roots of its success, they eventually became a source of difficult rather than advantage once their competitive environment had irreversibly shifted towards commodity computers and sophisticated software. Similar tales can be found in the retail sector where the rise of internet commerce has transformed the best high street locations into an expensive luxury which was often locked in place through long-term lease agreements.

Whilst this book offers advice on how to develop strategy, our focus is on looking at "how to do strategy" from the perspective of the strategist. Our reasoning is simple – it is strategists who do strategy, and the conceptual distinction between plans and emergence are reconciled in the actions of strategists. We do not hold a restrictive definition of the strategist as either the person at the top of the organization, or the individual with the official title of chief strategist. Anyone can do strategy – who does what is really a question of power on the one hand, and efforts on the part of some to balance control and creativity on the other. A good strategist, or a group of strategists, is capable of (re)developing strategy, yet a glance through the contents of many books on strategic management suggests that the habits and practices of good strategists represent something of a blind-spot. The curricula of many business school topics either overlook the relationship between strategists and strategy or compartmentalize them by offering separate courses on strategy and leadership. Perhaps the assumption is that armed with the right models and tools anyone can be a better strategist. Whilst the tools of strategy analysis play a role, our contention is that a focus on tools alone is necessary but not sufficient. A sculptor can produce intricate three-dimensional surfaces using only a hammer and chisel. The tools may be indispensable but the craft and inspiration come from the sculptor. We will, of course, present a range of strategy tools and most of them will be quite familiar. We think you will see the distinctiveness of our cumulative process for building a simple, succinct but coherent and comprehensive statement of strategy. It is an approach we have developed through hundreds of strategy workshops, it is based around the use of templates that capture disciplined logic and it works. However, this is not just another book about strategy tools. In our view the logic is important, necessary even. But good logic is certainly not sufficient in and of itself. Our primary purpose in this book is to bring the strategist centre stage. And we seek to bring them back as rounded human beings rather than intellectual machines. Our focus is on strategies as the products, processes and performances of strategists.

By the end of the book you will see how we present strategists as people who, on the one hand, employ disciplined analysis to formulate coherent plans – which they are ever ready to modify, radically alter or abandon; and, on the other, readily see, grasp and help to create the significance of new and emerging realities in which they involve others through a wide variety of means more traditionally associated with art and performance.

We will consider not just the analysis of markets and competitors but look to the nuances and the often decisive distinctions created by those doing the analysis. Our desire to write this book arises from our own experience of doing strategy and working with others on strategic development for two decades. Over the years we have detected subtle but significant shifts in the imagined practice of strategy. At one time it was more or less assumed that the primary task was an intellectual one of developing the "best" strategy and making top-level decisions that others would implement more or less mechanically. Over time, growing recognition of the importance of the "how" of strategy saw more sophisticated processes of participation and involvement occur. This was partly in line with the realization that competitive advantage often stems from voluntary actions that go beyond the mechanistic following of orders. Strategy thus became a more distributed activity with a less top-down flavour and more awareness of cultural issues. Today, we perceive a new shift towards a strategy process that combines and transcends the previous two phases. In a way, the importance of top-down influence is re-emerging, not in the form of intellectual decision-making but as a much richer social, emotional and intellectual dynamic which promotes cohesion and action – in short leadership whether in the form of a charismatic individual, a team or a more distributed process. At the same time, we are seeing a much more creative form of emergent, localized action that somehow coheres into often unexpected new patterns and success-stories. Such an approach makes strategy genuinely participative and creative. This new form of strategy is calling forth a different type of strategist. A new type of leadership.

Conceptual distinctions such as formulation and implementation or deliberate and emergent have acted as stumbling blocks for academics researching strategy and a source of (sometimes amused) puzzlement for many practitioners. As a result, senior scholars have repeatedly called for a more dynamic or holistic view of strategy. Perhaps the most influential strategy scholar of recent decades is Michael Porter. Based at Harvard Business School, Porter has created a whole new vocabulary for strategy and we shall examine some of his work in Section B of this book. He argues that the central question facing strategy researchers is why some firms fail whilst others flourish. He concluded in 1991 that we were some way short of a compelling explanation (see Porter, 1991).

In the decades since Porter made this observation, the nature of organizational and commercial life has changed beyond recognition. The impact of globalization, combined with dramatic changes in communication technologies, has been stark. A cursory examination of your own organization, and how it did business 20 years ago, is likely to produce the sensation that you are watching grainy, black and white footage of some far distant past. New products, processes, business models and industries have appeared. These, in turn, are fostering new attitudes and expectations amongst many stakeholder groups – from customers through to employees and suppliers. Rather worryingly, a recent examination of the contents of strategy classes in a range of international business schools[1] concluded that, despite these dramatic changes in the wider economy, we still default to materials and tools which have changed little since the middle 1980s. Our contention is not as simple as suggesting that the material is out of date. Rather, we argue that, since the context in which it is being deployed has changed so radically since much of it was first aired, we need a new take on strategy. In addition, strategy is making inroads into new spaces that are arguably even more complex and challenging than the issues to which it has hitherto addressed itself – pressing international difficulties such as climate-change, poverty, financial restructuring and energy shortages all calling forth collaborative, and inter-organizational, strategy making on an unprecedented scale.[2] So, in short, we need to innovate in our strategic thinking. This book is offered in that spirit.

In broad terms, we see strategy as a somewhat bizarre process of creating a plan which seems to galvanize collective action and then, often quietly, sees a seemingly unrelated reality take shape. Figure 1.1 below depicts the strategy cycle. At this stage, it may use language which is unfamiliar. As the book progresses we will revisit the components of **the strategy cycle** but for the time being we would draw your attention to the central row which suggests that we painstakingly develop a plan which then encounters the lived reality of our present circumstances and at this critical transition from planning to delivering, something highly creative occurs.

---

The **Strategy cycle** is an approach to strategic management which combines strategic logic (in the form of detailed plans) with the aesthetic, creative andinterpretive process of bringing a strategy to life.

---

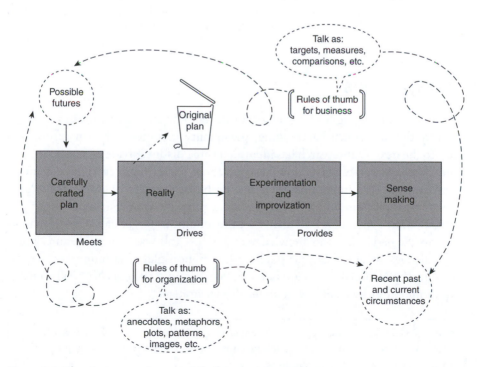

*Figure 1.1* The strategy cycle: a model of strategic management

Over the course of the book we aim to provide insights on both the tools and the discipline underpinning these two key processes – planning and emergence. We revisit many familiar planning tools to strip them down to what really counts; and we introduce some new ideas in a slightly more academic tone towards the end of the book to explain how emergence and planning rather than being alternatives are simply different sides of the same coin. In so doing we draw attention to some forgotten or overlooked practices that might help us see how emergence can be "stewarded" or managed in a new way.

Much of what you will encounter in Section B will be familiar. In Section C we adopt a different, more research-informed tone, to show how the collection of simple analytical tools presented in Section B, form the backdrop to a story about the strategy, told by strategists in an attempt to cajole, convince and inspire colleagues to implement new courses of action. This view of strategists as storytellers connects to ancient **Bardic** traditions where the past and present of organizations, institutions or tribes were woven together in ways which colour future possibilities.

---

**Bards** held a particular place in Gaelic and British society. In Scottish, Irish and Welsh history, the Bard was a poet and storyteller employed by the clan Chieftan. It was the Bard's responsibility to capture the history and tradition of the clan in song and poetry. They were also responsible for capturing current events and weaving these into the context of historical narratives. In so doing, they connected past, present and future in narrative forms which are sometimes referred to as epic. William Shakespeare is sometimes referred to as the Bard of Avon and this is seen as a significant compliment to his storytelling skills.

---

## Strategy styles

How we as strategists approach the task of developing strategy varies in much the same way that individual handwriting, personality or other traits vary from one person to the next. Our research has identified three distinct **strategy styles**. **Intent-driven strategists** place greater emphasis on those parts of strategy which relate to objectives, goals and intentions. They use ambitious targets or noble aspirations to generate inspiration and a sense of shared purpose amongst members of the organization. In 1961, John F Kennedy set the ambitious target of sending a man to the moon. He had little or no knowledge of whether this was achievable and significant challenges lay ahead but his public call to action played an important role in developing the National Aeronautics and Space Administration's (NASA's) strategy. In our terminology he would be an intent-driven strategist.

---

**Strategy styles:** The Stride App will allow you to get an indication of your own strategy style at no cost or you can complete a full diagnosis of your strategy style using our profiler. Both are available at www.stridesite.com.

---

A second strategy style is focused on developments, opportunities and threats in a firm's environment. **Trend-driven strategists** scan the horizon looking for advance notice of future tastes, trends and technologies. Using the market intelligence that they gather, they are able to position their organizations to capitalize on opportunities before others have time to react. Steve Jobs moved Apple[3] into the music industry with the release of iTunes and the iPod. Now it seems an obvious fit but at that point in time, Jobs was looking at developments in a number of key areas. Hard disks were becoming smaller, cheaper and had higher capacity. Digital music had been widely available in the form of CDs but technology developments meant there was a real possibility of convergence occurring between consumer electronics firms, especially those making stereos, and computing firms. Apple made a decisive move, opened significant new revenue streams and introduced a whole new group of customers to their products and services. We would describe Jobs as a trend-driven strategist. It is, of course, worth noting that early signals are often hard to read. Throughout the book we will examine salutary tales of strategists who have guessed wrong, leading their organizations to over-invest or come to market too early.

The third strategy style relates to those who pay attention to the internal skills, resources and capabilities of their organization. **Resource-driven strategists** look for opportunities to deploy existing skills and know how. Honda is often quoted as an example of a firm with a clear capability in engine technology. Whether the eventual product is a lawnmower, an outboard motor, a car or motorbike, there are key aspects of Honda's skill set which are being deployed and developed. Lessons learnt from one context are fed back into other contexts and strategy is in some ways the continuing search for opportunities to exploit core skills. It is no accident that Honda runs an advertising campaign that claims "everything we do goes into everything we do".

Our argument is that there is no definitive or correct way to build strategy. Rather, we suggest that individual strategists have default preferences and frame strategy work to foreground some issues whilst overlooking others. This book offers an overview of the main areas of strategy work and encourages you to recognize the strengths and limitations of your own biases in relation to strategy.

## How the book works

In the remainder of Section A we offer a brief historical review of strategy research. This will allow you to place particular schools of thought in their rightful place and to see the roots of some recurring tensions in the strategy literature. We then introduce three strategists and their organizations. Professor Sir Harry Burns was Scotland's most senior medical doctor from 2005 to 2014 and someone with significant influence over the strategy of the National Health Service in Scotland. Kate Buell-Armstrong was the founding Chief Executive of Confused.com which grew out of the Admiral Insurance Group Ltd, a Financial Times Stock Exchange (FTSE)-100 listed business with a presence in the UK, Canada, the USA, Europe and India.

Sandy Rowan is the Chief Executive Officer of Pointer Security Ltd., a family owned business which was founded in Glasgow and now has operations in the middle-East and Thailand. These three strategists operate in vastly different contexts covering the public sector, the corporate world and the small to medium sized enterprise sector. Throughout the remainder of the book, each strategist offers a commentary on the practicalities of strategy work in their own contexts.

Section B of the book provides the tools and techniques of strategy based on a simple sequence of analysis and decisions that we have developed through many years of running strategy workshops with several hundred firms. The emphasis is on what works, with supplementary material linking to the underpinning research and theory where appropriate. Many of the analytical tools that we present would be found in most other strategy texts. Distinctive to our presentation of these tools is a particular and cumulative structure which extracts maximum benefit and clarity from the analysis done. The analytical process culminates in crafting a simple, succinct statement of strategy covering 12 components. It is worth remembering that individual strategists tend to use these tools differently dependent upon their strategy style. Finally in Section B, we consider the conversion of these core ideas about strategy into strategy documents. Communicating strategy is challenging and strategy documents vary enormously in style, content and level of detail. In our experience, some are a triumph of presentation over substance. We present advice on moving from a simple, concise and robust strategy statement to a more elaborate and detailed account intended for other audiences.

Section C shifts tone and offers an attempt to place the practical approach we set out in Section B into a wider academic context. We therefore begin to elaborate on the challenges of both conceptualizing strategy and how different bodies of theory such as complexity theory may help reframe our understanding of both strategy and strategists. In so doing, we place our own views on strategy process and the role of the strategist into the wider context of the historical review set out in Chapter 2.

Section D contains four detailed case studies (Apple, Nokia, Nine Dragons and ABB) that afford an opportunity to apply the contents of the book to a range of different contexts. The four cases take a particular focus on the roles of key strategists in the story and will allow you to apply the ideas from the book to a variety of sectors, geographies and situations. Contrasting your own organizational setting with those of others is often instructive and we include shorter micro-examples within individual chapters, longer cases in Section D and running cases from our three strategists in public, corporate and family business settings. This combination of examples provides ample opportunity to see strategy in action.

Finally, the book contains three appendices. Appendix 1 collects the various analytical templates used in Section B into one place for convenience. When we are working with strategists we often use these individual templates as a form of workbook. Appendix 2 recognizes that strategists are often asked to produce a business plan based around their strategy and shows how to use the contents of this book to produce such a document. Appendix 3 recognizes that many of you reading this book will be studying towards a formal qualification and may need to write an essay or assignment on strategy. We have many years of experience of both teaching strategy and assessing coursework. Appendix 3 therefore contains some insights on how to approach a strategy assignment, case study, essay or exam.

The structure of the book is intended to allow you to read the text in a variety of ways. We hope that the book makes sense as a traditional sequence read from start to finish. Yet we also acknowledge that you may want to skip some parts or read in your own sequence. If for example, you want to understand how our view of strategy differs from existing bodies of work, then the history of strategy presented in Chapter 2 is helpful. If you want simply to focus on writing your own organization's strategy you can skip straight to Chapter 10.

We hope that you enjoy the book and we are confident that time spent thinking about strategists at work will help you to become a better strategist.

# A Brief History of Strategy and Strategists

We have already observed that strategy is not new. In this chapter we offer an overview of the literature on strategy in order to place the remainder of the book into an historical context. There is some debate surrounding the heritage of strategy (see e.g., Chris Carter's review, 2013). One view suggests that strategy can be legitimately traced back to seminal figures in the field of military or political strategy with Sun Tzu and Clausewitz cited under the former category, and Machiavelli cited under the latter. The opposing view holds that strategy is a thoroughly modern invention with a lineage that can be traced only as far as the key contributions of writers from the 1960s such as Chandler, Sloan, Andrews and Ansoff. What is undoubtedly true is that the explosion of writing about strategy in the last 30 years means that a particular grammar and vocabulary has grown up around organizational strategy, to the extent that Martin Kronberger and Stewart Clegg argue that the ability to speak strategically has to be learned (2011). We would extend this observation to suggest that many of today's strategy scholars have developed particular language and concepts in ways which serve both commercial and academic ends. Terms such as barriers to entry and core competence have moved from the pages of academic journals to common usage in modern organizations. Those who coin such terminology appropriate both reputational and financial benefits in terms of both book sales and consulting assignments. As the chapter progresses we will reflect on the subtle transitions that occasionally occur in the careers of key strategy scholars as they shift between roles as senior executives, senior academics and/or strategy consultants.

What follows is an abbreviated and partial summary of both the ancient and the modern roots of strategy. Our hope it to enable you to form your own opinion about the genesis of the subject but also to equip you with a grasp of key debates, schools of thought and disagreements within today's ever expanding strategy literature.

# Military and political strategy

Military combat has been a feature of most civilizations. Accounts of the heroes and villains of campaigns, battles and wars fought are the stuff of legend for those that follow. They offer rich storytelling potential to the Bards whose job it is to communicate the meaning of what happened. Further, such clashes offer rich insights to those studying strategy. Whether it is the clever deployment of troops, a cunning plan of attack or some unexpected manoeuvre that proved crucial, we are drawn to stories of success and failure both as entertainment and as a source of admiration. Those who draw lessons from antiquity suggest that insights are transferable since generals deploy troops whilst chief executives deploy resources.

Writing around 500 BC, Sun Tzu's *The Art of War* represents for many, the first definitive written set of ideas about strategy. The text offers advice on how and when to engage in combat. It has been translated many times and periodically resurfaces in popular culture (fictional mafia boss, Tony Soprano, quotes from the text in the HBO drama series The Sopranos, sales of the book rocketed immediately) and in management education. Taken in isolation, the quotable soundbites from the *The Art of War* sound both portentous and wise.

> Whoever is first in the field and awaits the coming enemy, will be fresh for the fight; whoever is second in the field and has to hasten to battle, will arrive exhausted.
>
> Sun Tzu, *The Art of War*
> (circa 500 BC)

However, it is often said that for every piece of such folklore, there exists a counter point. In more modern language, Sun Tzu may appear to be endorsing the idea of first mover advantage where firms put their competitors at a disadvantage by launching products or services that shape customer expectations. The counter observation is that many markets are dominated not by the first mover but by the first firm to perfect an offering. Apple was not the first firm to offer MP3 players, smartphones or tablet computers but their products represented a sophisticated packaging of existing technologies. Hence, whilst the "early bird catches the worm", one might countered that "all good things come to those who wait".

Despite this concern, many military stories form part of our awareness of strategy. In Chapter 5 we review one account of Alexander the Great's victory over the Persian Emperor Darius in 333 BC. One of today's most prominent strategy scholars, Richard Rumelt, gives a similarly vivid account of Hannibal's victory over the Roman army at Cannae in 215 BC, citing this as the first instance of strategy. Rumelt's account shows how Hannibal set out a plan for a battle where he was outnumbered. Describing the plan as premeditated, orchestrated, ruthless and clever, Rumelt concludes that this is the birth of strategic thinking.

Not all strategic insights are heroic. Tragic loss also informs our thinking. Figures such as General Custer (Battle of Little Big Horn, 1876) or General Haig (commander of British forces during the First World War) are heralded for having made grave strategic errors which led to lost battles as well as terrible loss of life. Yet, even these negative cases reinforce our fascination with military strategy. The underlying message is that military strategy is a subject worthy of detailed study. Carl von Clausewitz took this message seriously in his role as a military educator as he tried to help understand how to develop successful strategy in the midst of the fog of war. His is perhaps one of the most sophisticated conceptualizations of strategy.

> It would be disastrous to try to develop our understanding of strategy by analysing factors in isolation since they are usually interconnected in manifold and intricate ways
>
> Clausewitz, On War (1830)

His focus on a holistic view of strategy was based in part on his experience as a military officer during periods of conflict, but also by his later role as director of a military academy. Martin Kronberger (2013) suggests that, despite his popularity amongst modern strategists, the subtlety of Clausewitz's thinking has been diluted by a failure to engage with the original text of his writing.

A similar critique may apply to Machiavelli's "the Prince" (written circa 1513). It offers a treatise on the politics of power. In modern parlance, to be Machiavellian implies that we are behaving in a way which may not be entirely honourable because our immediate actions or intentions may not transparently connect to our eventual intentions. As Machiavelli states that the achievement of great things can be attributed to men who "have given their word lightly, who have known how to trick men with their cunning, and who, in the end, have overcome those abiding by honest principles" (1961: 65).

The insights generated by either military or political strategists from earlier eras have undoubtedly influenced the practice of strategists in the modern era. Such influence may be indirect, unattributed or subliminal but on closer examination it is often present. That said, it is far easier to see the explicit influence of the modern strategy scholars.

## Modern strategy

Having examined the military and political roots of strategy, we now turn our attention to the emergence of strategy as a formal, organizational discipline in the 1960s. As with our brief review of military strategy, our review of modern strategy is necessarily partial. We have chosen to focus on the contributions of a few seminal figures rather than to review the entirety of what is now a vast literature relating to strategy.

We begin by introducing Alfred Chandler, a business historian from Harvard University whose main works involved the study of large US organizations in the period 1850–1920. Most of his empirical work focused on four firms: Dupont, Sears, General Motors and Standard Oil. Each of these firms was in its own way, inventing a new way of doing business at scale. These firms were living through the invention of large, multi-site organizational forms. The industrial revolution meant that techniques of mass production were available to these firms and the development of railway infrastructure meant that it was possible to move both goods and people across large distances with relative ease. Individual businesses, fixed in one limited geographic catchment area were suddenly able to expand in ways, which had previously been unthinkable and modern organizational forms came into being. Chandler's landmark studies of the multi-divisional organization (or M-form organization) popularised and disseminated this new way of organizing large firms across multiple sites. Of particular note for our purposes, Chandler was an early advocate of the need to coordinate strategic planning from the corporate centre whilst acknowledging the importance of decentralization of other aspects of organizational life. This introduced the organizational separation of strategists based at a headquarters location and implementers based in the various locations or divisions of the firm. Furthermore, Chandler saw the health and effectiveness of the firm resting "almost entirely on the talents of its [top] administrators" (1962: 384).

> Structure Follows Strategy: Chandler's review of the firms he examined led him to conclude that organizational structures would be amended to follow the desired strategy of the firm. This conclusion sowed the seed of a view where strategy is centrally determined at headquarters then implemented throughout the other locations in which the firm operates.

Some point to a connection between Chandler and the second of our seminal figures in modern strategy, Alfred Sloan in that Chandler's work influenced Sloan's restructuring of General Motors during his tenure as President of that organization (Kennedy, 1991). Alfred Sloan was President of General Motors from the early 1920s through until the mid-1950s during which time he is credited with having revitalized the car maker. Sloan took on the role of running General Motors in 1921 when the organization was largely seen as failing. Within three years, he had turned the organization around. General Motors became America's leading automobile firm. His focus was on what he described as "federal decentralisation" that is autonomous sub-divisions acting within limits set in financial and policy terms by a relatively small corporate headquarters. The success of Sloan's approach to General Motors echoes across the years to more current fixations, which emphasize delayering and small HQs.

Before Sloan's tenure, General Motors comprised a loose amalgam of eight largely autonomous fiefdoms. The Ford Motor Company held 60% market share with a single product, the Model-T. General Motors offered eight models but held a total market share of just 12%. Worse, only two of their models returned a profit. By centralizing the strategic planning process, Sloan exerted control over a messy situation, and drove his clear agenda to coordinate an approach that would see the firm produce a car "for every purse and purpose". Rather than compete directly with Ford's standardized "any colour you want so long as it's black", Sloan pushed General Motors to introduce a new model every year with optional extras that allowed customers to customize. The relentless onslaught of new models inadvertently created the used car market as customers upgraded to current models rather than waiting for their vehicle to reach a state of disrepair.

Late in his career, Sloan switched from the role of senior executive to that of educator, penning his book "My Life with General Motors" (1963) as a means of passing on his accumulated wisdom. It betrayed the fact that he was a firm advocate of an impersonal, logical approach to strategy.

> "The strategic aim of a business is to earn a return on capital, and if in any particular case the return in the long run is not satisfactory, the deficiency should be corrected or the activity abandoned". (1963:49)

Political scientists had already begun to question the idea of analytically objective decisions associated with unambiguous goals (see Lindbloom, 1959) but the headlines were grabbed by the dominant voice of a captain of industry. Sloan's clinical and detached view of strategy eliminates two complications which we problematize later in the book. First, it assumes a singular and shared view of strategic intent, namely profit maximization. As we show in Chapter 5, we regard this as an impoverished view of intent since it overlooks other motivations or objectives. Second, Sloan is advocating a level of control which we would see as atypical since the authority to enforce strategic decisions is often illusory and more culturally bounded than one might like or expect (see Chapter 9). These reservations aside, it is worth noting that Sloan was seen as a credible commentator on strategy and was able to switch seamlessly from an executive role to a more academic one. It is questionable that such a transition would be possible today because a formal community of practice has established itself within the business school community.

The third seminal contributor to the modern (re)birth of strategy is Igor Ansoff. Placed at the height of the Cold War, Ansoff's is a fascinating biography. He was born in Vladivostock to a mother who was Russian mother and a father who was an American diplomat. Ansoff lived in the Soviet Union for the first 16 years of his life before studying mechanical engineering and physics. He worked at the RAND foundation, a think-tank specializing in military work, and he studied military strategic problems such as those facing North Atlantic Treaty Organization (NATO). He eventually found himself working on long range planning issues as a senior executive with the American firm Lockheed before joining the Carnegie Institute of Technology in 1963 to teach strategy. He introduced the phrase Corporate Strategy to the world with his 1965 book of that title. In it he set out a clear and structured approach to the development of strategy in five steps:

1 Establish a set of objectives
2 Undertake gap analysis that is where are we now; where do we need to be?
3 Develop courses of action
4 Test for "gap reducing qualities"
5 Select and implement

The impact of Ansoff's neat, tidy and linear strategy process is difficult to overstate. It persists, largely intact, in most strategy textbooks even today. Like Sloan, it is interesting to note that Ansoff also found it possible to switch from an industrial to an academic role. His view of strategy was understandably conditioned by the period in which he was writing. Large firms with limited international competition interacted with relatively stable sets of customers, technologies and regulation. His linear approach to strategic logic privileged senior executives by giving them responsibility for everything up to the point of implementation. This is a common theme across Chandler and Sloan too and sets in place the separation between planning and execution which troubled scholars in the decades to follow.

Finally, in the first wave of modern strategists, we would draw attention to Kenneth Andrews, whose 1965 book "Business Policy: text and cases" played an important part in formalizing the curriculum for strategy in business schools. Andrews is credited with the introduction of the **SWOT** analysis and for reinforcing the view that the formulation of strategy is analytically objective. This influence is still seen in the work of later scholars like Richard Rumelt (who suggests that if you are serious about strategy you **must** do your own analysis) and in our own approach (at least in Section B).

---

**SWOT** stands for strengths, weaknesses, opportunities and threats. It is one of the most commonly used strategy tools relating as it does the internal apparatus of the organization to the external environment. We return to SWOT analysis in Chapter 7.

---

The 1960s saw the establishment of a dominant view of organizational strategy and the emergence of business schools to train strategists. Military schools had existed and scholars like Clausewitz had wrestled with the challenge of translating practical experience into training materials. Also, the new organizational forms which were emerging shared similarities but also key differences to the competitive arena of wars between nation states. Organizational strategy had arrived, yet it is interesting to note that this is retrospectively characterized as "an era devoid of theory" (Floyd and Wooldridge, 2000: 7). The emergence of strategy as a profession might therefore be seen to have predated the emergence of a body of theory. Perhaps this is what led to the developments that followed from the 1970s onwards.

Whilst most of his contemporaries strived to correlate particular structures, decision making processes or market positions with financial returns, Henry Mintzberg approached the problem of strategy in a different way. He noticed that little or no research had been done to establish how strategists behaved in daily life. Rather than asking senior executives to offer a sanitized view of how decisions were reached in an interview, Mintzberg took the bold step of shadowing them as they conducted their business. By following five senior executives for a week he was able to challenge the perception of careful, rational and detached decision making. His findings suggested that senior executives lived busy, fragmented and confusing lives. His data suggested that they spent almost half their time on discussions that lasted nine minutes or less and spent more than an hour on a single issue only rarely. It is striking that this hectic and interrupted daily experience was recorded in a world which predated e-mail, mobile telephony and social media. It seems reasonable to assume that the working lives of senior executives have been further fragmented, confusing and challenging with the advent of 24/7 communication in recent years.

Mintzberg's body of work now spans several books and many more papers. His socially nuanced view of the strategy process has had a profound impact on both the academic and the managerial communities. He championed the idea of "emergent strategy" as a more realistic and honest account of the way in which strategy is crafted through a myriad of real-time decisions, sometimes intended, often opportunistic. From the work of Chandler, Sloan and Ansoff, the strategy literature featured a separation between formulation and implementation. Following Mintzberg's work, there existed a second dichotomy between his view of emergent strategy and the more conventional, rational and planned view of deliberate strategy. Others followed this more processual line of work, including key contributions from Quinn whose concept of logical incrementalism (1980) represents an early attempt to "conceptualise strategy as a social learning process" (Floyd and Wooldridge, 2000: xvii) and Andrew Pettigrew (see 1985) whose work combined history, anthropology, politics and a sensitivity to the influence of temporality.

In parallel to this more social and processual view of strategy, a different lineage is discernible in the literature drawing on industrial and applied economics. The key figure in this branch of the literature is Michael Porter. A Harvard professor, Porter's writings have earned him significant royalties from book sales and Monitor, the consultancy organization he founded in 1983, also earned large revenues. Where Ansoff introduced the term corporate strategy, Porter preferred competitive strategy which in his eyes was all about the pursuit of competitive advantage. He was intrigued by the relationship between market structures and individual firms. Porter was persuaded by the so-called "structure-conduct-performance" or SCP approach. In simple terms, SCP argues that the structure of a market, including issues such as the barriers that exist to stop firms entering or leaving a market, influences the conduct of firms within that market. In turn, the conduct of firms is seen to affect the performance outcomes that they achieve. But crucially, if structure influences conduct, and conduct influences performance, SCP posits that we can exclude firm conduct. The focus of attention shifts from how firms act to the relationship between market structure and performance outcomes.

One of the most commonly cited examples that Porter uses is the airline industry. It is expensive to start an airline. Planes are not cheap, nor are pilots, fuel or landing slots. Further, there are complex regulatory requirements. The very structure of the industry itself makes it hard to make good returns. For Porter, some industries are inherently attractive whilst others are not. In many ways the role of management is to either manipulate the structure of their industry to make it more favourable or to choose a more attractive industry. Perhaps his greatest achievement was to take the relatively dry subject of applied economics and communicate it in a series of simple frameworks that caught the attention of practising managers across the globe. We will use some of his frameworks in Section B of the book. Porter also demonstrated that it was possible for a career academic to travel in the opposite direction to Ansoff or Sloan and join the executive world as a senior practitioner. As founder of Monitor, he ran a significant global consulting business. The harsh realities of a competitive environment are clearly not amenable to formulaic answers though since Monitor filed for bankruptcy in November 2012.

## The role of resources

Whilst Porter was the highest profile and most heavily cited strategy scholars of his generation, there remained some dissatisfaction with the fixation on industry structure and pure economic logic. Some argued that it missed the point. Crucially, the strategist was marginalized and the SCP view underplayed the central role of good management. If industry structure was all that mattered, why did some firms dramatically outperform others within the same industry? If the airline industry is so unattractive, why do firms such as Ryanair and Southwest airlines buck the trend and report significant profits. The answer must lie within the firm itself.

The so-called resource-based view (RBV) of the firm can trace its roots back to the writings of Edith Penrose in the 1950s. In her seminal book "The Theory of the Growth of the Firm" published in 1959, Penrose sought to examine the ways in which firms developed specific resources which helped them to engage with their external environment. At the time, her work was seen as radical. Perhaps this explains why it was overlooked by the mainstream strategy literature for several decades. It was not until Birger Wernerfelt published the RBV of the Firm in 1984 that significant attention began to be paid to this more inward looking take of strategy. Further elaboration took place when Jay Barney published a landmark paper in Journal of Management (1991). Barney suggests that firms can build competitive advantage if they nurture resources which are valuable, rare and difficult to imitate. We explore this in more detail in Chapter 7 but here it is sufficient to note that scholars advocating a resource-based perspective on strategy are amongst the most heavily cited in the literature.

Success breeds both followers and critics. Richard Priem and John Butler developed a comprehensive critique of the RBV (see 2001) arguing that it was weak not least because it was tautological. For example, Priem and Butler argue that the RBV defines competitive advantage in terms of value and rarity yet also argues that the characteristics which generate competitiveness are value and rarity. Hence, a circular argument is framed in a way which cannot be tested or falsified. Nevertheless, the RBV proved popular and other scholars developed a new variant of resource-based theorizing, which focuses on the dynamic capabilities of a firm. Researchers such as David Teece (see 2007), Margaret Peteraf, Connie Helfat and Kathy Eisenhardt argue that dynamic capabilities help enable long-term competitiveness. Sidney

Winters (2003) offers a simple distinction between two types of capability that a firm might possess. Zero order capabilities represent the ways in which a firm earns money today. These might include the ways in which it designs and delivers current products and services. However, since markets, tastes, technologies and consumers change, zero order capabilities can only take you so far. What is needed is a new concept. Dynamic capabilities then describe the ways in which a firm extends, modifies or creates new zero order capabilities.

## A focus on the strategist

In more recent years there has been a resurgence of interest in the role of the strategist. The strategy-as-practice movement was launched in 2001 in a bid to draw analytical attention toward what strategists actually do when they craft strategy. It is therefore something of a return to the themes and methods used by Mintzberg. Senior scholars argued that there was a need to establish a micro perspective for strategy as a discipline (Johnson et al., 2003). In sharp contrast to those economists who studied industry structure, practice scholars sought to study the mundane, day-to-day practices in which strategists became engaged. Building on Mintzberg's earlier work the so-called "practice turn" in strategy moves beyond merely observing how strategists spend their time and tries to theorize about the consequences of the behaviours, habits and routines which are observed. One simple example is the practice of conducting strategy workshops. Many management teams will periodically hold a strategy workshop perhaps on an annual or an ad hoc basis. The purpose of the workshop is ostensibly to take time out and to rethink the strategy of the organization. Such workshops are often held off-site and are frequently facilitated by external consultants. Workshops have become the subject of several key studies. Gerry Johnson and colleagues examined workshops from an anthropological perspective treating them as rites of passage and as such suggesting that they represented a ritual in modern organizational life (Johnson et al., 2010). Our own study of workshops (see MacIntosh et al., 2010) suggests that one off workshops tend to fail precisely because they are seen as separate from daily organizational life. However, a series of workshops can bridge the gap between the off-site away day and regular organizational life and effect significant change to strategy.

This move toward a practice perspective has generated a virtual **community** and, as is often the case, a critical response from others in the field. The critical response to the strategy as practice movement includes the observation that earlier social theory

The strategy-as-practice **community** have established an online network of over 2,000 scholars and research students as well as a presence at a number of major international conferences. Professional bodies such as the Strategic Management Society and the European Group for Organization Studies regularly feature practice streams in their annual conferences. For more details see www.strategy-as-practice.org

relating to practice is not always fully reflected in the research published under the practice banner. Indeed, the strategy as practice community have been accused of taking a colonialist perspective "discovering an already peopled continent, for whose existing inhabitants is given scant regard" (Carter et al., 2008: 85). Those seeking new insights into strategy occasionally encounter challenges on two fronts; first they have overlooked some more ancient wisdom from military or political strategy and second that they have not fully incorporated insights from some earlier branch of social theory or pragmatist philosophy.

With great trepidation therefore, we introduce one final view in the literature which regards strategy as socially constructed. This view of strategy as fantasy suggests that senior managers operate with a necessarily and inevitably incomplete view of circumstances leading to a situation where individuals imagine a plausible explanation of what is happening (MacIntosh and Beech, 2011). Ultimately it matters little whether facts are or can be verified by senior managers since perceptions become reality at least in as much as they colour the actions of those involved. One such example relates to a situation where a large corporation acquired a series of small technology firms. The management team of the corporation were impressed by the entrepreneurial flair of a firm they had acquired. Over an extended period an awkward stasis was generated. The corporate team were determined not to undermine the autonomy of their newly acquired firm, hoping that entrepreneurial behaviours might cross-contaminate their own much larger and more established organization. Meanwhile the management team in the acquired firm were of the view that there must be "a plan" which there was little point in second guessing. Hence, for many months they waited to for their new colleagues to announce a direction of travel. Both groups operated with a fantasized view of the other (we have no plan for them other than to allow them to continue to act entrepreneurially; there must be a plan and there's no point doing anything until it is revealed). These fantasies, whilst unacknowledged, allowed an extended period of dissatisfaction to occur.

## Who to read

A number of scholars have produced more extensive overviews of the strategy literature than the abbreviated history offered above. Two in particular merit closer examination. First, Richard Whittington's "What is strategy and does it matter?" offers a thorough examination of the foundations of the discipline. Second, Henry Mintzberg, Bruce Ahlstrand and Joe Lampel collaborated in 2008 to produce their text "Strategy Safari" which sets out ten major schools of thought within the strategy literature. Although it is possible to take issue with the subdivisions they create, it remains a highly readable overview.

# CHAPTER 3

# The Running Cases

ase studies are a familiar way of developing our understanding of strategy. Almost every textbook on strategic management features a range of cases and we have included four such cases in Section D of this book. However, cases are often written in ways that illustrate the use of models, techniques or frameworks. Indeed, cases are typically chosen because they offer particularly telling insights about some specific aspect of strategy. To supplement the four cases in Section D, we now introduce three running cases. Each refers to a very different setting and our intention is to allow you, the reader, to hear directly from strategists operating within these organizations. These strategists vary in their approach to strategy by, for example, attaching greater importance to some issues than others and by sequencing the kinds of strategic analysis which they have undertaken.

It seems obvious that the role of the strategist will differ in public, private and family organizations. The running cases presented here offer the chance to see both how and why strategy is a context-dependent activity. Section B contains a range of analytical frameworks that we find useful in the conduct of strategy work. As each framework is presented you will hear our three strategists discussing how these ideas were translated into the development of strategy in their particular circumstances. Our objective is to provide a glimpse of the lived-reality of strategy work. Sometimes the strategists disagree. Often what is important to one context or individual barely registers with another. This very messiness is precisely what we wanted to display, since it captures the sense in which strategy is as much an art as a science.

## Running case #1: Confused.com

Kate Buell-Armstrong started with a degree in Biochemistry and her transition to roles in information technology (IT) and marketing in the insurance industry wasn't planned. Having been responsible for setting up the IT systems of other UK insurance firms, she was recruited to the start-up team who launched Admiral Insurance in the UK. Founded in 1993, Admiral Insurance grew rapidly and now employs over

6000 people to handle the 3.6 million customers who generate a turnover in excess of £2 billion. As the wider insurance industry moved from the high street to postal services, then the phone and finally the internet, the strategy at Admiral changed to reflect these opportunities. By 2002, Kate saw the opportunity to revolutionize the insurance market by creating Confused.com as the UK's first internet-based aggregator. The underlying driver for Confused.com was the observation in multiple focus group settings that customers found the whole business of buying car insurance confusing and time consuming. Nobody liked the amount of time and effort involved in sourcing multiple car insurance quotes. Equally, customers were worried that they weren't getting a good deal and struggled to compare one provider with another in any meaningful way.

In 2002, Kate stumbled across a piece of technology that would allow her to turn the insurance industry up-side down. The Confused.com proposition was simple. Capture the customer's details once, then use these to generate quotes from multiple providers. Today the price-comparison marketplace is crowded and competition is fierce but in the early years Confused.com was the only player. Convincing their parent company, Admiral Insurance, to place their own quotes next to those of competitors wasn't easy but a compelling case was made. Even if customers chose an alternative provider for their insurance, Confused.com would be able to secure some value from its role as a relationship broker. The vast majority of car insurance in the UK is now sold through intermediary organizations like Confused.com.

**Kate:** I have an MBA and so do many of my colleagues but, like most organizations, we tend not to use the word "strategy" in the same sense that academics do. We tend to just do it. The whole management team can feed into the process as everyone has specialized knowledge and everyone "sweats the small stuff". We have a set of key indicators that tell us how the business is performing, we know how those indicators developed over time, and of course everyone knows their own areas in more detail. In the parent company, Admiral, everyone is wired into the external environment. There's a natural focus on your own particular area of expertise but the executive directors have a very wide remit. This external knowledge comes from our networks of colleagues, industry journals and seminars. Keeping close to the customer is key. Our senior managers and directors spend time reading the comment forms returned by customers. They also spend time attending focus groups with customers, and are expected to speak to customers and staff when they visit the service floors. Our senior people then have a great opportunity to listen in on customer conversations as a great way of keeping their finger on the pulse of the organization. This is just one part of our staff-development process.

Swapping information at Admiral tends to be informal, although there are structured meetings of the senior management where the discussion tends to be more formal but our culture is one where we'll talk to a colleague over lunch or as you walk past their desk. The informal stuff can be very instructive. No one waits for a formal meeting if they have an issue someone else can help with. Strategy is decided amongst the executive directors although other relevant managers can contribute to shaping a direction and the people in those roles are very adept at seeing things happening in the market, which will be threats/opportunities for the company. But, we have a very organic and bottom-up culture where people at all levels feel comfortable with raising new ideas direct with the CEO. Ideas and opportunities might relate to new technology or new legislation, new ways of processing data, new things our competitors are doing, or simply brainstorming "what do we need to do next to increase value in this company".

One of our key challenges has been to keep feeling like a small start-up despite growing to a size where many of our competitors become bogged down in procedures and structures. Once a strategic direction is determined, it is debated in the wider management group: how wide depends on the scope of the change needed and ideas for implementation are honed but implementation is swift. We prize our ability to move quickly and our ability to mitigate the risk of these big strategic changes (and in fact any change) through a process of "test and control". Essentially, we strive to create a control loop. A change is made, and preferably tested if that is at all possible. Measures are devised to check progress against the objective. These measures are reviewed at a senior level regularly and if further tweaks are required they are implemented; if progress is satisfactory, things continue unchanged or rolled out to a larger test group and if the measures indicate that the strategy is not working then it gets abandoned and the firm learns lessons and moves on.

This emergent process is dependent on having people in the organization who constantly innovate and recognize opportunities. We have people in the wider Admiral business who are good at change and we populated Confused.com with those people. The business seems to have developed a number of simple guiding principles which trigger change, discussion and debate. When any of these rules are broken, action occurs and because the firm's managers are very sensitive to small fluctuations in trends they tend to act before performance deteriorates too far. The strategy per se tends to be a well-understood maxim in the business which is "to be the most profitable company in the UK" and that encompasses success financially and success for its staff to work and develop in a positive environment. When we launched Confused.com, I made a point of writing out our strategy with the management team. It was important at that point because we were a new team and many of the management teams were in a senior role for the first time. It worked well for us then, but over time we've reduced the amount that we write down. Neither the rules nor the overarching vision are written down today. Our current group of managers understands what it is they are trying to achieve and our more informal approach works for us.

## Running case #2: Scottish health policy

Professor Sir Harry Burns graduated in medicine from the University of Glasgow in 1974. He trained as a surgeon and spent time in the operating theatres and wards of Glasgow's hospitals. Glasgow's economy had once been dominated by shipbuilding, locomotive construction and other heavy engineering industries. These industries gradually collapsed in the 20th century leaving a void in the lives of many working men and women in Glasgow. As de-industrialization swept through the city, some areas were marked by very high levels of unemployment whilst others remained affluent. As a young surgeon, Harry was intrigued by differences in the ways that patients would recover from surgery. Those from more affluent socio-economic groups appeared to recover both more effectively and more quickly than their counterparts in lower income groups. This started a life-long interest in the relationship between social issues and health. He completed a masters' degree in Public Health in 1990 and became Director of Public Health for Greater Glasgow Health Board where he continued to research the social determinants of health. In 2005, he became Chief Medical Officer for Scotland and found himself with a role at the heart of the Scottish Government. His remit as Chief Medical Officer gave him an overview of the whole of the National Health Service (NHS) in Scotland. Importantly, health is an issue devolved to the Scottish parliament and the Scottish NHS had reacted differently to issues such as the introduction of an internal market which occurred in other parts of the UK NHS. Harry's view was that a new strategy was required for healthcare and he played a key role in engaging a wider range of stakeholders from other areas of government in rethinking the approach to health. He received a knighthood in 2011 in recognition of his contribution to healthcare.

**Harry:** For many people, the definition of health is simply the absence of disease. Framed in this way, improving the health the population becomes is determined by the availability and effectiveness of healthcare for that population. Very quickly that framing leads to a conversation about creating more doctors, nurses and hospitals.

The World Health Organization offers a wider definition of health, suggesting that "health is a state of complete physical, mental and social wellbeing, not merely the absence of disease of infirmity". I prefer this definition in that it offers a positive view of health but even this remains inadequate. By suggesting that health is a *state*, it proposes a binary view of health. A person is either in the state of health or is in the state of non-health.

Our everyday experience suggests that our sense of being healthy is complex. The patient with incurable cancer who is pain free and actively enjoying life is objectively unhealthy but may have a strong sense of subjective well-being. The Olympic athlete, in a state of peak fitness, might become depressed and anxious because the weather has interrupted their training plans. For me, health is an emergent property generated by a complex set of physical, psychological, social and environmental determinants.

As Chief Medical Officer for Scotland, I was in a unique position to influence the strategy of the Scottish Government in ways which might improve the health of an entire population. This is not without its dangers. Anyone tampering with health in a society has huge responsibilities and little right to make mistakes. There is a commonly held view that Scots are unhealthy. Their smoking, eating and drinking habits are the subject of commentary in the media and it is assumed that their love of fatty foods, whisky and tobacco is the cause of their poor health. Empirically, the

Scots do have a lower life expectancy than most neighbouring European countries, but this observation cannot be attributed to conventional explanations.

A number of studies have shown that Scots probably smoke less than other European populations. Finland is often held up as an example of a country which took radical action to improve the diet of its population in the 1970s. Yet, Scots have experienced the same dramatic fall in heart disease mortality as the Finns. Scots have a high level of mortality from alcoholic liver disease but this is a problem which has only been observed in the last 30 years. Prior to that, Scots had one of the lowest death rates from liver disease in Europe. A review of trends shows that Scotland's relatively poor life expectancy is a recent phenomenon and, prior to the 1960s, Scottish life expectancy was similar to that of other Western European countries. Since then, there has been an ever-widening gap in life expectancy between the rich and poor in Scotland. The rich have kept pace with the rest of Europe whilst life expectancy in the poorest sections of Scotland has not improved as rapidly. In my estimation, Scotland's relatively poor health is fundamentally a function of the health of the poor.

Like other countries, Scotland has gone through the traditional, and largely ineffective, process of "health promotion". This has largely consisted of efforts to persuade individuals living in poor circumstances to give up harmful lifestyles. Such efforts usually result in widening the gap in health between rich and poor since the so-called worried-well from the more affluent parts of society are those most likely to respond to such information. Others have argued that the only way to increase growth in the health of the poor is to redistribute wealth and power in society. While such sentiments are laudable they are largely impracticable in a democratic country where public health does not control the entirety of the political agenda.

The strategy we developed in Scotland combines improvement science with the recognition that healthcare is a complex system. In adopting that approach, we have been very lucky in having the support of [government] ministers who understand and have been persuaded by the science underlying our strategy. The strategy consists of four phases.

## Phase 1. Assemble the knowledge

Our first step in developing a strategy to improve the health of the population of Scotland was to gain as comprehensive an understanding of the problem as possible. Everyone has an opinion about health. However, few of those opinions appeared to be based on evidence. The assumption that Scotland had always been unhealthy, and that the ill-health was largely due to unhealthy behaviours, could not be substantiated. Instead, the science suggested a very different set of drivers for health inequality across the population. Research suggested that our capacity for well-being across a number of dimensions of life, not just health, is laid down mainly, but not exclusively in early years. Hence, our thinking was that efforts to improve well-being should include attention to the well-being of children and families.

## Phase 2. Build the will for change

The scientific analysis left little room for doubt about the complex set of drivers of ill-health in deprived communities. Initially there was disagreement as to the action required to make the necessary improvements but there was little doubt about the need to do something. Agreement on this point was achieved through wide dissemination across Scottish society of the evidence of the impact of adverse social circumstances on complex biological processes. Without data, all you have are opinions. We had data, so consensus on the need for change became easier to achieve.

## Phase 3. Decide what needs to be changed

Our analysis of the drivers of ill-health suggested that adverse events in early life were a major factor in increasing the risk of poor physical and mental health in later life as well as childhood. Other events in later life were also identified as important but our initial effort was concentrated on transforming life in childhood. Wanting to make a transformational change in society is a common enough aspiration. Having a method for change, however, is usually an insuperable difficulty.

## Phase 4. Implement the agreed actions

Our model of change was that used by the Institute for Healthcare Improvement in Boston to transform safety in US hospitals. It has been applied effectively as part of the Scottish Patient Safety Programme in Scottish hospitals. We adapted the model for use in improving early years. We began by getting a wide section of the community together to decide on aims. This process brought together 800 people from every local authority and health board in Scotland to determine what they wanted to change, by how much and by when. These aims were specific, measurable and involved agreeing reductions in key areas like infant mortality and improvements in developmental milestones across the whole of Scotland. Next, teams developed ideas for interventions that might produce the desired changes. They brought together their own knowledge as well as the insights of others. A critical part of the process is selecting quantitative measures to determine if a particular change actually results in an improvement.

Finally, the changes are tested in a real-life setting using the familiar Plan-Do-Study-Act (PDSA) cycle. This led to a diverse range of stakeholders in the healthcare arena and beyond planning something, trying it, observing the results, and acting on what was learnt. As evidence emerges that changes are being successful, the effective ones are progressively refined and the learning from this small-scale process is then being shared across the whole of Scotland. Critical to this strategy has been a very large group of frontline staff who design, test and implement the changes. Strategy, which is planned in committee rooms and communicated to the front line by documents and memos, has not worked in the past and our estimation was that they would not be successful given the challenge that we face. By making those who are implementing the change as the designers of what they are doing so that they can also see it working through the results generated by PDSA cycles, the new strategy becomes part of the routine way of working.

## Running case #3: Pointer Ltd

Sandy Rowan was born and brought up in Scotland, graduating with an MA in Economic History from Edinburgh University before joining automotive firm Austin-Rover in a variety of roles in sales and marketing. He later switched to Mercedes-Benz UK before finally joining Pointer Ltd. in 1991 as the Branch Manager for Glasgow.

Pointer was established in 1972 by Bob Rowan and Jimmy Mowat supplying intruder alarms to homes and independent retailers in the Glasgow area. It remains a privately owned business and Sandy succeeded his father as Chief Executive of the firm in 2007. Over the first ten years of its existence, Pointer achieved steady growth in both its domestic and commercial markets. As the firm grew, it developed a strong tradition of staff training and development. The first apprentices were recruited to the firm in 1979 and the Pointer apprentice programme has been recognized by many external bodies. Many of the current management team started with Pointer as apprentices and staff turnover is low.

Today, Pointer has operations in the UK, Oman, Thailand and the Philippines providing sophisticated electronic security services to blue chip organizations. Technology in the security industry has been changing rapidly from traditional closed circuit television to modern integrated systems offering Internet Protocol (IP)-based video, access control and fire detection. Pointer offers services that cover design, project management, installation, testing, commissioning, training, service, maintenance and services. Monitoring services include a 24-hour control room and the ability to remotely service systems for clients.

The market for security systems in the UK grew as insurance companies began to demand that customers used them. By working with local businesses that were expanding, Pointer began to win business from local and regional retail chains rather than individual customers. Firms such as American District Telegraph (ADT) and Chubb operate in multiple geographies but Pointer quickly became one of the largest independent players in the security market.

**Sandy:** We're a reasonably small organization with ambitions to grow. I was proud of our Scottish roots but it became clear that we had hit the limits of growth in our local market. We've begun to expand with significant successes in niche industries like the prison services and water utilities in the UK. We still have a steady stream of smaller scale customers but the real challenge has been to take our high levels of service and apply them to larger corporate customers. We began to bid for larger projects which meant that we began to need skills which we learnt by trial and error in the early days.

It was becoming increasingly clear that our traditional intruder alarm market had become commoditized. There were very low barriers to entry and we faced low cost competition from a set of micro-businesses. Moving into the project business took us away from that price pressure, and the barriers to entry operated in our favour because we were one of the few providers that could design and integrate complex systems for clients. Profit margins are lower on larger projects but total "cash" profit is higher. We reinvested our profits in our internal training resources so that we could train our existing staff in new technical skills. It hasn't always been a comfortable ride but as our home and small retailer client base has contracted, we've offset this with new work in the corporate sector.

Our combination of deep technical knowledge and strong customer relationships helped us build a reputation for delivering complex projects successfully on a consistent basis. Sometimes we describe ourselves as a boutique hotel. Whilst our competitors are in the main much larger businesses covering all parts of the market, much like the global hotel chains with brands at different price points that we all recognize, Pointer concentrates on a specific niche and delivers what matters to those customers. It helps that we have a culture which recognizes the importance of looking after our customers, taking pride in our work and investing in our staff to enable them to do just that. Many of them have been with us for a long time and that helps embed this culture of customer care. It can, however, lead to complacency and a sense of being too inward looking. So, we've tried to recruit experienced staff from other businesses to counter these tendencies by offering an alternative view of the world.

Our strategy has been to try and exploit the technological changes that are occurring as the security industry converges with the wider, larger and better resourced world of computing and IT. I sometimes describe the security world as existing on its own island, essentially looked after by its own dedicated suppliers providing it with specialist recording units, specialist cameras, specialist monitors. I don't believe a lot of it was shared in other areas of business. The advent of IP meant a growing area of activity and the IT industry has spread as costs have come down, whether it's been into consumer electronics, phones, computers, tablets or commerce. CCTV by its very name means a closed circuit, an island mentality. But all that those cameras are collecting is data which were not available readily to other parties unless they had access to the closed circuit. What IT enables you to do is bring it into open circuit, the data becomes instead of images, 1 and 0 like every other piece of data and can, therefore, be shared. So, going back to the analogy of the island, the security island is sitting there and what's creeping out over our shores is the world of IT which will eventually end up absorbing security as it has other industries. If you're on the security island, you either adapt to what IT wants or you go the way of the dinosaurs.

We partnered with a major IT company, Cisco, in their initial foray into the security market. That was a statement of intent both externally and internally for Pointer. This convergence between our industry and IT was going to happen. There were heavyweight players in the IT world who were interested in our part of the market so we've tried to move faster and further than our competitors in the security industry and to embrace what was happening around us.

# Summary

It is evident from the descriptions above that both the contexts and the individuals vary. Placed in the same organizational setting, each of our three strategists would likely act differently based on their own interests, strategic style and prior experiences. These differences are then exacerbated when they are placed in very different contexts across public, corporate and family business settings. Finally, another layer of variation is added when we realize that each organization is trying to achieve something different. Each of our strategists identifies changes in their environment and makes choices about how to frame the challenge that these changes represent. As we move into Section B we begin to introduce a step-by-step process for developing strategy. It should be obvious that these steps will produce radically different strategies dependent upon the preferences of the strategist, the context in which they are operating and the challenges that they are facing in that context. In each of the analytical chapters in Section B, we will return to the running cases to see these three strategists at work. Their views don't always coincide and our aspiration is that, rather than confusing you, this will act as an encouragement to you as you develop your own views and your own practises in relation to strategy.

**SECTION**

# B

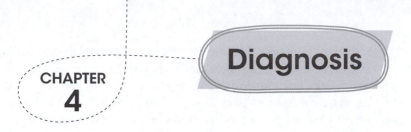

# Diagnosis

trategies shouldn't exist in a vacuum. Rather, a strategy should be developed as a response to a particular set of circumstances. When Steve Jobs returned to Apple in September 1997 the firm was facing a challenging set of circumstances. Bankruptcy was a real possibility. Apple's market share had eroded over a number of years and, by 1997, the firm was seen as a marginal player in the Windows-Intel dominated personal computer market. Mobile telephony, tablet devices and MP3 players were not yet part of the Apple offering and Jobs needed to perform an accurate diagnosis of what was wrong before establishing a strategy for the firm. The early months of his second term as CEO suggest that his diagnosis was that Apple's very survival was at stake. Dramatic simplification of the product range for both desktop and portable computers were matched by reductions in inventory and the scaling back of development activities. Perhaps most surprising of all, he struck a deal with Microsoft to secure the investment needed to rebuild Apple.[1]

In this chapter, we will show how the diagnosis of an organization's circumstances needs to consider three key issues: business issues, cultural issues and the political dynamics of current, past and/or potential strategists. By examining each of these three areas independently and in relation to each other it is possible to build a solid understanding of what is happening. Armed with this diagnosis, it becomes significantly easier to build strategy because both purpose and direction of travel are established.

However, diagnosis is not as objective as might first appear to be the case. Think of the process of visiting a clinician with a set of symptoms. Ideally your condition would be subjected to rigorous and objective scrutiny in order to arrive at an accurate diagnosis of your situation. Worryingly, studies of clinical diagnosis suggest that "who you see is what you get" (Cherkin et al., 1994). Some cases are simple; a patient with severe blood loss from a wound sustained in a fall or accident evidently needs to stop the blood loss as a first priority. The absence of such dramatic and obvious signals creates circumstances where individual biases can come to the fore. If you're seen by a rheumatologist they may call for blood tests and their attention may be drawn to small anomalies in the results of those tests. Meanwhile, the same patient meeting with a neurologist may be sent for a series of scans to assess the condition of their brain. In many healthcare systems, the first round of diagnosis is conducted by a general practitioner (GP) who can treat routine cases there and then or refer the patient on to colleagues with specialist knowledge and skills. In theory this is a sensible approach but GPs are often confronted by patients with vague, poorly differentiated or rare symptoms. Where a specialist may treat several cases of a particular disorder every day, a GP may only see one or two patients a year with the condition. Spotting those patients is difficult and there are several studies which raise questions about the reliability of the diagnostic process (see Kings Fund, 2010 for a summary).

In organizational terms, the strategist faces a similar dilemma when attempting diagnosis. A range of specialists are usually at hand with disciplinary expertise in areas like marketing, finance, operations, human resources, etc. The same vague symptoms, for example falling market share, might be diagnosed as a marketing problem. However, it could equally be caused by poor logistics and distribution generating poor customer experiences such that the eventual outcome is falling market share. Another parallel can be found in terms of infrequent but important events such as changes to industry boundaries. The advent of new technologies or regulatory changes may go unnoticed since the strategist concerned doesn't encounter such circumstances often enough to recognize the symptoms. Indeed, Weick observes that "problems do not present themselves [to managers] as givens" but rather converting a problematic situation to a problem requires "a certain kind of work" (1995: 9). Although problem solving is a well-established field (Baer et al., 2013), the kind of diagnostic to which Weick refers is not well understood (see Lyles and Mitroff, 1980 or Dutton, 1993 for rare examples of scholars studying this important but under-developed area of work). Yet problem framing or problem setting is vital.

Diagnosis then, is fraught with difficulties. Unfortunately, misdiagnosis has two distinct consequences over time. First, diagnosis leads naturally to specifying treatment. Hence misdiagnosis often results in an inappropriate course of treatment. Whether in medical or organizational settings, being treated for something that isn't actually there is rarely neutral. Rather, the treatment itself may cause changes, which are potentially harmful or dangerous in their own right, whilst there may also be side-effects with which to contend. Second, whilst the wrong issue is being treated, the actual and original problem is likely to deteriorate if left unattended. In combination, these two consequences of misdiagnosis highlight the fact that diagnosis is rarely harmless. It can make the situation better or worse but it is unlikely to leave the situation unchanged. In particular, the early stages of the diagnostic process set in train a series of decisions which often have far reaching consequences as we draw attention to some data whilst overlooking or downplaying others.

In organizational terms it is suggested that open and closed framing approaches represent two different approaches to diagnosis (Beech and MacIntosh, 2012). **Open framing**, involves diagnosing the situation in ways allows others to read the problem based on their own experiences and particular organizational perspective. This generates multiple views and can foster creative and unexpected solutions. A diagnosis framed as "needing to regain our position as market leader" offers the potential for some consensus to emerge over the end game, whilst permitting competing or even contradictory solutions to emerge. In contrast, **closed framing** implies that some prior diagnostic work has already been undertaken since a closed framing tends to link the articulation of the problem to courses of action which will improve the situation. A closed framing of the earlier problem might specify that there is a "need to regain our position as market leader by developing products with superior features and performance within the next two years". Closed framing usually identifies one or more dimensions of the situation such as what needs to be achieved, the means to achieve it and/or the timescale within which this has to occur. Hence, diagnosis which develops a closed framing of the situation tends to produce a more unitary account of that situation as well as implying a particular way of moving forward. Closed framing is achieved by working iteratively between analysis and diagnosis in much the same way that a clinician will refine their diagnosis as various test results become available.

In the next section, we introduce three key ways of diagnosing an organization's current situation.

## Business issues

When diagnosing an organization rather than a patient, there are still a handful of vital signs on which it is helpful to have data. Turnover, profitability, sales figures, return on equity, market share, levels of innovation, rate of staff turnover, rate of market growth and a host of other measures offer an insight into the performance of the organization. Typically, most organizations hold a few such measures as being more important than others and monitor these so-called key performance indicators (KPIs) closely. These are often captured and communicated as **rules of thumb**. Whatever the local nuances in your own organization, knowing what these rules of thumb are, how the measures that they relate to are calculated and how those measures have been shifting over time is vital. Trends are more important than absolute values. Knowing that market share is currently 15% is a start. However, recent performance looks very different dependent upon whether the last five years have seen market share double each year from a very low starting point, or collapse from a dominant position of having held a much larger market share five years ago. This temporal dimension of diagnosis (see Figure 4.1) is often overlooked. It draws into focus a central question: do current measures imply that things are getting better or worse?

> **Business Rules of Thumb** may include issues of profitability (e.g. only engaging in work that achieves a particular level of profit), growth (e.g. a focus on growth by acquisition) amongst many others. These simple guides or heuristics allow strategists to make decisions when bombarded with information.

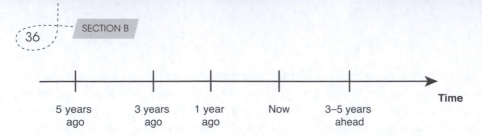

*Figure 4.1* The temporal dimension of strategy

## Cultural issues

Assuming that you have assessed the kinds of business issues discussed above, the second aspect of diagnosis explores the cultural fabric of the organization. We know from our own experience of organizational life that organizations are social systems. As such, different organizations within the same sector and offering the same product or service can feature dramatically different cultures. Perhaps the most commonly cited definition of culture is "the way we do things round here" (Drennan, 1992) and when we enter a new organizational setting as a member or visitor, our attention focuses on those processes, practices and routines which seem unusual. Culture then, connotes something about membership, acceptance and participation. Think about being a new member of staff in an organization. How do you react when something has gone wrong? You may display anger, apportion blame, conduct a post-mortem or try to move on as quickly as possible. The actual choice you make will be influenced by your own habits and characteristics but also by what you see as the norms of your new organizational home. These cultural norms are often expressed, either explicitly or implicitly, as **cultural rules of thumb.** Over time, we become socialized into our organizational settings such that we no longer need to think about the nuances of acceptable behaviour. Perhaps this is why Hall argues that "culture hides much more than it reveals, and strangely enough what it hides, it hides most effectively from its own participants" (1959: 53). Thus, organizational culture gradually recedes from the view of those most familiar with it, yet culture can also change subtly over time. It is therefore prudent to diagnose the organization's culture.

> **Cultural Rules of Thumb:** These perform a similar purpose to their business counterparts but act to inform how people relate to each other within the organization. They may set out the types of individuals that are recruited, how conflict is resolved, how decisions are taken, etc. They are also heuristics and tend to capture "how we do things round here".

Trying to capture a description of something as elusive as culture is challenging. The culture web attempts to summarize organizational culture by capturing observations about the physical, symbolic and social/organizational aspects of a specific setting. The model uses six overlapping but separate dimensions as a means of establishing a sense of the **organizational culture**. These six dimensions represent a set of interlocking activities, beliefs and structures that form a cultural web. The metaphor of a web conveys a view of culture as interwoven as well as indicating that changing one aspect of culture in isolation may not be enough to break the web of interconnections currently in place (Johnson et al., 2013) (Figure 4.2).

Organizations quickly develop ways of doing business and these become embedded as **routines**, which avoid the need to reinvent the wheel for each new customer or transaction. How firms recruit staff, develop products, manage suppliers, etc., might be conceptualized as routines and these routines characterize and form part of the organization's culture as the routine is repeated again and again over time. Some routines represent commonplace and everyday activity, whilst others carry more significance. Hence, there are some **rituals**, which we might describe as special events, which highlight or reaffirm aspects of the organization's culture. Such rituals might include strategy away days, promotion rounds, the announcement of annual results, etc. Rituals of this type are repeated though less frequently than routines, and are often associated with rites of passage, celebration or reprimand.

These routines and rituals often form important aspects of the **stories** which circulate within the organization. Story telling in organizations is an established area of research and scholars argue that stories need to be succinct enough to be retold, have some memorable point or moral and be engaging or entertaining. Larger complex narratives are summarized down into snippets[2] to facilitate story-telling (Sims et al., 2009). The most powerful stories are viral. You don't need to have been there to interpret the story of a young entrepreneur striking a deal with a global firm and redrawing the map of an entire industry. Only a handful of individuals were actually involved in the interactions between a young Bill Gates and IBM, but many of us

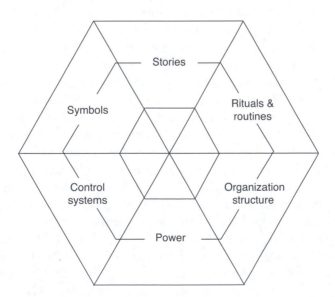

*Figure 4.2* The culture web

have subsequently heard snippets of the story where he convinced IBM to allow a then fledgling Microsoft to provide the operating system for personal computers. Stories usually feature heroes and villains who may be interchangeable depending upon which stakeholder group is telling the tale. The stories that are retold tell you something about the culture of the organization.

Next, the culture web draws our attention to the symbolic aspects of the organization. These **symbols** are likely to be artefacts or events that hold meaning beyond their functional purpose. On one level, a named parking space ensures that you can always get parked outside the office, but on a cultural level it symbolizes importance and status. Company credit cards, frequent flyer lounges, numbers of direct reports, the use of first names or nicknames and jargon all operate at a symbolic level. Hence many other aspects of the culture web, such as organizational structure, also operate symbolically to reinforce the culture and paradigm of the organization.

These first three parts of the culture web (Rituals and Routines, Stories and Symbols) are common to all members of the organization. In many ways, these three aspects of organizational culture pervade organizational life. However, the next three (Power Structures, Organizational Structures and Control Systems) tend to be more prominent in the minds of those in managerial positions. **Power Structures** say something about the extent to which individuals, teams or groups can exert influence on others within the organization. These power structures are likely to be reflected in the relative positioning of stakeholders. Influence here could be formal and directive (e.g., I am giving you an order) or informal and coercive (e.g., I am persuading you that this is the right thing to do). Power structures are therefore related to but distinct from organizational structures. Someone further up the organizational hierarchy may have formal power over a more junior group of staff, whilst in reality being unable to use that power. **Organizational Structure** then relates to the formal organograms that set out which groups and individuals report to each other as a means of capturing roles, responsibilities and authority. Organizational structure also says something about the number or frequency of meetings, who attends those meetings, etc. Again, it may be that in formal terms, key decisions are taken a monthly management meetings but informally everyone acknowledges that these formal proceedings simply rubber stamp outcomes agreed in some other forum. Hence, the sixth and final category in the culture web is that of **Control Systems.** These are the mechanisms which formally and informally monitor behaviours and outcomes throughout the organization. Examples might include performance indicators, bonus systems, promotion procedures, etc. Again this highlights the interconnected nature of strategy since rewards are usually structured to reinforce the values of the firm and stories, rituals and routines often centre on conformance to, or rejection of, these formal structures and processes.

The culture web offers a rudimentary account of a sophisticated phenomenon. Culture may not be not uniform throughout the organization. One common variation is for the sales and commercial parts of an organization to feature one culture, whilst those in operations, engineering or delivery roles to share a different culture. Another common variation is hierarchical where senior staff and/or owners have one culture, whilst those in junior roles have another. Professional allegiances, length of service and organizational role may all produce cultural differentiation rather than uniformity. That said, there may be some common values which transcend such internal boundaries. Nevertheless, the culture web forms the basis of a useful discussion about the organization's circumstances despite its limitations. It also acts as a useful way into a discussion about an organization's cultural rules of thumb.

## Political dynamics amongst current, past and potential strategists

The third and final aspect of diagnosis is to consider the political power of the group of strategists or strategic influencers involved in the situation. In private sector firms it is likely that the owners and the managers of the organization will monitor performance. In some firms ownership and management coincide, whilst in other settings, owners and managers are completely separate. Consider the case of listed versus family owned businesses. In all commercial organizations, managers may hold shares in the business but the majority owners may be third parties, pension funds or individual investors. In the case of public organizations, the concept of ownership is more complex but the idea of sponsors, funders or regulators may still apply. Regardless of organization type and setting, the reality is that organizational performance will be assessed by a mix of shareholders (i.e., those with some form of ownership) and stakeholders (i.e., a wider grouping of those who take an interest in the organization). Some examples of stakeholders would definitely include owners and managers as already discussed. Other stakeholders might include employees, customers, suppliers, regulators, commentators, competitors, trade organizations, unions, etc. Very quickly it becomes apparent that an organization's stakeholders can be a very diverse group. There are ways to shorten this list. First, consider whether to deal with aggregate or disaggregate categories. It may make some sense to think of customers as a singular and unified group in some cases. You may have many thousands of customers, yet typically some customers are more important than others. In purely practical terms it makes for a shorter list of stakeholders if you use aggregate labels. Set against this simplicity is the observation that in reality we usually interact with individuals and small groups. Hence, disaggregating large groups by thinking about influence, importance or priority tends to draw attention to a smaller number of more significant stakeholders. Given our particular purpose, a second way to shorten the list of stakeholders is to focus solely on those who are, or could be, strategic influencers. Stakeholder mapping is one way of thinking about who to prioritize by contrasting how much power or influence individuals or groups have relative to their interest level.

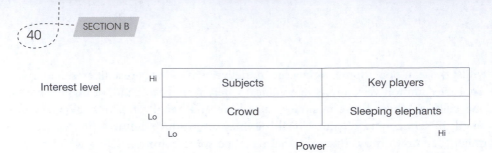

*Figure 4.3* **Stakeholder mapping**

As shown in Figure 4.3, stakeholder mapping usually works with four categories. Those individuals or groups with high power and high interest are the **key players** in the situation. These stakeholders can block or enable initiatives directly. The **sleeping elephants** are those who hold considerable power but are not currently interested in the situation. These stakeholders could be very influential should their interest be drawn to the particular issue or agenda under discussion. The **subjects** are those with low power but high interest because they are often subjected to the outcome of decisions by the key players or sleeping elephants. Finally, the **crowd** have low interest and low power yet such stakeholders are often large in number and could provide a real resource if mobilized effectively.

In terms of diagnosis, think of the most significant strategic influencers with particular emphasis on the key players and sleeping elephants. Now, for each strategic influencer that you identify, ask yourself how they might read the performance data that you have gathered. As performance indicators and stakeholder perceptions are brought into some sort of proximity what usually becomes clear is that seemingly objective performance data is read differently by different individuals. Some will see falling market share as a short-term blip. Others will see it as a crucial error in need of immediate attention, whilst others still will see it as unimportant because their attention is focused on profitability rather than scale. Understanding this political dynamic will help make sense of the situation that the organization faces. In turn, this helps see potential responses to that situation as either appropriate or inappropriate (we return to this topic in Chapter 9 when we discuss evaluation).

## Developing a diagnosis

Returning now to the circumstances Steve Jobs faced when he returned to Apple, it is possible to think about business issues, cultural issues and strategic influencers both independently and as a set. In performance terms Apple was struggling. Market share had collapsed to somewhere below 10%, staff had recently been laid off, arch-rival Microsoft had mimicked many of Apple's distinctive features with the recent release of Windows 3.0 and the firm had a product portfolio with a bewildering array of choices that even Jobs himself couldn't fathom.

If the performance data looked bad, there has been open conflict within the organization in terms of potential future direction. Issues such as whether to pursue the new handheld market with the Newton product range or to allow third parties to manufacture Apple compatible equipment under licence were contentious. When Jobs convinced Microsoft to invest $150M in Apple, at least three key stakeholder groups were involved: the senior management of Apple, their counterparts in Microsoft and regulators in the US government's Department of Justice who were concerned with Microsoft's dominance of the computing industry. Each of these strategic influencers read Apple's current performance differently.

Also, in cultural terms, Apple had a distinctive approach based on a history of innovation and design which developed "insanely great products". Shunning the mainstream personal computer market and controlling hardware, software, manufacturing and design such that each was fully integrated to the others and each was to Apple's own high standards had led to spectacular early successes. By the time Jobs was reappointed, the same culture had been responsible for Apple's gradual decline.

The strategy which Jobs deployed in the short term was to scale back the product range and strike a deal with Microsoft for investment. Whilst sensible in the context of a failing business, this strategy sat uncomfortably with Apple's staff and their loyal fan base. In all likelihood, this strategy in isolation would have led to the eventual failure, break-up or sale of Apple to a rival firm such as Sun Microsystems. However, Jobs saw these initial survival steps as part of a trajectory which would clearly focus Apple back on distinctive, user-friendly products with a strong design emphasis. He managed to marry short term survival measures with nurturing the underlying culture in Apple which focused on being different, being distinctive and more than anything else, being cool. Using precious resources from the reduction of the product range to invest in a smaller number of outstanding products, such as the new iMacs, helped Apple turn the corner. As revenues and confidence recovered, Apple moved from personal computing to music with the launch of iPod and iTunes. Subsequent moves into mobile telephony and tablet computing would make Apple the most valuable company on the planet by 2011 but none of this would have been possible without a sound diagnosis of the firm's original circumstances and a strategy developed to deal with those circumstances.

## Articulating your strategy

The first step when articulating a strategy is to identify the challenge which must be overcome by that strategy. When attempting to conduct diagnosis of this sort in a complex, multifaceted organizational setting it is possible to become overwhelmed the detail. The approach set out below focuses attention on three themes and offers a means of structuring your thinking about the situation you are facing. The three themes are:

**Business issues**: Select up to three prominent measures of sustainable performance in your organization. Typical examples might include turnover, margins, profit, staff satisfaction, staff turnover, product development lead-times, innovation measures, production yields, dividend payments, training, reviews and industry ranking or awards. Use the template to map performance over the last five years.

**Cultural issues**: Describe the organization in terms of its cultural rules of thumb. Typical examples might include incentive systems, structures, values, routines, norms, etc.

**Political issues**: Identify the key strategic influencers and map their interest in, and/or power over, the performance, behaviour, health and sustainability of your organization. Use the template to consider any cause and effect relationships between culture, performance and politics.

| | Year 1 | Year 2 | Year 3 | Year 4 | Year 5 |
|---|---|---|---|---|---|
| Measure 1 | | | | | |
| Measure 2 | | | | | |
| Measure n | | | | | |
| Business diagnostic | What do changes in key performance measures over time tell you about competitive positioning for the firm? Are there any product/ market/customer issues arising from this? Can you identify any business rules of thumb that underpin the organization's performance? | | | | |
| Cultural rule of thumb 1 | | | | | |
| Cultural rule of thumb 2 | | | | | |
| Cultural rule of thumb n | | | | | |
| Cultural diagnostic | Are there any obvious tensions between the business and cultural rules of thumb within the organization? | | | | |
| Strategic influencer 1 | | | | | |
| Strategic influencer 2 | | | | | |
| Strategic influencer n | | | | | |
| Political diagnostic | By mapping the strategic influencers we get a sense of the political dynamics of the firm's current situation. Ask how strategic influencer will react to the performance measures set out above. Who, if anyone, is generating political pressure for change? | | | | |
| Diagnostic summary | A one paragraph summary of the organization's current situation and the challenge it needs to overcome. | | | | |

Figure 4.4 shows an example of the diagnostic template based on Apple's circumstances in 1997–1998 when Steve Jobs returned as CEO

Having used the diagnostic template shown in Figure 4.3, you should now be able to articulate the challenge facing the organization in a single and simple statement such as the one below:

The challenge we face is... [insert a short diagnostic summary].

## Strategists at work: ABB

ABB is a major international engineering and technology firm. Formed in 1988 from the merger of Asea and a rival firm, Brown Boveri, it grew rapidly through an aggressive process of acquisitions. In five years ABB acquired 200 firms at a cost of some $5bn. When the founding CEO stepped down ABB struggled to keep up with the rate of growth. Eventually in 2005 Fred Kindle took on the role of CEO and made a clear diagnosis. ABB had been growing so rapidly that it had failed to stabilize.

| Apple | | | | | |
|---|---|---|---|---|---|
| **Business issues** | | | | | |
| | 1994 | 1995 | 1996 | 1997 | 1998 |
| Net sales | $9,189M | $11,062M | $9,833M | $7,081M | $5,941M |
| Net income | $310M | $424M | ($816M) | ($1,045M) | $309M |
| R&D expenditure | $564M | $614M | $604M | $485M | $303M |
| Business diagnostic | Falling sales and growing losses were not good news. Apple's 1997 annual report also acknowledges the worry of being marginalized by a declining share of the personal computer market. | | | | |
| **Cultural rules of thumb** | | | | | |
| 1 | We're design led | | | | |
| 2 | We think differently | | | | |
| 3 | We make insanely great products | | | | |
| Apple | | | | | |
| **Business issues** | | | | | |
| | 1994 | 1995 | 1996 | 1997 | 1998 |
| Cultural diagnostic | Apple's culture had drifted in the absence of Jobs. There is a fine line between being different and being irrelevant. A succession of so-so products and falling market share was in danger of making Apple just another computing firm. Confidence within the firm was at an all-time low. | | | | |
| **Political issues** | | | | | |
| Strategic influencer 1 | Steve jobs | | | | |
| Strategic influencer 2 | Apple board members | | | | |
| Strategic influencer 3 | Regulators | | | | |
| Political diagnostic | Shareholders were growing increasingly concerned in the face of deteriorating performance. The decision to rehire Steve Jobs was born of desperation. It would help reengage Apple's loyal but dwindling group of customers. Notably, Microsoft even extended financial support to Apple to help prevent it disappearing altogether. This surprising act was probably motivated by self-interest. Microsoft needed at least one competitor to help convince regulators that their monopoly position wasn't absolute. | | | | |
| Diagnostic summary | On his return to Apple, the diagnosis from Steve Jobs was clear. The firm's survival was under threat. Apple could not take on the then dominant Windows-Intel platform head on. Jobs cut expenditure on R&D, effected a rapid and radical reduction of the product range but critically, he then reintroduced design flair with the iMac range. Apple was smaller but profitable again. Jobs reconnected with Apple's culture of building "insanely great products" in the eyes of both colleagues and customers. With Apple stabilized, he waited for an opportunity to redefine the basis of competition. Almost four years passed before digital music gave Apple the opportunity to leverage its design flair in a new market. The iPod was launched, Apple switched from being a computing firm to a consumer electronics firm and the rest, as they say, is history. | | | | |

*Figure 4.4* **Diagnosis for Apple circa 1997**

Some of the acquisitions made before Kindle took office had become embroiled in asbestos claims and the organization was no longer the darling of the stock exchange. Kindle focused his attention on switching one crucial business rule of thumb when he stopped growth by acquisition and focused instead on organic growth. A detailed account of the ABB story is offered in Section D.

## Strategists at work: the running cases

**RMacI:**  Tell me how you set about defining the challenge that you were each facing in your organizations.

**Kate:**  Confused.com was trying to solve a perennial problem in the car insurance business. Nobody wants to deal with insurance, they all go "I hate it" but equally they all say "why do I have to spend so much time to get the cheapest price". So we were trying to reinvent an industry and as soon as I saw insurance companies embracing the internet and moving from information sites to online quoting I had a light bulb moment. I could suddenly see a way of giving customers what they wanted which was everybody's prices in one place. Perfect. Of course, because we were first to do it you couldn't really tell what your competitors were up to but our strategy was focused on trying to find a way to solve a genuine customer problem.

**Harry:**  Well I faced a very different kind of problem and I started with the realization that there had been successive failures to improve health. People assumed that there were simple explanations for inequality in health. Poor people smoked more, which they do; poor people eat more fatty food, which perhaps they do; and the behaviours that predicted health were commoner amongst poor people; therefore, all we had to do was change behaviour. That was patent nonsense. Whenever you began to unravel what the problem was, whenever you went beyond just assuming the simple and simplistic explanations, you began to see that it was more complicated. What we found was that instead of the caricature of the Scots being an unhealthy race we found that Scots, up until a few decades ago, were as healthy as anywhere in Europe. Then, we began to see a widening in inequality between rich and poor and the cause of that widening was more people dying prematurely from things like drug abuse and alcohol and so on. So, it was a very particular set of explanations that had their roots in psychological and social drivers. So our challenge was to improve the health of the people of Scotland in ways that didn't just engage the healthcare service but which began to join up social care, education, criminal justice, the fire service and basically anyone else in the public services that impacted on peoples' quality of life.

**DMacL:**  And what about Pointer, Sandy?

**Sandy:**  Pointer had always thought of itself as a security business and for many years the security industry existed on its own island, essentially looked after by its own dedicated suppliers providing it with specialist recording units, specialist cameras, specialist monitors. Our world began to change when non-security people began to realize that you can stick a webcam on a network and join everything up. So what has been happening is that the security industry was finally been drawn into the world of IT and it was moving from an analogue environment to a digital one to where devices were being attached to networks. It has happened in many other trades but now it was happening to ours and we faced a challenge to either move with the times or go the way of the dinosaurs.

*RMacI:* So that was your challenge, to not go extinct?

*Sandy:* Well that and the fact that if you're an optimist there was a potential for some land grab to be had as well.

## Dos and don'ts

Before working on your strategy, diagnose the organization's current circumstances. This will involve gathering a mix of empirical evidence and anecdotal opinion. The diagnostic template (Figure 4.3) helps structure these data.

### Do

1 Source facts and figures over a reasonable time frame (we suggest five years).
2 Share these facts and figures with colleagues and gauge their reaction.
3 Crystallize your diagnosis in a few sentences...what is the headline message here?

### Don't

1 Base your diagnosis purely on opinion and anecdote...what do the facts say?
2 Exclude your competitors. Gather similar performance data for both current and potential competitors to see how your organization is doing in both absolute and relative terms.

## Who to read?

**Ian Mitroff** trained originally as an engineer before moving on to a wide-ranging academic career that drew insights from a range of different disciplines. Now an emeritus professor at UCLA Berkley, Mitroff says that during his earlier career he "realized that he loved engineering but grew not to love engineers" and in his later career believed that "there are two types of people in the world; people who think there are two types of people and people who don't". His early contributions to the field of problem formulation can be traced back to the 1980s and his recent book outputs include "Dirty Rotten Strategies" (2009) and a number of other approaches to dealing with messy situations.

**Jerome Groopman** is a professor at the Harvard Medical School and his book "How Doctors Think" considers the advantages and disadvantages of structured diagnostic processes such as those used to train doctors. His eloquent account of diagnosis emphasizes the importance of questioning, listening, observing and daring to think differently.

# CHAPTER 5

# Strategic Intent

Strategy is often associated with the idea of securing a significant, long-term objective. As described in Chapter 2, this is at least partly explained by tracing the roots of organizational strategy back to military strategy. Whilst victory in a military context is a reasonably singular objective, organizations often need to deliver complex, multi-dimensional objectives to a diverse range of stakeholders. For this reason, the diagnostic process set out in Chapter 4 is a sensible precursor to establishing clarity on strategic intent.

Whilst acknowledging that absolute clarity may be unattainable, our ideal is that organizations should be clear about *what* exactly is to be achieved and that this should be linked to a diagnosis of the situation in which the organization finds itself. Our own view is that strategy should be developed in response to a particular challenge yet we know that organizations may develop strategy because a particular set of timings are in place for example when the five year strategy is about to expire, or through habit. Strategy developed through habit or mimicry is rarely effective. Instead, we recommend an approach which starts by connecting intent to diagnosis. This starts by addressing three related questions which flow directly from the previous chapter:

1 What do you want to achieve in response to the challenges and opportunities that you face?
2 Within what time frame will your achievement(s) be delivered?
3 How will the achievement of your intent affect the organization? for example will you be market leader, the most profitable or some similar relative positioning?

## The vision thing and other related concepts

In the lead-up to the 1988 Presidential election, George Bush is reported to have responded to a suggestion that he spend a few days thinking through plans for his campaign by saying "Oh, the vision thing". For us, intent sits in a conceptual space which also includes mission statements, visions, values and other related terms.

Our view is quite simple. We think strategic intent is a more useful concept than these more nebulous terms because it tends to promote focused, purposeful, collective action. We recognize, that vision and related concepts have their place in certain circumstances. In particular, a compelling vision in the hands of a genuinely skilled leader can help win hearts and minds over to a picture of a brighter future. Nevertheless, our experience suggests that they are prone to difficulty. We have encountered too many situations where visions are so concerned with what the leader would like the organization to "be" that no one is quite sure about what to "do" in order to get there. Likewise, mission statements that are either so orthodox and dull as to be meaningless (e.g. we know of one well-known bank which aimed "to be a professional provider of high quality financial services"), so complicated as to be completely beyond recall, or so vague as to be unlikely to inform any decision. Perhaps more controversially, we are sceptical of organizations who institute "values programs" with the belief that those working within the organization will straight-forwardly adopt the requisite values. A value is less something that one can choose to have (or not have) and more something that one has to have in order to make choices in the first place. As such, values rarely originate in corporate programs. We return to the relationship between strategic change, values and business logic in Section C; for the time-being we repeat simply that in our experience, the best way to approach the issue of strategic purpose and collective will is via the concept of strategic intent.

## "Kill Darius"

Military history is littered with stories of great victories and unexpected defeats. One example in particular shows the impact that strategists have on the delivery of intent. Whilst accounts of Alexander the Great's victory over the Persian emperor Darius vary markedly, they appear to agree on a couple of key factors – leadership and a highly focussed strategic intent.

In November of the year 333 BC, Alexander and his generals were engrossed in a pensive discussion of a very real and immediate danger. Their army of around 50,000 men had finally come face to face with the vast army of Darius of Persia. The Persians had more and better resources, including a much larger cavalry. The odds of victory were, to say the least, not in Alexander's favour. In diagnostic terms, they were outnumbered and under-resourced. A strategy that dealt with the particular challenges they faced was their only hope.

What could be done? What advantages did, or could, they have? Alexander's forces were relatively small in number, but they were therefore more nimble. They were also battle hardened as a result of their young leader's ambitious pursuit of empire and success. Alexander's army broke the mould – it was organized and professional, the prototype for subsequent armies through to Napoleonic times. It employed new tactics and weaponry, rejecting the largely defensive tactics of many armies includ-ing the Persians who they now faced. Alexander's army often advanced aggressively on enemy lines using sophisticated and deadly weaponry. When Darius's cavalry charged, Alexander's reinforcements to his left flank managed to repel the charge whilst his own legendary phalanx of infantry attempted to puncture Darius's army's left flank. Alexander had instructed his troops to remember their discipline, advance in silence and then let out a mighty, terrifying roar. He is noted as one of the last of the great generals to lead his men from the front. He led his cavalry towards Darius's chariot in a direct assault, realizing that if the enemy king was toppled, his army of conscripts would collapse and flee. He halted this process to assist his infantry phalanx which has become surrounded by the enemy and impeded by rough ground. Achieving this, all of his men were now able to resume the advance – on Darius. Next, Alexander's men, without exception, joined in a single drumming chorus:

"Kill Darius"
"Kill Darius"
"Kill Darius"

Casualties were inevitable but as Alexander's lead soldiers were slain, others took their place and they maintained formation. Even if those in Alexander's phalanx continued at its current rate, Darius could see that it was only a matter of minutes until they would reach him.

Suddenly the perceived odds changed. Whilst Darius still commanded a much larger force, his army contained mercenaries and men from a vast number of conquered tribes. Different languages and different cultures produced differing levels of commitment to the cause. Darius now saw a highly personalized risk as 50,000 soldiers pursued him as an individual. He retreated from the battlefield for his own safety but panic and disintegration quickly spread through his own forces. Understandably, many of Darius's men fled. Those who didn't paid the price. Alexander won a victory, which would be retold both in the immediate aftermath and in the centuries that followed.

Running a modern organization is not directly analogous to commanding an army in 333 BC. And, of course, the brutality of war presents an unappealing context. Nevertheless, as a narrative laced with some poetic licence, key aspects of good strategy shine through this account. Ingenuity, innovation, using scarce resources and capabilities to best effect, capitalizing on anything the environment had to offer in pursuit of success. But perhaps most of all, the message that comes through loudest and most clearly from this example relates to the power of leadership and a focused and united strategic intent – kill Darius. There are even parallels in the modern business era. The then fledgling Japanese firm Fuji Film are alleged to have used "Kill Kodak" as a statement of intent. It may not solely be because of the actions of Fuji Film but Eastman Kodak filed for bankruptcy in 2012.

## Strategic intent in business

Most of us recognize the hallmarks of a focused strategic intent in business. Think Easyjet or Ryanair both of whom might appear to have focused their intent not simply on corporate goals but on redefining an industry. Indeed one might say the same of many of the newer players in any given industry. In 2012 internet streaming service Netflix began making its own content, setting aside a $300M budget for original programming, Chief Content Officer Ted Sarandos was clear, "our goal is to become HBO faster than HBO can become us." Amazon, with its early "get big fast" philosophy (Management Today, 2012) in which intent clearly prioritized growth over profitability, is another prime example of focused strategic intent. But there are more conventional examples. Intel's desire to get a chip inside every personal computer heralded phenomenal growth for the firm. UK supermarket giant Tesco's obvious intent to overtake all of its competitors and dominate the market saw them develop from a somewhat downmarket chain of smaller stores to the undisputed leader in the course of a decade or two.

It doesn't always work as planned. British Petroleum's (BP's) desire to move "Beyond Petroleum" would appear to have faltered. But perhaps this is simply a case of intent "on the move". In Chapter 1, we drew attention to the subtle differences between the notion of intent and the more processual orientation of behaving intentionally. Intent can, and perhaps, should be allowed to evolve. It shouldn't hang like an albatross around the neck. In our view, a dynamic and processual sense of intent is far superior to no sense of intent at all. BP is still a successful company despite difficulties in moving beyond petroleum and the reputational damage caused by the Deepwater Horizon leak of 2010.

## A sense of purpose

Our experience suggests that the most powerful statements of intent are set within some deeper sense of purpose, which captures the "why" of the organization. With most successful organizations it is reasonably easy to describe what the organization does. Ryan Air is in the low-cost flight business. Tesco is a supermarket. Amazon is an internet retailer. Yet scratch beneath the surface and there may also be a deeper purpose at play. Amazon holds an impressive array of data about customers. The ability to recommend products based on the algorithm "people who bought this also bought..." allows Amazon to cross-sell. The business also presents consumers with detailed product reviews generated by previous customers. If you're considering buying anything from a lawn mower to camera, Amazon is likely to be able to give you recent and detailed accounts of what the product is actually like to live with. As well as the obvious observation that it is an internet retailer, Amazon could equally argue that it acts as an information provider, creating a space in which customers and buyers can interact. In this deeper sense, Amazon is in the trust business and the firm's aim to be the "Earth's most customer-centric organization"[1] in the world is a significant part of this hidden purpose. Amazon sells its skill in designing and managing web-sites to third parties. It would be reasonably easy to create another internet retailing site, but it would be a much larger challenge to take Amazon on in the trust business. Considered in purely economic terms, the firm may respond to recent public scrutiny of its corporation tax payments to the UK government as a matter of tax efficiency. However, in terms of its aspirations to be seen as a trusted friend to consumers, there may be more at stake than simply the monies eventually paid to Her Majesty's Revenue and Customs.

A similar line of thinking about the deeper, less obvious purpose behind a firm's strategy could be applied to Tesco, Ryan Air or a host of other firms. Articulating the purpose behind your own organization is a helpful first step in shaping a statement of intent. For example, it could shed new light on decisions which might otherwise seem strange. Ryan Air periodically presents itself as a "no fares" airline emphasizing its role in economic development and tourism for regional airports. Tesco may use data from its customer loyalty scheme (the Tesco Clubcard) to cross-sell mobile telephony, financial services and other product offerings of its own, or of partner organizations. John Kay argues that all complex goals are best approached indirectly. Individuals who pursue something that they are passionate about tend to be happy, whilst those who pursue happiness directly tend not to achieve their aim. Similarly, organizations which pursue some purpose beyond immediate financial outcomes, tend to perform well in economic terms over the longer term. Kay calls this concept **obliquity** (2011) and suggests a paradoxical relationship between what we strive to achieve and the means of its achievement. Michael Porter's recent interest in the development of shared value is driven by the same observation that a focus on short term financial outcomes produces poorer results in the longer term (Porter and Kramer, 2011).

> **Obliquity:** John Kay's counter-intuitive message is that complex goals are best approached in an oblique manner i.e. indirectly.

## Specifying intent

In light of the suggestion that we should approach goals indirectly, crafting a statement of intent might seem problematic. On one level, our strategy cycle model (see Chapter 1) accounts for this by acknowledging the iterative nature of the process and we will revisit this problematic issue in Section C. In the meantime, we recognize that producing a statement of strategic intent can be challenging, particularly for those new to an organization. It is not untypical to feel that you cannot and perhaps should not be specifying intent until you have become familiar with some of the key dimensions of your organization and its environment. However, our strategy cycle opens with the diagnosis of a challenge (see Chapter 4) and the specification of intent. Our experience has been that these form a useful platform from which to scan the environment and thereafter there is an iterative process at play where what you are looking for informs your ability to narrow your search.

As with any complex and unstructured task, the very act of writing something down can itself be difficult. Richard Rumelt argues that the bullet point format afforded by modern word processing and presentation software has produced a tendency to compartmentalize and decompose issues. His view is that asking a group to set aside bullet points and write coherently produces a step change. "Having to link your thoughts, giving reasons and qualifications makes you a more careful thinker" (Rumelt, 2007).

These may be just some of the reasons that we experience a sense of writer's block when it comes to intent. We know at the outset that attempting to frame a simple unifying statement of intent may engage some whilst alienating others. Nevertheless, crafting a first iteration of a statement of intent is part of an on-going process of shaping our intentions. Diversity is, of course, essential to a healthy ecosystem but clarity of purpose is vital to good strategy. The political debate which flows from an attempt to craft intent could, if handled skillfully, be the very exchanges that forge a joint commitment, a fellowship and a company. Good leadership does not shrink back from this challenge. It keeps going until a "critical mass" of people heading in roughly the same direction has been established.

There is the nagging worry that something beyond our control changes in ways which render our original intent meaningless. We worked with a firm in the food industry that, having just framed intent around growth in its meat products business, had suddenly to contend with the impact of the Bovine spongiform encephalopathy (BSE)[2] crisis in the UK. Rather than giving up, they redeveloped their strategic intent, changed direction and went on to become the largest player in their national markets. Intent shifts and evolves like a bird in flight. The observation that intent evolves should not be read as an invitation to adopt an unintentional stance.

The second challenge of writing a specific statement of intent is that in many ways it requires you to have done some prior work. For example, in order to know that the magnitude of the cost reduction required is 35% within two years, or that generating 50% increase in turnover over a five year period from adjacent geographical territories, is sensible, those involved would probably have done some work on the problem beforehand. Whilst this is true, the fact of the matter is that the formation of strategic intent is an on-going cyclical and iterative, process. You have to start somewhere. We advocate an initial statement that by its very nature casts light on areas where work will be needed to clarify and focus things further (much of which will be covered in subsequent chapters).

In order to structure a reasonably succinct statement of intent, we suggest that there are four themes to consider. These are some *desired outcome* which is amenable to calibration and measurement; the internal *resources, capabilities or processes* that are likely to be involved; an indication of some aspect of the *external context* that you are addressing, typically in the form of a potentially beneficial development or hazard and the *time frame* within which the objective should be reached. These four key components can be set out in the form WXYZ as shown in Figure 5.1 below.

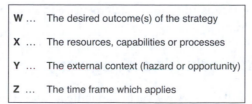

**W** ...   The desired outcome(s) of the strategy

**X** ...   The resources, capabilities or processes

**Y** ...   The external context (hazard or opportunity)

**Z** ...   The time frame which applies

*Figure 5.1* **Articulating strategic intent using WXYZ**

Our suggestion is that a statement of intent using this approach should run to no more than fifty words. Though this is not cast in stone, we find it a useful upper target. In a firm which manufactured vacuum cleaners, these four themes were specified as $W$ = a 35% reduction in costs within a time frame ($Z$) of two years. The external opportunity ($Y$) was the growing trend to outsource manufacturing to economies with lower wage costs and the capabilities involved ($X$) were training and quality assurance. Hence, the statement of intent became

> We aim to reduce total costs by **35%** within **two years**. To achieve this we will exploit our **ability to train new staff** to establish a new manufacturing facility in **Eastern Europe** working to our established QA processes.

Since specifying intent is an iterative process, it is easy to see how the pieces of such a statement might fall into place over time. Indeed Chapters 6 and 7 will offer insights on specifying opportunities in the external environment and organizational resources respectively. Even so, it is not always possible to tie down all themes components at the outset. Paradoxically, this statement of intent is both the beginning and end of the strategy process. A first iteration, though partial and perhaps inaccurate, plays an important part in getting the process started. A more settled and final version plays an important part in allowing those involved to agree that objectives are close to being met and the process can begin again.

## Articulating your strategy

It should be possible to specify intent in one of two ways, as set out below.

1   We will achieve [intent statement] by [timeframe or deadline].

The intent statement embedded above may be a simple and measurable (such as a particular level of market share), more abstract (such as being seen as a market leader) or indirect (such as a proximate focus on innovation which is intended to deliver higher margins in the medium term). Regardless of the type of strategic intent specified, you can further elaborate this statement of strategic intent using the strategic intent format that is set out in Figure 5.1 above. Subsequent chapters will help refine these early attempts to specify intent. However, even at this early stage, it is possible to begin to craft a rudimentary articulation of strategy by linking a statement of intent with the diagnosis of the challenge facing the organization from Chapter 4.

2   The challenge we face is [diagnostic statement] and our strategy is to achieve [intent] by [timeframe].

## Strategists at work: nine dragons

Zhang Yin is queen of all she surveys, yet her appetite is not yet sated. As the founder of Nine Dragons Paper, she has a fortune estimated at over $3bn. She was the first woman to top China's annual rich-list and she runs a firm which has become the world's largest recovered paper manufacturer. Her original idea was simple but effective. The US was producing large volumes of waste paper but had no particular plans for dealing with it. Nine Dragons imported waste to China and processed it to produce paper-based products from the recycled material. The business model meant that the firm got paid twice. Once to take the material away, and a second time when it sold the newly recycled end products. Zhang Yin had set out with the clear intent to become "the world's largest and leading recycled based paper manufacturer".[3] When she entered the market with machinery that had quadruple the capacity of rival firms and she continued with this aggressive approach. Profits were reinvested in larger and more efficient recycling facilities and she was soon the dominant player. Having achieved the title of "queen of trash" in the popular press, Zhang is already thinking of the next objective. A glimpse of her latest statement of intent came in a rare public statement where she said, "someday I'd like to be known as the queen of containerboards". An extended account of Nine Dragons Paper is offered in Case 4 in Section D.

## Strategists at work in the running cases

*RMacI:*  Turning our attention to strategic intent, I want to hear how you framed objectives and goals in your own organizations. Harry, we've heard your argument that Scotland's problem wasn't poor health in general but rather, the health of the poor in particular. So, how do you translate this into a strategic intent?

*Harry:*  As Chief Medical Officer, I was in a privileged position and I was trying to reach out to other parts of the government beyond just health because I felt that health is just one emergent outcome from the way society organizes itself. Other emergent outcomes are low crime rate, high educational attainment rate, fit and independent elderly people, all of these things that you would want to happen in a society will come when we get the interrelationships right. So, to be blunt, if you want to recruit the Justice Ministry in a country you point to the fact that what you're trying to do to improve health will also improve offending behaviour. For me, it wasn't just about improving health, I am in no doubt that if we get this right we will be able to close prisons.

*DMacL:*  Not quite what you might expect to hear but, it counts as intent certainly.

*Kate:*  For us, the first thing with Confused.com was to get the funding in place to allow us to launch this new business. I think if you go back and look at the early documents we presented to the Board (of Admiral Insurance) our intent was really expressed in financial terms. What I said to them was that we wanted to be a company worth four billion in ten years and in some ways, you know, it was just a number that came out of nothing. But, it did at least make it clear: "look, this can be a very valuable asset to the firm".

*DMacL:*  What about Pointer?

*Sandy:*  We'd been talking about IP for five or six years. So, it wasn't a surprise that it was coming. We had already partnered with a major IT company, Cisco, in their initial foray into the marketplace and so that, I guess was our statement of intent both externally and internally within the business. This is going to happen. We're no longer a security business, we're going to get on board with the world of IT and be at the front of that wave, not under it.

## Do's and don'ts

Working to articulate a statement of intent for your organization can be challenging. We've found that good strategists understand their own strategic management style and those of their colleagues. This knowledge can be used to engage others in what can be a lengthy set of negotiations about trade-offs between both the logical and cultural aspects of organization. Convincing others that you have a sound diagnosis of the organization's current situation and that you can explain how key internal decisions and external events have led to that situation will help. The strategy cycle suggests that you should use conversations with colleagues as an opportunity to build a plausible and compelling version of the organization's story so far. Identify key characters, an overarching plotline and link events to a pressing problem in the eyes of key stakeholders.

### Do

1  Write it down in no more than 50 words.
2  Link your statement of intent to the opportunities, problems and challenges highlighted in your diagnosis.
3  Think about capabilities, or gaps therein, when specifying what you are trying to achieve.
4  Engage others and work iteratively to gradually refine your statement of intent.
5  Stretch rather than daunt those on whom implementation depends.

### Don't

1  Create verbiage. Try to be clear, precise by avoiding fluffy or ambiguous phrases.
2  Assume that other stakeholders will see the same problem that you see.
3  Focus solely on numeric targets. Think about the wider characteristics of your organization as it delivers on specific and measurable targets.

## Who to read

**John Kay's** work on objectives and aspirations is instructive and insightful. He teases apart two things which are often interwoven, outcome measures and processes by which these are delivered. Although not strictly a strategy text, his book "Obliquity" is worth reading as is **Richard Rumelt's** "Good Strategy, Bad Strategy" because it also gives an account of what he calls "proximate objectives".

# Trends and Opportunities

F ew strategists working in public, private or third sector organizations would describe their operating environment as stable. Indeed, we hear so often that today's operating environment is changing faster than ever before that the assertion is rarely questioned. The internet revolution of the last 15 years or so has further compounded pre-existing trend towards the globalization of trade. Global brands, supported by global supply chains mean that consumers can find Starbucks, McDonalds, Apple and many other providers wherever their travels take them. Yet the industrial revolution changed society in ways which could be viewed as at least as significant as anything that has happened in the new millennium. Setting aside the scale of change that we are living through, the pace of change has undeniably quickened. Scottish inventor John Logie Baird gave the first public demonstrations of his rudimentary television in 1926 it was heralded as a scientific marvel, but the transition to mass market status occurred slowly and incrementally. The British Broadcasting Corporation launched a national television service in 1932 just six years after Logie Baird's breakthrough. Yet a further 13 years passed before television reached an audience of 50 million viewers. When Google+ was launched in 2011 as a competitor to Facebook, the service achieved an audience of 50 million users within three months.

The American academic Richard D'Aveni describes dynamic industries, such as the provision of social media services, as hyper-competitive (1994) in the sense that innovations and competitive moves occur with such frequency that any advantage is only temporary. Indeed, such fast moving and fluid conditions led Gary Hamel to conclude that competition is no longer between products and services but between business models and strategies. From airlines to music, new approaches and new competitors have begun to appear as technology leads whole industries to **converge**.

**Convergence** is the process by which the boundaries between previously separate industries begin to erode. One such example is timekeeping. In order to accurately track time watchmakers invested in precision engineering to make ever smaller and more reliable mechanical devices. The use of quartz produced an order of magnitude improvement over the best mechanical timepieces and introduced a range of new competitors. More recent innovations have included time pieces which can syncrhonize with radio transmissions from the atomic clock in Greenwich. When convergence of this sort occurs, both the basis and the boundaries of competition shift. It is therefore vital to interpret and exploit the early signals of such changes in order to either defend against them or exploit the momentum that they provide. A recent survey suggests that two-thirds of executives in the Swiss watch industry don't see smart-watches as a threat. As computing, mobile telephony and consumer electronics converge individual firms are having to make assumptions about the shape of their industry and the identity of their competitors.

In the previous chapter, we considered the ways in which strategists can frame strategic intent. For the moment we will assume a simple and linear transition from establishing intent to an examination of the operating environment. The ideal outcome in such a transition would be to match internal resources to opportunities spotted in the changing operating environment (i.e., factors external to the business). If this is achieved early, it confers significant advantage over current or potential competitors. One way to think of the strategist's role then is to consider the relationship between ends, means and conditions. With some particular end in mind, strategists are able to assess the means at their disposal and the conditions in, or through, which they are likely to be operating. In this chapter we introduce some simple approaches to assessing what the operating environment may have in store. Critically, this requires that we develop not only a view of both the nature and timing of changes that may occur but also, that we are able to tap into external sources of energy and opportunity in order to propel us towards our desired outcomes.

Predicting the future is fraught with dangers and history offers salutary warnings. Daimler once predicted a very limited market for cars because they felt that there were very few trained chauffeurs. IBM predicted a restricted market for what were at that point, hugely expensive and prototype computers. On perfecting the telephone, Alexander Graham Bell imagined that there would eventually be one phone in every major city. With hindsight, these predictions look laughable yet they were made on the basis of careful consideration of the available data filtered through the lens of prevalent ways of seeing the world. The signs of impending crises or huge new opportunities are usually hidden in plain sight.

Before proceeding, there are two observations which are worth making. First, for many strategy scholars the starting point for the whole strategy journey would be a scan of the external environment. Read in isolation, this chapter suggests a different starting point in that we advocate moving from a diagnosis of the challenges presented by the organization's present circumstances (Chapter 4), which leads to an emergent statement of strategic intent (Chapter 5) before an assessment of the external environment begins. Second, read in the context of our wider approach, the strategy cycle readily acknowledges that the assumption of a simple and linear transition from intent to reviewing opportunities and threats in the environment brings with it limitations. In reality, strategic intent, the search for opportunities in the environment and an assessment of available resources interact in a messier, more iterative way, than is implied in this chapter alone. We may not know what we're looking for; predicting the future becomes progressively more fraught the further ahead one looks; absolute clarity is unattainable even with a relatively short time horizon in mind; what we perceive in the operating environment is likely to shape our goal. We return to this messier reality when setting out a fuller account of the strategy cycle in Chapter 11. In the meantime, we are convinced that a pragmatic approach implies that the difficulty associated with reading the future should not be allowed to deter us from trying to build better strategy. Hence, our ideal is that strategists are clear about the forecasts they are making, what guesses they are taking (and with what risks) to maximize the chances that everyone is heading in the same direction in pursuit of growth or in the face of external threats.

> **The Chicken-Egg Problem.** Some of the world's greatest minds have been troubled by the question, which came first, the chicken or the egg? Both are in a circular relationship with each other and yet the challenge remains that you have to start somewhere. In our context, this problem manifests itself as the relationship between an understanding of the external environment and clarity over what you are trying to achieve. The strategy cycle foregrounds the need to know what you are looking for, at least initially.

As a starting point then, we would suggest that it is worth examining the changing environment to try to develop a shared response to a set of simple questions. Of the external developments which we can see, which are you going to target as opportunities given the nature of your strategic intent? William Cohen draws attention to the fact that the opportunities and threats facing an organization always outweigh the resources available to respond (2006). Thus strategy inevitably involves prioritizing. Related to the search for attractive opportunities is the more pointed question of defending yourself against potential threats. In both cases, timing matters. The energy crisis means that there is broad consensus on the need for car manufacturers to switch from the internal combustion engine to some greener technology. UK entrepreneur Sir Clive Sinclair introduced the C5 as an electric vehicle in 1985 and was probably right in his assessment of a market opportunity but wrong in the timing of his product launch. Had the C5 been introduced today it may have succeeded. Dealing with trends too early is just as dangerous as dealing with them too late.

## Working with trends

Just as was the case with intent, most of us recognize the hallmarks of a foresight in business. Think again of the way in which new entrants such as Ryanair or Amazon redefined the industries in which they participated. This didn't happen in a vacuum.

Visionary drive on the part of key individuals plays a part but equally, incumbent firms as well as other potential players had access to the same signs of opportunity emerging in the broader environment. Many of today's successful firms spotted, exploited and perhaps contributed to trends such as the development of computers, e-mail and the internet; growing numbers of middle class consumers in emerging markets, increased business and holiday driven by low cost travel to regional airports, increased demand for higher education, etc. Likewise, many formerly successful firms missed the transition from one business model to another and found themselves marginalized from a seemingly dominant position. Amazon's early "get big fast" philosophy (Management Today, 2012) played into the explosion of internet usage. Jeff Bezos claims that the trigger point for Amazon was his observation of internet usage growing at 2300% per annum. Similar spectacular growth is now occurring in smartphone usage around the world. In a related industry, Intel's desire to get a chip inside every personal computer was partly predicated on what the company's strategists foresaw in the art of the possible with increasing miniaturization and cost reduction in electronic chips.

One of the most common ways of structuring an assessment is to use Political, Economic, Social and Technological changes (**PEST**) analysis (see Figure 6.1).

> **PEST** is an approach commonly used to study operating environments. It stands for **P**olitical, **E**conomic, **S**ocial and **T**echnological changes. Francis Aguilar (1967) was one of the first to refer to this model in his book "Scanning the Business Environment" though he referred to it as ETPS.

| Political trends, for example: | Economic trends, for example: |
|---|---|
| ➢ Stability<br>  ➢ Local<br>  ➢ National<br>  ➢ Alliance (e.g. EU)<br>➢ Taxation policy<br>➢ Foreign trade regulations<br>➢ Regulatory environment<br>  ➢ Ownership<br>➢ Employment law | ➢ Business cycle for example growth or recession<br>➢ GDP trends<br>➢ Interest rates<br>➢ Money supply<br>➢ Inflation<br>➢ Unemployment levels<br>➢ Average incomes<br>➢ Property prices |
| Social trends, for example: | Technological trends, for example: |
| ➢ Demographics<br>➢ Income distribution<br>➢ Social mobility and networking<br>➢ Values and norms<br>➢ Work and leisure patterns<br>➢ Consumer preferences<br>➢ Levels of education | ➢ R&D investment<br>  ➢ Governmental<br>  ➢ Firm level<br>➢ Patents rates<br>➢ Product introduction rates<br>➢ Adoption rates<br>➢ Scientific breakthroughs<br>➢ Rates of obsolescence<br>➢ Convergence |

*Figure 6.1* **PEST analysis**

Using PEST, introduces some structure to an otherwise overwhelming range of external factors. The lists given in Figure 6.1 are not exhaustive but give some indication of common themes which merit attention. Gathering and assessing data about these or other trends is a necessary pre-condition to developing deep insights about where your organization could and should head. Gathering data is sometimes straightforward. Take healthcare as one example. When trying to examine future demand patterns, there are reasonably robust data sources that can be tracked such as birth rates. In some countries, children are given vaccinations for diseases like polio or measles at specific ages. Therefore, if one knows the number of births in a given year, it should theoretically be straightforward to predict the number of vaccinations required for children of a particular age group at a specific future date. Of course, other factors confound such precision. Political changes might dictate that formerly free vaccinations are charged for, or vice versa. Economic changes might drive migration into or out of particular geographies as countries and industries decline or prosper. Social changes might alter parental willingness to engage with vaccination programmes, as happened in the UK with measles, mumps and rubella (MMR) vaccination[1]. Technological changes might lead to new treatments and delivery methods. Thus, accurate prediction becomes problematic because the individual components of a PEST analysis can also interact to generate new and unexpected dynamics. PEST analysis is therefore unlikely to generate new insights if undertaken as an exercise in generating lengthy lists but there are things, which can be done to improve the quality of the insights that PEST can generate.

Where data are available, it is important to be as thorough and objective as possible but it is worth remembering that publicly available data will also be visible to your competitors. Whilst they may be privy to the same observations they may not be able to infer the same quality of insight from the data. Where data is limited it may also be worth looking for proxy data that is, data about something else from which you can indirectly observe a trend that is of interest. For example, if you cannot gather on the scale of the market for a new product or service it may be possible to infer valuable insights from measurements of related or complementary services. The sale of electric vehicles and the number of available charging stations are likely correlated in some way. Data on one may serve as a useful proxy for data on the other, though this is an assumption that would warrant careful justification.

Two further issues arise when studying changes in the operating environment using a technique like PEST. First, it is helpful to consider not just the magnitude of any change observed but also the rate at which it is occurring. Seemingly modest changes become more interesting when they are growing or shrinking rapidly. A segment of the market which is doubling every year will become significant quickly, even from a very low starting point. The second issue to note is that the individual components of a PEST analysis interact to reinforce each other, as was the case with the MMR vaccination example used earlier. Despite its limitations, PEST analysis represents a useful first step in trying to read the implications of longer-term changes in the broad business environment. Just as with weather forecasting, the further ahead one looks the harder it is to be precise. Yet these broad changes will shape the behaviour of customers, competitors, suppliers or other stakeholders over the medium to long term. These stakeholders occupy what we term the operating environment. The American academic Mary Coulter suggests, that the process of scanning and evaluating an organization's various external sectors to determine positive and negative trends that could impact organizational performance is how strategists determine the opportunities and threats, which face their organization (2009: 66). In practical terms then, we suggest a three-stage process. First, work through each of the categories in Figure 6.1 to produce a preliminary list of factors which may be changing. Second, revisit this initial analysis and assess the available data. This should help with calibration and will make your insights more robust since it is one thing to say "more and more customers are choosing this service" and another to note that "demand for this service is predicted to grow at 20% per annum for the next ten years". The third and final stage in developing insight from a PEST analysis is to work through the list one last time giving each item a score of high medium or low in terms of the impact it could have on your business, then in terms of the probability of them actually happening. Your attention should be focused on those issues which appear to be high impact, high probability and you can make a note of these using the template in Figure 6.2.

The left hand column of Figure 6.2 should contain a limited number of important and impactful trends that you have gleaned from a careful analysis of the operating environment. The right hand column then takes these observations and translates them into actions. It is important to think about the dynamics and timing of any moves, investments, changes that your organization must make since we have already noted that moving too early, or too late is unwise.

In some senses PEST analysis is analogous to the process of weather forecasting. Long-term changes such as, those prompted by climate change must be translated into decisions about when and how to respond. Sailors are often said to "keep a weather eye" on things because it is good practice to look over the upwind side of the boat in order to glimpse what the weather is likely to deliver next. Microsoft, Dell and other firms in the personal computing industry have been able to see market data that suggest change in their industry. By 2011, smartphone sales had outstripped personal computer sales and tablet devices quickly followed suit. The kind of structured approach to PEST analysis described offer strategists some early warning signals about such "upwind" developments. Nevertheless, good sailors cannot predict the weather, far less control it. The ability to "see what's coming" and perhaps

| From PEST analysis: | Given our strategic intent: |
|---|---|
| Trends in the operating environment | Implied strategic moves |
| 1. | 1. |
| 2. | 2. |
| 3. | 3. |

*Figure 6.2*   The PEST template

more critically, "when it's coming" is a help, not a guarantee. Better forward visibility creates time to prepare for changes. For sailors, engaged in competitive racing, the ability to read the weather can be more influential than the boat and handling when it comes to winning. For organizational strategists it can make the difference between exploiting the energy available from some new development in the environment and being swept away by them.[2]

## Working with uncertainty

Whilst PEST analysis is intended to extract insights from observable and long-term trends in the operating environment, some issues are not amenable to this way of thinking. Hence, alongside observable trends, a second aspect of the operating environment relates to uncertainties where strategists have no way of judging which way the dice will fall. Issues such as an election result, a policy change, which technology standard will be adopted or regulatory changes are specific uncertainties rather than long-term trends. The response to such specific uncertainties is neither to handle them through PEST analysis nor to ignore them. Rather, something closer to creative writing is called for. Scenario planning is one such approach and one of the influential scholars in this field, Paul Shoemaker, describes scenario-based approaches as more art than science (1995). Royal Dutch Shell used scenario planning in 1971 as a means of preparing for unexpected situations. Pierre Wack (1985) offers a neat overview of the process that Royal Dutch Shell used. Trend data such as predicted oil reserves and changes in oil production volumes across various countries were available and helped shape decisions processes about investment in new oil fields, etc. However, specific uncertainties also existed. Two such uncertainties were considered in detail. First, whether oil markets would remain liberalized or, through a series of policy interventions, would they become more regulated? Second, would natural gas, which was then emerging as an alternative energy source, turn out to be a major competitor or would retain its current position where it represented only a small percentage of overall energy supply?

The answer to both questions was unclear, but Royal Dutch Shell moved forward by combining the binary yes/no answers to both questions to prepare four distinct possible futures, or scenarios. For example, regulated markets with significant natural gas supply or liberalized markets with small volumes of natural gas. What then followed was a process of creatively imagining how Royal Dutch Shell would fare in each of these four scenarios. Who would their competitors be? How suited was their current strategy to the scenarios? Clearly, what would work well in some scenarios might be a bad idea in others. Wack notes that the main benefit of scenario work was the realization that "business as usual decisions would no longer suffice" (1985: 89). Inevitably, dealing with uncertainty involves risk. Sometimes things

---

Rather than predicting the future, **scenarios** offer multiple plausible views of how fundamental uncertainties might play out thus allowing strategists to take more informed decisions.

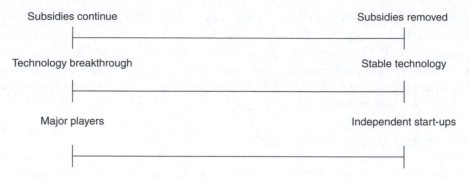

*Figure 6.3*  **The scenarios template**

take an unexpected turn. Royal Dutch Shell is still in the energy business; IBM is a radically different company from its origins in computer manufacture. Foresight played a role in the outcomes achieved by both firms. Some may feel that in periods of turbulent social change, such as the one driven by globalization and communications technologies, it is madness to try and predict what will happen next. In our view it is madness not to.

Figure 6.3 shows one approach to generating scenarios for the renewable energy sector. It proposes three specific uncertainties for a firm considering an investment in marine energy technology. First, government subsidies could persist in the form of green energy taxes, or these could be removed over coming years. Second, energy technology could feature some radical new solution or the continued, incremental improvement of existing technologies could prevail. Third, major energy firms may consolidate their position in the industry by buying up smaller competitors, or the marine energy sector could come to be dominated by an independent start-up. Ideally, each of these uncertainties would be independent of the others but it may be that, for example, government subsidy creates conditions that allow smaller start-up firms to remain viable.

## Understanding industry structures

Having scanned the operating environment, a strategist may have gleaned some information about the possible futures, which their organization may face. A second level of analysis, relating to industry level dynamics, is also helpful. In Chapter 2 we introduced the influential strategy scholar, Michael Porter. He suggests that industries, and therefore competition, are shaped by five competitive forces (see Porter 1980). He argues that understanding "the competitive forces, and their underlying causes, reveals the roots of an industry's current profitability while providing a framework for anticipating and influencing competition (and profitability) over time" (Porter, 2008: 80).

The **five forces model** was originally developed to assess industry attractiveness. The underlying assumption it makes is that in industries where the five competitive forces are high, all firms will struggle to achieve high returns because the industry is

> **Porter's Five Forces Model**. The forces which define competitiveness in an industry are:
> 1 The bargaining power of customers
> 2 The bargaining power of suppliers
> 3 The degree of competitive rivalry
> 4 The threat of new entrants
> 5 The threat of substitution

inherently unattractive. Such industries are prone to restructuring events to alleviate the pressures caused by the high competitive forces. Airlines and car insurance are often cited as examples of unattractive industries. Conversely, where the industry is inherently attractive, all players tend to perform well.

Examining each of Porter's five forces in turn offers a useful starting point. The first and second forces relate to the supply chain. Most firms use suppliers of materials, labour or other inputs and sell on to other customers. The relative **bargaining power of customers and suppliers** can have significant consequences for firms in any given industry. Where your customers are much larger than you, or where your customers can choose from a wide variety of suppliers, the power in your relationship is skewed in your customers' favour. As a result, they are more likely to dictate terms that suit their needs on issues such as price, risk, lead time, etc. Large supermarkets are often accused of abusing their power in relation to farmers and other providers. Of course, this power differential is not set in stone and farmers may choose to operate in a cooperative way in an effort to equalize or offset the benefits that scale confers on their customers. A similar logic applies when you consider your relationship to your suppliers. For example, if you wish to repair a jet engine, you will likely have to go to a single supplier to source key components such as turbine blades. This creates a situation where the supplier holds the bulk of the power in the relationship and can set prices accordingly. Suppliers with such monopoly situations tend to charge high prices and make good returns whilst their customers struggle to maintain margins. These first two forces demonstrate the ways in which competitive pressures and relative amounts of power influence the competitiveness of not just one firm, but a whole industry.

Next, Porter argues that the **degree of competitive rivalry** also has a bearing on industry competitiveness. Here, the argument runs that competitive rivalry is highest when a limited number of similarly sized competitors are chasing customers in a maturing market. Compare the circumstances in a rapidly expanding market such as the early days of the smartphone industry. Demand grows at such a pace that there are ample growth opportunities for all players. Today however, the smartphone market is maturing with a limited number of key players (Apple, Research in Motion, Samsung, HTC and Nokia) all competing for the attention of existing customers who are replacing their handset rather a steady flow of new customers buying a smartphone for the first time. The resulting rivalry drives up competition and tends to suppress margins for everyone. Where competitive rivalry is high, firms may attempt to alleviate these pressures through consolidation or alliancing, such as the recent partnership struck between Nokia and Microsoft.[3]

Finally, two types of threat impact on competitiveness. First, **the threat of new entrants** impacts on the attractiveness of an industry. Notice that new entrants don't necessarily have to appear, it is merely the threat that this may occur which counts. Porter's language of describing "barriers to entry" has passed into common usage in business conversations. Barriers may take many forms. For example, in capital-intensive industries, it is more difficult for new players to join the market whereas if entry costs are low many new players may join the market. The threat of new entrants therefore acts as a deterrent to individual firms who may be tempted to raise prices. Again, these circumstances are not a given. Coffee shops are sometimes used to demonstrate the point that low barriers to entry increase the threat of new rivals opening next door. However, global chains such as Starbucks spend significant amounts on branding, prime locations and other resources to defend their position and differentiate their offering.

Finally, **the threat of substitution** operates when your product or service could be replicated by some other offering. The introduction of the Eurostar train service from London to mainland Europe in 1994 offered a substitutable service to existing air and sea routes. The net result was to heighten competition in the marketplace with consumers able to check ferry, train and air fares before making a decision on which service to use. As with new entrants, the implied threat of substitution is enough to increase competition even where substitute products or services are not being used in significant volumes.

Taken as a set, these five forces are commonly used to examine the operating environment in search of possible changes, opportunities and threats. The intention is to seek out strategic moves that might benefit one firm over the others. Since the model was first introduced there have been claims that it is either ill-equipped to deal with the internet era or that it overlooks issues such as complementary products (see Margetta, 2012). Porter himself refutes these claims (see Porter, 2008). For our purposes, we would suggest that each of Porter's five forces offers a useful "window" onto industry dynamics. Firms such as Intel have manipulated the forces in their industry to ensure their future success. End users of personal computers would be unlikely to recognize the latest Intel processor let alone understand its operation. There are other providers of chips such as AMD and theoretically, Intel should be operating in an unattractive market. Strategic moves over a period of time have reversed that situation. Intel relentlessly brand their products such that almost all the major computing firms will have products bearing the "Intel inside" logo. Further, they invest heavily in research and development to improve product performance and stay ahead of the competition. In so doing, they have increased their power, whilst eroding those of competitors and customers.

Our suggestion is that a structured scan of the more localized business environment, using the five forces model, adds significant new insights to the wider PEST scan described earlier. Figure 6.4 describes a particular structure that we use to

|  | Strength | Trend | Opportunity/Threat? | Possible action |
|---|---|---|---|---|
| Customers |  |  |  |  |
| Suppliers |  |  |  |  |
| Rivalry |  |  |  |  |
| Entrants |  |  |  |  |
| Substitutes |  |  |  |  |
| Summary |  |  |  |  |

*Figure 6.4* The five forces template

extract insight from a five forces analysis. Take each force in turn and rate its strength. A rudimentary scale of high, medium or low is sufficiently accurate. Next, over time, we ask is the force in question strengthening or weakening and does any trend create an opportunity or a threat to your organization? Finally, we suggest that you make a note of any potential strategic moves that might follow. For example, faced with powerful customers in the supermarket sector, farmers could form co-operatives to bargain collectively and offset an otherwise problematic power differential.

Taken as a set, the PEST analysis, scenarios analysis and five forces analysis described above offer a fairly comprehensive review of the operating environment for an organization. We would make two observations. First, whilst PEST and scenario analysis apply straightforwardly to a variety of organizations, five forces analysis is more problematic in the context of public organizations. Second, use of any or all of these techniques does not guarantee future success but nevertheless, represents a prudent investment of managerial time and attention.

It is not just high technology firms that need to understand their operating environment, some of the world's longest standing industries are beset by similar challenges. Mining engineer Bob Buchan founded Kinross Gold in 1993, later diversifying into copper mining. Speaking about the future of his industry, Buchan notes "the yield from a copper mine if you look back 20 years was at somewhere between 4% and 6%". Today that yield level is 0.5%. You need to dig a much bigger hole in the ground and shift a lot more material to get the same amount of copper out these days. Demand for copper continues to grow because China, India and the other growth markets all have burgeoning middle classes who want products and services that require copper. The one thing this means is that the price of copper is going up because the cost of extracting it is going up. Buchan faces both trend data (e.g., changing yields over time) and specific uncertainties. For example, will new deposits be discovered that revert back to higher yield levels or will new technology allow base minerals to be extracted from different sources. Buchan acknowledges that "you could extract copper from sea water but using today's technology, the energy costs of doing so aren't viable. Who knows, someone somewhere might find a different material that conducts as well as copper. When you're making an invest-ment decision, you're laying a bet that a new solution won't come along and alter the economics".

In this chapter, we have tried to set out a structured way of militating against the risks that uncertainty brings. Of course, circumstances always exist where these types of analysis are confounded. For example, Brian McBride, the then CEO of Amazon. co.uk recalls his reaction to an early prototype of the hugely successful Kindle.

> I saw the mock ups of the Kindle, I thought they looked clunky. I said to Jeff [Besos] "why are we in this business? Why don't we let Sony or someone do the industrial design and we stick to what we know?"... he was right and I was wrong. There would have been no point in bringing a 100 people together to ask them what they wanted in that space because the Kindle didn't exist yet.
>
> Brian McBride

Nevertheless, we would argue that even with breakthrough products or technologies, valuable insights would be gained by performing a structured assessment of the operating and competitive environments.

## Articulating your strategy

From earlier chapters, you should now have a view of the challenge facing the organization and a rudimentary strategy statement that specifies strategic intent. In opening this chapter we have temporarily assumed a linear flow from diagnosis to intent to trend spotting in the operating environment. Whilst this can happen, it is more likely that an iterative process occurs. For example, our intent may draw attention to particular trends in the operating environment but equally, a thorough environmental scanning exercise may throw up new information that causes us to reframe our intent. We will return to that iterative process more fully in Chapter 11 when we discuss the strategy cycle. In the meantime, one important aspect of such iterating is the process of writing and rewriting drafts of your strategy statement. It should now be possible to further elaborate your strategy in two ways.

1   We will exploit [trend statement or opportunity from environmental scan].

The trend may be a growing new market segment, the reducing cost of some service, lower regulatory barriers or some other dynamic. This can then be linked to the statements of intent and diagnosis developed in earlier chapters.

2   The challenge we face is [diagnostic statement] and our strategy is to achieve [intent] by [timeframe] by exploiting [opportunity].

## Strategists at work: Apple

According to Richard Rumelt, Apple's decision to enter the digital music market was crucial to the firm's recovery from the brink of bankruptcy. As discussed in Chapter 4, Steve Jobs waited four years to make a decisive move into the music industry. He was perhaps influenced by earlier experiences since his view was that "one of our biggest insights [years ago] was that we didn't want to get into any business where we didn't own or control the primary technology because you'll get your head handed to you". Having scanned the external environment, Jobs focused on music for two primary reasons. First, it represented a large and global target market. Second, there were a mix of smaller firms, like Creative, and larger ones, like Sony, who hadn't yet found the recipe for success with their own offerings. As Jobs said in 2001 at the launch of the first iPod product, "not only has no one found the recipe but we think that the Apple brand is going to be fantastic, because people trust the Apple brand". As a strategist, Jobs was actively seeking opportunities in the market and could see key trends like miniaturization, increasing penetration of broadband speeds, improving battery life and progressively larger hard disk capacities. He got the timing right. As with many Apple products, the iPod was not first to market but when it did arrive the market had reached sufficient maturity to offer high volumes of which Apple captured the lion's share because their product was perceived as superior. A more detailed account of Apple's long-term strategy, including the firm's development in the post-Jobs period, is offered in Case study 1 in Section D.

## Strategists at work in the running cases

*DMacL:* So next we're going to look at trends and opportunities. How did you each approach the problem of scanning the environment?

*Sandy:* Well, I supposed in Pointer, much of that is down to me. I read a lot, I go to trade fairs, I'm always looking at things, some of which don't immediately seem connected to the business. In terms of the changes in our industry, what was clear was that there were an increasing number of sales of IP, camera units and NVRs as opposed to DVRs. At the point that I noticed it, the cost of IP related kit was still higher than the cost of traditional products but it was already offering better quality. The broadband infrastructure on a national scale in the UK was still lagging behind and it wasn't yet of sufficient quality to deliver consistent video transmission. The third barrier, or at least a barrier in the UK was that there was a very large legacy estate of analogue product whereas countries which had been slower to develop security systems in the past were now moving faster than our developed market because they didn't have the issue of trying to integrate IP into an analogue environment. But, you could see what had happened. So, it wasn't a case of *if* IT was going to happen to our industry, it was just a case of when it was going to happen.

*RMacI:* and in terms of timing, where are you ?

*Sandy:* Probably ahead of most of our peers in the earliest days but people are definitely beginning to catch on to it now.

*Harry:* In the health service you could easily drown in a sea of data. Technical change comes frequently because there are always new drugs, new surgical procedures and so on. There's a big drive now with digital approaches to things, and the use of remote monitoring to begin to see how you can detect things earlier. There's definitely some potential there but the difficulty is often that [the] introduction of these things are done in the old style, you know. It becomes a big project, a three-year investment and at the end of the day not everyone agrees to use the same system, and it just all falls apart. Then there's a wealth of stuff on changes in the population, like the increasing number of elderly. One of the things we're trying to do is see how we can reduce dependency in the elderly. There are two big ideas there for improvement, keeping elderly people connected socially and keeping them physically active. So I suppose that connects back to trying to improve the health of the population as a whole and trying to prioritize things that make a difference. A great example would be the work we're doing around improving childhood. The week after we got the health service together to try to do this, one local authority tweeted the results of its first test of change. It was just an A4 sheet of paper and an ink marker that they used to draw a graph of their results. Someone photographed it and sent it on Twitter. So, you can be very low tech in all of this. For me, it's more about what you are doing and how often you are doing it and how you are measuring it than the technology that's involved.

**Kate:**  External market intelligence was probably one of the key parts of how we formulated strategy.

**RMacI:**  So what kinds of things were you looking at?

**Kate:**  Well, when we first started the things that we were using to put together a business case were how internet usage was growing, people shopping, people buying on the internet, their resistance initially to buying was degrading quite quickly. You could see that commerce itself was taking off. People weren't just looking for information they were actually looking now to transact and so there were lots of numbers about that. What was interesting then was that you could then look at those statistics which were produced externally and it would be broken down for you by socio-economic group, by propensity to buy, by socio-demographics with cool names like Silver Surfers, Empty-nesters, Impoverished Youths but what was really interesting to us, given that we were a part of the wider Admiral group, was the fact that the people who were most likely, at that current time: we are talking early 2002, to buy and transact were people who were actually in Admiral's target market so paying slightly more for their car insurance. That helped us shape our strategy around what was going on out there.

## Do's and don'ts

Developing and articulating foresight and target opportunities for your organization can be daunting and even embarrassing sometimes. We have to stick our neck out and reveal our view of the future – the way we think, what excites us and, perhaps most difficult, try to justify what might in cases be guesses, gut feel and even a dash of wishful thinking. Not only that, it can open up arguments, conflict and even expose us to ridicule. More often than not, if strategists hold back from "going public" it's because they feel they haven't sufficient information, or even conviction, to back up their claims. In our view however, this is a reason for working through the issues – not reversing away from them. Leadership can create and foster the right atmosphere for this kind of exploration, conflicting views can be turned into healthy contestation which helps build the appetite to find out more and help disperse the mist of uncertainty – if not about the future, then at least about the organization's chosen view of it and how to approach it. It is vital that we "get over" these feelings and get on with it.

In Chapter 1 we argued that good strategists understand their own strategic management style and those of their colleagues. Some will be naturally comfortable with uncertainty, some will want facts and data. Some will like trying to spot trends and scan externally; others will devote their energies to internal "facts". You will never have enough data to eliminate all the uncertainty. If you did, there would be no risk. No business would ever flourish and none would fail. We believe that the essence of good strategic management lies in making winning decisions in the face of imperfect information.

Good strategists will use their understanding of these differences to engage others in what can be a lengthy set of negotiations about trade-offs between both the logical and cultural aspects of organization – for example its ideal positioning, its flexibility (the more flexible, the less important prediction may be) and its attitude towards risk. Convincing others that you have a sound diagnosis of the organization's current environment and that you can explain how key internal decisions relate to it will help. Use conversations with colleagues as an opportunity to build a plausible and compelling interpretation of the environment and your desired position in it.

## Do

1 Write down your target opportunities – three or four – with timings and implied strategic moves (filling resource gaps, reconfiguring the organization, making investments, etc.).
2 Provide a one or two sentence rationale that links these opportunities to the achievement of your intent and (eventually) your capabilities.
3 Think about any threats your analysis might have revealed and what you need to do about them.
4 Engage others and work iteratively to gradually refine your foresight. Allow others to play to their strengths (scanning, playing devil's advocate, etc.).
5 Blend rationality, intuition and imagination – start with a blue-sky approach and whittle your list down. Think about reinforcing feedback loops linking individual trends into more significant waves of change.

## Don't

1 Create verbiage and ridiculously long lists. Try to be clear, succinct, precise and convincing.
2 Assume that other stakeholders will see the environment that you see.
3 Broadcast your ivory-tower findings and expect colleagues to buy them.

# Who to read

**Kees van der Heijden** worked for Royal Dutch Shell as Head of the Business Environment Division in London before moving into an academic role. He is now an emeritus professor at the University of Strathclyde. His book "Scenarios: the art of strategic conversation" gives an overview of the history or scenario thinking as well as some practical guidance on the ways in which firms can attempt to glimpse possible futures.

# CHAPTER 7

# Resources and Capability

I f strategy is essentially about competition, it is natural that strategy scholars have been fixated with the study of how organizations compete. In order to succeed, it is essential that organizations are better at something which customers value either directly, like the ability to launch exciting new products, or indirectly, such as the ability to recruit and retain leading designers. The nature of the "something" at which you choose to excel can vary, but the generic label used in the strategy literature would be **capability**. When reviewing the wider strategy literature in Chapter 2 we described this focus on capability as part of the so-called resource-based view (RBV) of organizations. And, in our own definition of strategy we highlight the importance of nurturing a capability over the medium to long term. This then represents the next stage of the strategy cycle.

A number of terms are used almost interchangeably in the strategy literature. There are subtle distinctions between distinctive competencies (Selznick, 1957), core capabilities (Leonard-Barton, 1992) and core competence (Prahalad and Hamel, 1990) and distinctive capabilities (Kay, 1990) but for our purposes we will emphasize the areas of commonality between these terms rather than their differences. One notable distinction is however, worth drawing out. The RBV has been critiqued for providing a static view, and more recent work focused on dynamic capabilities is intended to overcome this limitation since this introduces a relationship between operational capabilities (how we earn a living today, see Winter, 2003: 992) and dynamic capabilities (which represent our "ability to change or reconfigure" operational capabilities (Zahra et al., 2006).

In practical terms, if you want to offer low cost air travel you would likely need capabilities which allow you to excel at a range of tasks that reduce operating costs. Everything from baggage handling and employment contracts to web hosting, and landing costs might contribute to your ability to offer lower prices than your competitors whilst still making a healthy profit. Yet price is not always decisive. Perhaps it is service, reliability, speed, design flair, location or some combination of criteria that really matters to potential customers. Monopolistic markets are of course, an exception since customers have no, or at least no comparable, alternate provider.

For us, a key distinction is that between **resources,** which an organization might possess, and **capabilities,** which represent the ways in which organizations are able to deploy resources in order to generate value for customers. Resources themselves may be tangible (e.g., equipment) or intangible (e.g., brand) but importantly, resources can be bought and sold. Within the wider strategy literature, resources are therefore rarely seen as the source of competitiveness. In contrast, resource bundles delivered through an interlocking set of organizational capabilities are often seen as "the essence of superior performance" (Grant, 2010: 127).

To begin analysing organizational capabilities, it is worth considering how seemingly ordinary individuals reach exceptional levels of skill and performance in settings ranging from sports to music. Studies indicate that exceptional skill is not exclusively down to talent or some inherited genetic advantage. Rather, it results from the combined effects of repeated and purposeful practice, access to skilled coaching or facilities and an innate persistence born of a determination to succeed. The received wisdom is that it takes an investment in the region of 10,000 hours practising to attain world-class performance levels in any given discipline. The psychologist Anders Ericsson studied violin players, his fellow psychologists Herbert Simon and William Chase studied chess players.[1] Both found similar results. Exceptional skill is the product of hard work rather than luck, talent or genetics.

How one responds to the idea that world-class performance is available to anyone with the patience is revealing. For some it is an empowering insight that levels the playing field. For others, the slow realization that there are no short cuts acts as a disincentive. Before deciding which reaction fits you, we must first make a leap from individual to organizational examples. In making that leap, something challenging occurs when we make a claims such as organization A offers world-class customer service and is noticeably better than organizations B or C. Whilst we tend to attribute service experiences to organizations, in practical terms we interact with people. Organizations are therefore something of an abstraction. It would therefore be more precise to say that staff from organization A deliver better customer service than staff from organizations B and C. This subtle distinction serves an important purpose. What if the particular individual you deal with leaves organization A? Will their replacement reach the same standard of customer service? What if they leave organization A and join organization B or C, will they then take with them the standards of customer service required to make a difference? We will return to this need for precision in thinking about capability and we will continue to explore the consequences of such nuances as the chapter unfolds.

As a final introductory comment, it should be noted that capabilities are not regarded as universally good or indeed, good for all time. In organizational terms, Stanford graduate Jim Collins, argues that the good is the enemy of great. "Just because you've been doing something which is core to your business for years, does not necessarily mean you can be the best in the world at it" (2001: 13). Harvard professor Dorothy Leonard goes further, claiming that core competences can become core rigidities over time (Leonard Barton, 1992) that actually hold businesses back.

Canadian scholar Danny Miller echoes Leonard's sentiments, which he describes as the Icarus Paradox (see Miller, 1991). In essence, Miller argues that the seeds of an organization's eventual demise are often rooted in the causes of earlier success.

## Current capability

Perhaps the most common way to think about capability is to think of the strengths and weaknesses of a business. Kenneth Andrews was one of the pioneers of strategic management and is credited with the development of Strengths, Weaknesses, Opportunities and Threats (SWOT) analysis. By considering the strengths, weaknesses, opportunities and threats facing an organization, Andrews argued that we generate insights about what to do next. Figure 7.1 below summarizes the way in which SWOT analysis connects the internal apparatus of the organization to its external environment to generate insights about key issues and challenges.

SWOT analysis can be helpful but is prone to difficulties. First, there is an overwhelming temptation to generate volume. From a lengthy set of bullet points it can be hard to sift important data from the noise. As Kees van der Heijden notes, a wealth of information creates a poverty of attention (2005: 55).[2] Further, the items in a SWOT analysis do not necessarily carry equal weight or urgency. SWOT tends to compartmentalize thinking and loses the effect of feedback loops where items interact within and across the boundaries in the model. Finally of course, perceptions matter. Whether, a low market share represents an opportunity or a threat depends on whether a number of assumptions. Is this a market where you want to hold a large share? Is it a market, which is shrinking or growing? Is it a market, which tends to feature high margins, reputational or other benefits that link to your stated intent? Too often, SWOT analysis is undertaken in isolation without recourse to the very themes that would allow a more detailed and grounded set of judgements about the differences between opportunities and threats, strengths and weaknesses.

That said, those areas where an organization claims some particular strength appears to offer a reasonable starting point when analysing capability. Indeed, one

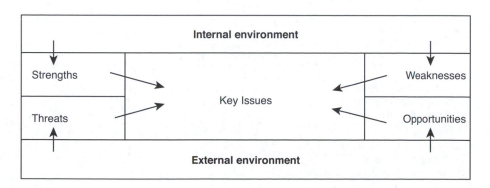

*Figure 7.1* **SWOT analysis**

of the most frequently cited theorists in the RBV of strategy suggests that resources can be "anything which could be thought of as a strength or weakness" (Wernerfelt, 1984: 172). Whilst it is not intended to be exhaustive, Figure 7.2 is drawn from our experiences using SWOT with many hundreds of managers in workshop settings. Using language from those workshops, we have summarized common claims that managers make when reviewing the strengths of their organization.

Using Figure 7.2 it is possible to focus attention quickly on those areas, which may represent key capabilities for your organization. The list contains commonly cited answers but you may wish to add others that are specific to your own organization's circumstances. Once complete, the next step should be to check that you would be able to defend each individual claim selected from Figure 7.2. For example, can you provide comparative data to suggest that you are measurably better than your peer group? If so, it is even better if you can track changes in such comparative data over time. You may currently have higher market share than your competitors but that advantage may be stable, shrinking or growing over time. A snapshot offers less insight than a trend.

| Current strengths |
| --- |
| Our history:<br>  We have a great reputation ☐<br>  We have loyal customers ☐<br>  We have a large customer base ☐<br>  We have a strong brand ☐ |
| Our people:<br>  We have experienced/knowledgeable staff ☐<br>  We have highly skilled staff ☐<br>  We are trusted ☐<br>  We have strong relationships with customers/suppliers ☐<br>  We have innovators on our team ☐ |
| Our technology:<br>  We have great products/services ☐<br>  We have great reliability ☐<br>  We have good quality ☐<br>  We have excellent processes ☐ |
| Our contracts:<br>  We have licence(s) ☐<br>  We hold patents for our products/services/processes ☐<br>  We have exclusivity (e.g., products/territories/time periods) ☐ |
| Our physical assets:<br>  We have prime location(s) ☐<br>  We own valuable assets ☐<br>  We have great facilities ☐ |
| Our finances:<br>  We have financial reserves ☐<br>  We make good margins ☐<br>  We achieve efficiencies of scale/scope ☐ |

*Figure 7.2* **Generic strengths**

If you can secure robust data, compare yourself with key competitors and track changes in performance over time then your SWOT analysis is already substantially better than the default outcome, which is a lengthy list of items. Yet there remain inherent difficulties that render SWOT analysis inadequate when studying capability. To make progress, we need to move beyond a form of language based on the present tense and possessive statements embedded in Figure 7.2 since these obscure the generative processes which led to current strengths or weaknesses. The phrasing used was deliberately possessive and present tense since this is almost universally how managers articulate capability. It seems natural when asked, "what are the strengths of your organization?" to respond by saying something like "we have great products". Unfortunately, this tends to focus attention on the here and now and thus provides only a partial explanation of competitiveness. Almost inevitably, one or more cumulative and generative processes will have underpinned current strengths. Whenever we see firms excelling today it is worth recognizing that investments of time, money and attention will likely have been made at some prior point in time.

Current superiority in a specific area, such the customer service levels attributed earlier to organization A, is rarely an accident. Usually it results from training investments, incentive systems and recruitment processes designed and implemented years earlier. Similarly, innovative products are rarely an instantaneous breakthrough. The first Dyson vacuum cleaner revolutionized its product category but it followed 5,126 prototypes. Excellence, whether in product performance or service experiences, usually results from the careful accumulation of expertise. This is often rooted in developmental processes, which can be traced to actions and practices that express particular aspects of organizational culture or corporate values. This temporal linkage between the development of capability over time and its current configuration forms an important basis for understanding capability and is completely overlooked by a simple SWOT analysis.

John Gemmill worked in a variety of senior roles including periods with Unilever, Inchcape and Scottish Power before moving into consultancy and recruitment. He makes a simple but insightful observation about the way in which language shapes the way we engage with concepts. By taking the possessive statements in Figure 7.2 and translating these into active statements something subtle, but significant occurs. Figure 7.3 below shows the rubric that Gemmill suggests using.

This simple linguistic shift draws attention to the generative process rather than the eventual outcome. In the research literature Brown and Duguid use examples from Xerox to develop a similar distinction between what they describe as an "epistemology of possession" and an "epistemology of action" (see Brown and

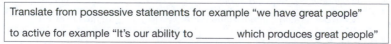

Translate from possessive statements for example "we have great people"

to active for example "It's our ability to _____ which produces great people"

*Figure 7.3*  **An active description of capability**

Duguid, 2001). In simpler terms, a switch from nouns to verbs emphasizes the same shift from *what we've got* to *what we do*. The shift to a more active perspective forces analytical attention to be paid to the temporal relationship between historic investments, ongoing practice and current performance. In many ways, this is at the heart of our message: strategy is best conceptualized as something that results from strategists at work, rather than something that an organization possesses. A logical consequence of Gemmill's linguistic observation is that one of the core concepts in strategy (capability), should always be expressed in terms of activity. This is important not least because we manage things that we do; for example we leverage, deploy, showcase, curate, steward or neglect things. Value is added, or indeed destroyed, in the doing rather than the owning. In the example given in Figure 7.3, the blank in the statement may relate to selection processes, training programmes, incentive systems or a host of other contributory factors. In fact, it is possible to undertake a recursive assessment of capability in a search for **root causes**.

The "Five Whys" is an approach first developed by Sakichi Toyoda for the Toyota Motor Company. It involves repeatedly asking the question "why?" until **root causes** are surfaced. For example, why does a finished product feature a particular defect? The answer may be that a component has failed. The next question would be to ask why that particular component failed? The answer may be that the component had been outsourced. This in turn, raises another question "why was the component outsourced?". The eventual answer may lie some way distant from the surface level enquiry. Toyoda argued that within five questions root causes are typically visible.

Mansour Javidan is better known as an international business scholar, but his article in Long Range Planning (1998) offers a practical approach, which we adapt here to help sharpen our focus on capabilities. In essence, he challenges us to be more discriminating in our assessment of potential capabilities. Each of the strengths identified from the list in Figure 7.2 represents a potential capability for an organization. Yet most organizations are thought to have only a few core capabilities. Javidan's tests offer a way of sifting possible from actual capabilities and is summarized in Figure 7.4 below.

| Q1. | It's our ability to _____ that means we do _____ very well. |
|-----|---------------------------------------------------------------|
| Q2. | Is this ability embedded in every part of our business? |
| Q3. | Is our ability to _____ demonstrably superior to that of our competitors? |
| Q4. | Does this specific ability result in outcomes, which matter to our customers? |
| Q5. | Is our advantage here durable? |
| Q6. | Given our strategic intent, does our ability to _____ remain relevant? |

*Figure 7.4* **Identifying capabilities**
*Source*: Adapted from Javidan (1998).

For Javidan, a capability assumes greater importance if it is embedded in every part of the organization. Other scholars would call this a core capability or core competence, arguing these core capabilities inform and infuse everything that the organization does. Amazon prides itself on its deep knowledge of customers and markets. The following exchange took place at a seminar given by the then CEO of Amazon. co.uk, Brian McBride.

*B McB:*  We know our customers very well and we're very good at reading the market
*R MacI:*  How many people do you employ in market research?
*B McB:*  About half of one post
*R MacI:*  Okay, let's ask that differently. How many people look at market data?
*B McB:*  Pretty much everyone looks at the numbers, pretty much all the time

This short exchange offers a good example of the way in which capabilities become deeply embedded in an organization such that the organization is no longer reliant on a single individual for exceptional performance in a particular area. If Amazon can answer yes to each of the subsequent questions in Figure 7.4, it has identified a particular capability. For example, it may be that Amazon's ability to monitor market data makes it the most customer responsive organization in the world (which is one of the stated intentions of the business).[3]

One final view of capabilities merits attention. Jay Barney is perhaps the most heavily cited strategy scholars of our times and his breakthrough paper on the RBV (1991) is credited with reinvigorating interest in the ways in which internal resources create and sustain competitive advantage. For Barney, resources build competitive advantage when they meet four criteria. First, they must be **valuable**. This is consistent with the view set out by Javidan that resources should be important to customers. Second, Barney argues that resources should be **rare**. Intuitively this chimes with everyday experience since commonly available resources will also be easily available to your competitors. Third, resources should be **imperfectly imitable**. There are many tablet computers available but Apple's iPad has a look, feel and user interface that renders competitor products an imperfect imitation of the original. Finally, resources should be **non-substitutable**. If no other product or service meets the customer's needs then advantage is conferred on the owner of those specific resources that can meet those needs. The so-called **valuable, rare, imperfectly imitable, and non-substitutable (VRIN)** test is a useful additional way of thinking about resources. Barney's characteristics act as a reinforcing set since rare resources are usually valuable and are rare precisely because they cannot be imitated or copied. Barney and other RBV scholars argue that resources are heterogeneous across organizations.

In summary then, we would draw attention to two key points, which will help you identify and manage capabilities within your own organization. First, we would suggest that capabilities are the product of many years of development in circumstances specific to one organization. Just as with individual excellence, the nuances of organizational circumstance and biographies matter but are unique to that particular organization. It therefore helps enormously to start by looking for distinctive aspects of your organization's history. The second point, draws upon our earlier argument that adopting an active orientation when describing capabilities i.e., "the ability to do something," is helpful since this focuses on practices that generate strengths.

## Articulating your strategy

Most organizations survive precisely because they are good enough at things which customers value. It is therefore clear that an explicit knowledge of capabilities is not a prerequisite for successful performance. We have worked with the management teams of many successful organizations which cannot articulate the capabilities practiced by their organization. If however, you cannot offer a satisfactory explanation of the generative sources of your organization's capabilities then there is a significant risk that decisions will be taken that damage them over time, particularly during periods where changes to strategic intent are being considered.

Capabilities are organic and are sustained by something akin to the root system of a plant. Damage to this root system will not necessarily translate instantly to visible damage in the plant above the surface of the soil. Rather, small signals of deterioration will occur and, by the time these are noticed, irreparable damage may have been caused.[4] Capabilities take time to develop and are sensitive to significant changes in both intent and the operating environment. Hence, the definition of strategy we introduced in Chapter 1 drew attention to the role of "genuine capabilities cultivated over the medium to long term".

To understand capability, we would suggest the following analytical sequence. First, review the strengths of your organization (see Figure 7.2). Next, translate each strength into the linguistic form "it's our ability to ____" (see Figure 7.3). Finally, apply each of Javidan's test criteria (see Figure 7.4). What remains after this rigorous examination process are the core capabilities of your organization.

These capabilities must be related to both the strategic intent and external environment. Thus capability can be expressed in the context of a wider strategy statement using the format set out below.

> The challenge we face is [diagnostic statement] and our strategy is to achieve [intent] by [timeframe] by using our superior ability to [capability statement] to address [opportunity].

This latest articulation of a strategy statement represents the minimum specification required for a comprehensive strategy in that it sets out ends (intent), means (capability) and conditions (opportunity). In subsequent chapters we will further elaborate on this structure but we have now arrived at a robust and coherent strategy.

## Strategists at work: Twitter

Ev Williams is a serial innovator with serious pedigree in Silicon Valley. Having already co-founded the blog tool "Blogger.com" and sold it to Google in 2003 for an undisclosed sum. The idea behind Twitter emerged from the booming social media revolution, which was happening by 2006. Central to Twitter is the ability to follow someone without the need for this to be reciprocated. Messages were limited to 140 characters and this "SMS for the internet" mindset was developed in proto-type format very quickly. At launch, there was scepticism about both the basic idea and the restrictions on message length. Interviewed at the time of Twitter's launch, Williams argued that he had ambitious plans to monetize the service. "Rather than attach advertising to a personal communication channel, we want to make it a benefit…we think those things have potential, so as the userbase grows we'll flesh out which of those things work and the business model and revenue will fit in". The story of Twitter offers a classic case of building something first then figuring out how to make it commercially viable. Williams wasn't sure where Twitter would lead yet he helped build a business that was worth £11bn when it was floated and handles more than 500 million tweets each day. It has influenced both global communications and everyday language with terms like "hashtag" and "retweet" becoming part of our everyday conversations. Further, Twitter has become one of the developments, which has influenced the wider news industry both in print and other media.

## Strategists at work in the running cases

*RMacI:*  Resources, skills, capabilities are the next theme. What is your organization particularly, perhaps even uncommonly and unnaturally, good at?

*Kate:*  The fusion of marketing knowledge, of IT, specifically the internet, and knowledge about customers. We were big on what they [customers] wanted and about delivering it through technology. So, at Confused.com it was a particular skill set and it was actually quite difficult to find people with that skill set. I have a background in both Marketing and IT and what I did was surround myself with young, IT geeks who hadn't worked too long in the industry so weren't stuck in a mould where they could say something wasn't going to be possible. I wanted people who were fresh and had the sort of behavioural trait and desire to seek out, look for new things, find new ways of doing things.

*RMacI:*  In our language then, it was your ability to combine a deep knowledge of how the car insurance industry works with insights from the emerging world of web-technology?

*DMacL:*  or, maybe, your ability to spot talent and develop the requisite industry knowledge after the fact?

*Kate:*  Yeah, they both work.

*Sandy:*  For our business, it's the ability to integrate fairly complex systems and bits of kit. To bring more to the installation than just installation because we've got the experience and knowledge to say "you could be doing it this way, you could be combining these other activities; this is the smart way of doing it". How do we nurture that skill? Well, it's training. It's the fact that we have an apprentice programme and that we can take someone right from the basics, to the cutting edge of technology and give them practical experiences whilst they're doing that.

And, I suppose, taking a further step back it's a skill that's got nothing to do with security per se but it's about project management and just simply being able to operate in the project marketplace and being able to deliver projects and to manage the intricacies of projects in a contractor dominated environment. That's what wins us business.

*Harry:*  A lot of my life has been spent talking to doctors, and doctors are pretty smart people. Over the years they've become accustomed to change in the way their system's are managed. I think two things need to happen. The government needs to settle down and not cause too much system disruption; and, secondly, we need to doctors and other health professionals more involved in designing the change. What doctors do is spend a lot of NHS money and, therefore, they've tended to be very managed over the past few decades. I think that's been to the detriment of effectiveness and efficiency in the service. We're getting a view now of an improvement methodology

*RMacI:*  which you've largely borrowed from other industries

*Harry:*  yes, but we need to make it part of clinical training. We now have a whole cadre of hospital doctors, in Scotland, who have done the patient safety programme using this technique and they see it and they understand it and they just have to be given the opportunity to go and apply it elsewhere. But, the kind of thing I do is about getting teachers and social workers and so on beginning to think this way. It would be something about creating an ability to get the evidence of what works out onto the table and then get out of their way. The whole point is these initiatives are not designed in committee rooms, they're designed by the people who have to deliver them.

*DMacL:*  So, you don't need permission?

*Harry:*  No, you just tell them to go out and do it. There's that quote I use, a guy from MIT I think it was who said: you can't expect people to be committed to something that they've no hand in designing.

## Dos and don'ts

Our experience suggests that developing a firm grasp on capability is challenging. Demonstrating capability or justifying a claim to capability is arguably one of the most challenging tasks facing any strategist. It is no overstatement to say that the majority of businesses we deal with find our easiest concept to be the simple assertion that "to win at something you have to better at something". Yet the same people probably experience more difficulty in articulating the generative source of their superior capability than they do in addressing any of the other questions or challenges posed by the strategy cycle. Vital clues about capability are distributed across time and therefore rely on unpacking the collective organizational memory. Habits and processes relating to capability are likely to be culturally embedded and therefore can be hidden from view. However, a clear understanding of capability, its development and, perhaps as importantly, recognizing and dealing with capability gaps is essential. Remember that assessing capabilities is more difficult, though not impossible, from the outside of the organization.

## Do

1 Be persistent. Surface level views of capability are rarely the whole story.
2 Demand that claims are substantiated with real data.
3 Express capability using verbs rather than nouns.
4 Repeat the same analytical process for both current and potential competitors.
5 Think about the capabilities you might need going forward and how these will be developed within your organization.

## Don't

1 Settle for a present tense account of "strengths".
2 Assume that your colleagues have already thought this through. They rarely have.
3 Attempt to rush capability analysis; it takes time and iteration to get traction.

# Who to read

There are many writers who consider the ways in which resources build competitiveness. A useful starting point is the work of **C K Prahalad** and **Gary Hamel**. Whilst their work appears in some significant academic journals, they were also able to communicate their ideas in a series of books and Harvard Business Review articles in a form that was accessible to non-academics. Their 1990 article "The core competence of the organization" is a good starting point.

# CHAPTER 8

# Strategic Options

Thus far we have combined strategic intent with an assessment of both the operating environment and organizational capabilities to craft a rudimentary but complete view of strategy. We would argue that this is a minimal but complete view of strategy since it covers the essential issues of ends, means and conditions. Whilst, it may be minimally complete, it is not yet a singular view of strategy since there may be multiple ways in which the strategy could be delivered. Key questions such who to compete with and the basis on which to engage in competition remain unanswered at this point. To think and act strategically we suggest that it is necessary to develop explicit answers to such questions and, in the remainder of this chapter we set out a structured process based on five key decision points which help specify **strategic options**.

> **Strategic options** are defined here as plausible courses of action which would deliver the particular combination of ends, means and conditions articulated in the strategy statements developed thus far. The presence of at least one plausible alternative strategy implies a process of evaluating options which is covered in the next chapter.

First, it is helpful to specify the aim of the strategy. Eventually, most organizations find themselves in the situation where one product, service or division declines and something new hopefully emerges in its place. This natural life cycle is observed both at the level of individual products or services within a single organization, and at the level of operating divisions or companies within a larger corporate setting. The Boston Consulting Group (BCG) developed a matrix, which maps activities in terms of market share and rate of market growth in order to visualize this natural cycle. Often referred to as the Boston Box, BCG matrix or growth-share matrix, it is responsible for introducing key terms such as cash cows to everyday business usage. Figure 8.1 below shows the model.

Cash cows typically generate surplus profits that should be used to turn current stars into future cash cows. Question marks will either turn into stars or dogs and

*Figure 8.1* **The growth share matrix**

*Source*: Adapted from The BCG Portfolio Matrix from the Product Portfolio Matrix, ©1970, The Boston Consulting Group (BCG).

are likely to require funding. Dogs tend to draw in both cash and managerial atten-tion for little reward. The BCG matrix should therefore see a clockwise tendency for surplus profits generated by cash cows to be redistributed. As Figure 8.1 implies, in using the BCG matrix it is important to establish a sense of market share **relative** to competitors and the rate at which the market is growing **relative** to the broader economic cycle and other comparable markets. What seems at first glance to be a simple model can therefore become challenging to use because issues such as industry and product boundaries can blur, as can one's sense of timescale. These difficulties aside, the BCG matrix often forms a useful starting point when thinking about the aim of the strategy. Put simply, there are three fundamental choices avail-able since organizations must either achieve **growth**, **retrenchment** or **consolida-tion**. If, for example, strategic intent has already been crafted in explicit and directly measurable terms, outcomes may be obvious. An intention to achieve 20% higher market share implies growth which may come from the expansion of a cash cow, or the conversion of a star or question mark into a future cash cow. However, the link between intent and outcome is not always as obvious. A stated intent to achieve particular profit margins could be achieved by retrenching from the less profitable market segments, or by consolidating a position in particular markets, or even by growing the proportion of revenue from high margin segments. Our experience has been that the simple act of specifying one of the three intended outcomes (growth, retrenchment or consolidation) removes the possibility for ambiguity even when indirect or proximate strategic goals have been set.

The majority of the strategists that we have worked with have been interested in growth and this is, in many ways, only to be expected since private organizations are usually tasked with expansion of scope and scale. Therefore, the second set of choices facing strategists relate their choice of how to engage with products, services and markets. Igor Ansoff, who featured in the review of history given in Chapter 2, developed a simple two by two matrix to summarize differing approaches to achiev-ing growth. The so-called Ansoff Matrix focuses on two key questions when deciding which tactic to pursue. First, do you plan to persist with your existing offering or develop new products and services? Second, will you seek to sell these products and services to new or existing customers? These questions combine to produce four possible outcomes as summarized in Figure 8.2 below.

Hypothetically, your strategy could define intent, specify opportunities in the operating environment and suggest which capabilities you will use to address those opportunities whilst being executed in any of the four tactics suggested in Ansoff's Matrix. **Market penetration** suggests that you already occupy a successful niche with the right offering servicing the right kinds of customers. Therefore, your strategy sees you aspiring to find ways of doing more of the same. Supermarkets building more or bigger stores selling their existing product range to existing customers are pursuing their strategy by means of market penetration. However, the introduction of home delivery services by supermarkets could be interpreted as **service development**, whilst Apple's regular introduction of the iPod nano or touch would represent **product development.** In both cases existing customers are being presented with new, or at least modified, products or services. When attempting **market development,** organizations are looking to find new customers for existing offerings. In some cases this is effected by expanding into a new geographic territory,[1] in others something more subtle is involved. A handful of firms manage to find secondary audiences for their products or services. The North Face has manufactured a range of outdoor equipment including waterproofs, thermal clothing and footwear for over 40 years with the strapline that they are serving "athletes that never stop exploring". However, many of their products are worn by customers in search of what is sometimes referred to as "wilderness-chic". Such customers would probably not describe themselves as athletes let alone explorers, nevertheless, there are many more of these customers than there are elite athletes. Thus, market development may represent a very lucrative strategic move. Finally, the Ansoff Matrix suggests that firms engage in **diversification** when they develop new products or services for new customers. The distinction between related and unrelated diversification can sometimes be difficult especially when existing customers unexpectedly buy the new product or service. As agriculture has become less economically attractive, some land owners have switched from farming to property development or leisure pursuits. The only connection to their previous activities may be the land used, but customers who bought foodstuffs may return to buy clay pigeon shooting lessons.

|  | Products and services | |
|  | Existing | New |
| Customers — Existing | Market penetration | Product / Service development |
| Customers — New | Market development | Diversification |

*Figure 8.2* **The Ansoff Matrix**

*Source:* Adapted from Ansoff (1957).

Diversification is often portrayed as the riskiest tactic available since it introduces uncertainties in two dimensions simultaneously. In our experience, diversification is undertaken by two distinct groups of organizations. One group is hugely success-ful and is seeking to harvest revenue from existing business activities in the hope of creating future success. The other group tends to consist of organizations, which are in serious difficulty and thus see diversification as something of a last throw of the dice. In truth, there are risks attached to all four tactics and careful consideration is required.

Logically, it should be noted that an aim of consolidation or retrenchment is consistent with the tactic of persisting with existing customers and existing products or services (namely market penetration). Growth could be delivered by any of the four tactics set out in Figure 8.2, or indeed by combinations of these tactics.

A third set of choices relates to the **method** used to execute the strategy. Here we identify three simple choices. The first is to pursue **organic growth** where the organization remains entirely responsible for all new business activity. An organic approach is usually seen as the least problematic way to proceed in that it does not involve reliance on third parties, but even organic growth can introduce challenges, particularly in circumstances where the organization is expanding rapidly. The second approach is to achieve strategic aims by **acquisition**. This can speed up devel-opment by, for example, allowing an organization to instantly develop a presence in new technologies, markets, geographies or segments. Again, acquisition is not with-out its challenges since in the medium term issues such as alignment of cultures and consolidating shared resources, services or locations can lead to difficult decisions. It is notable that it was the acquisition of ABN Amro in 2007 that many cite as the deal, which led to the eventual collapse of the Royal Bank of Scotland. Pursuing a strategy of growth by acquisition may lead to a situation where an ability to conduct due diligence may either be, or need to become, a core capability (see for example, the ABB Case in Section D). Finally, if an acquisition is seen as to drastic, expensive, risky or final a solution, organizations can choose to collaborate to achieve strategic aims. This approach to **partnership** is supposed to allow both parties to leverage their own skill set whilst exploiting the complementary skills of their partner(s). In practice, many organizations enter partnerships with an unspoken agenda to inter-nalise the skills of their partners and the consensus in the collaboration literature is that partnerships are typically more time consuming, controversial and problematic first anticipated (see Huxham and Vangen, 2005).

---

Corporate Strategy: This book is primarily concerned with strategy at the level of the individual organization. A separate sub-discipline exists relating to corporate strategy that is strategy when multiple sub-units, divisions or subsidiaries are collected together into a corporation. It would be an oversimplification to suggest that corporate strategy is simply the aggregation of individual business level strategies but many of the same concepts and challenges do arise when crafting corporate strategy.

Having specified an aim, tactic(s) and method, a fourth choice relates to the basis on which an organization chooses to compete. There are a number of ways to think about this **competitive stance**. Michael Porter suggests that although firms have unique features, in competitive terms there were a limited number of generic strategies available (see Porter, 1980). He argues that firms must choose to compete on costs or on the basis of differentiation. So-called cost leaders win customers on the basis of the economy of their offering which is available at lower prices than achieved by competitors. To remain profitable, such firms must therefore maintain lower operating costs and higher efficiencies than their competitors. Ryan Air is often heralded as an archetypal example of this cost-led strategy and has regularly been the most profitable airline in Europe. Ryan Air's passengers are not expecting luxury but accept that a basic service meets their needs given the low price paid. If customers cannot be won on the basis of price alone, then some form of differentiation is required. Apple has never won customers on the basis of low pricing and despite rumours of low cost variants of successful products like the iPhone, its products remain relatively more expensive than those of key competitors. They claim to justify a price premium by offering features, service levels or benefits that make the additional cost to the customer seem worthwhile. Porter argues that it is a serious mistake to attempt to straddle both cost leadership and differentiation. "The firm stuck in the middle is almost guaranteed low profitability ... and also probably suffers from a blurred corporate culture and a conflicting set of organizational arrangements and motivation system" (Porter, 1980: 42). We have adapted Porter's model to introduce two other generic strategies.

The first of these is a premium strategy adapted from Cliff Bowman's view of Porter's focused differentiation.[2] Luxury, high performance, heritage, rarity or some combination of these three features are common in firms following a premium strategy. Typically a significant price premium is justified by outstanding product or service performance. Firms such as Ferrari, Gucci, Rolex and others could be seen as differentiators but they do so in such specific segments that grouping them together with mass market differentiators overlooks subtle but significant differences.

Our second addition recognizes the innovative competitive strategy suggested by Insead researchers, W. Chan Kim and Renée Mauborgne in their 2005 book, *Blue Ocean Strategy*. Paradoxically, Kim and Mauborgne suggest that "the only way to beat the competition is to stop trying to beat the competition". They suggest breaking the traditional assumption that cost and value are locked in a linear relationship, i.e., as costs rise, so the value of the product rises and as a consequence, selling price also likely to rise. Instead, a *Blue Ocean Strategy* features high value delivered at low costs to mass markets. Rather than competing in a contested market space which they suggest will run red with the blood spilt through competition, their ideal is to find a Blue Ocean untainted by competition since what is being offered is so unusual that the very idea of competition becomes an irrelevance, at least for the time being. They suggest looking beyond current customers to non-customers in order to navigate toward such uncontested space. One example they offer is the Nintendo Wii console.

Rather than engage in direct competition with existing players Sony (Playstation) and Microsoft (Xbox), Nintendo looked to create a new type of gaming experience that would appeal to a far wider audience. Traditionally, gaming was the preserve of younger people, mostly male and mostly engaged in highly specific forms of platform, simulator or strategy gaming. By creating games which required physical movement on the part of the gamer, Nintendo managed to attract customers across the generations and across the gender divide with whole families engaging in bowling, tennis, boxing and other sport-related gaming. This new demographic were never likely to be customers of existing providers no matter how much more sophisticated the graphics became. By offering high value at low costs, a *Blue Ocean Strategy* creates a new market and the combination of high value and low costs makes it difficult for other firms to enter the space. By definition, a *Blue Ocean Strategy* should create a strategic group of one, for a time at least. Of course, other firms will see the opportunities of entering this blue ocean space and will soon begin the process of copying or mimicking the original innovator.

Figure 8.3 shows the four competitive stances that we suggest are available to an organization. We are sympathetic to Porter's suggestion about the dangers of trying to straddle more than one orientation. It is also worth considering the challenges of switching competitive stance. A move from economy to premium, or vice versa, may be hypothetically possible it is difficult to think of firms that have successfully managed the transition in a single step. More likely, there would be an intermediate step involved. Also, switches in competitive stance are not easy to reverse. Once you let go of a premium orientation it may be difficult to regain credibility in that space, at least in the short term. Various airlines attempted unsuccessfully to launch low cost carrier brands that were intended to run in parallel to their existing offering. Most ended badly.

The final decision point relates an organization's choice of peer group. This choice of who to compete with is clearly linked to the previous decision which sets out the

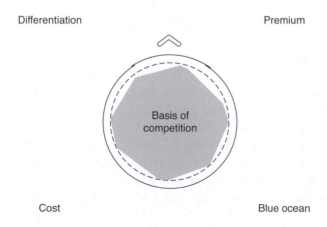

*Figure 8.3* **Competitive stance**

basis on which you will compete. In most cases where multiple providers of a given product or service exist, there key distinctions between those providers. Take the newspaper industry as one example. The industry generates revenues of over £5bn annually in the UK alone but has been in decline globally for a number of years. The emergence of 24-hour news channels combined with the growing trend for citizen reportage via Twitter (see Chapter 7) and other social media has led many commentators to predict the demise of newspapers at least in print form. In the UK there are over 300 titles on sale ranging from so-called broadsheets like the Times and the Guardian, to tabloids like the Daily Mail and the Daily Express. There are also specialist publications like the Financial Times as well as Sunday papers, regional and local papers, etc. Existing players in the newspaper industry have taken different approaches to their web-presence with some offering free access whilst others have introduced subscription-based services. Clearly any new entrant to the UK newspaper market would be unlikely to compete directly with all 300 existing titles. **Strategic Group Analysis** is a technique which operates somewhere between industry level analysis and individual firms. Michael Hunt first coined the phrase strategic group (1972)[3] and noted that the competitive challenges faced by individual organizations varied dependent upon the group to which they belonged. In simple terms a strategic group is defined as that subset of groups within a given industry that have similar characteristics, are competing for similar customers and are typically competing on the same basis as other members of the same group. Hence luxury car makers such as Ferrari and Aston Martin have more in common with each other than they do with Fiat, Ford or Skoda. The basis of competition often changes as you move from one strategic group to another and, consequently, there are often **mobility barriers**, which act to inhibit movement between strategic groups.

> **Mobility barriers** inhibit the movement of firms from one strategic group to another. When Toyota decided to enter the luxury car market it chose to develop the brand name Lexus (which supposedly stood for **Lux**ury **EX**ecutive **US**) as a way to overcome the barriers that it encountered when trying to move into a new strategic group.

When trying to identify strategic groups the first step is to look for features which distinguish one competitor from another. Some means of comparing competitors within the same market are reasonably objective and in the public domain, such as sales price. Others may be objective but individual organizations may jealously guard what they see as sensitive data such sales volume, profit margins, etc. Others still may be more subjective such as journalistic quality of a newspaper. In this latter category, proxy variables may be helpful. For example, when trying to assess journalistic quality you could look at industry awards, numbers of journalists employed, the average word count of articles or some amalgam of such measures.

The conduct of strategic group analysis is a relatively straightforward and is set out in Figure 8.4 below:

1  Identify a complete list of all current providers in the market
2  Identify several criteria that differentiate between the providers on this list
3  Check whether you can source public domain and/or proxy data for each of the criteria
4  Combine two criteria to produce a strategic map
5  Map individual firms in relation to axes chosen
6  Look for strategic groups (i.e., clusters of firms)
7  If the strategic groups aren't meaningful, repeat the process with new axes

*Figure 8.4*  **Steps in strategic group analysis**

Applying this process to the UK's newspaper industry could produce multiple views of strategic groups dependent upon which criteria are used to produce the strategic map. Two possible outcomes arise. If each new pair of axes places your organization in a different strategic group, this suggests that the industry is relatively immature with both customers and suppliers viewing the basis of competition as fluid. In these circumstances, strategists face significant choices about how to frame their industry, which grouping of competitors offers the most favourable outcomes and the basis on which to engage those competitors. If however, your organization remains in the same strategic group even when multiple different axes are chosen then your industry is reasonably mature. Faced with stable competitive groups, strategists must decide whether to persist within their current strategic group or seek to enter another. Finally, strategic group analysis can also highlight **strategic spaces** where no competitors currently exist. A strategic space could either be vacant because it has not yet been spotted as a viable or lucrative gap, or because other players have ruled it out.

To illustrate strategic group analysis, we consider one mapping of the UK newspaper industry, which compares titles on the basis of word count and coverage (see Figure 8.5 below). Word count might be interpreted as a proxy for journalistic depth, rigour or quality with longer articles signalling the kinds of extensive and investigative reporting, editorials and opinion pieces generally written with a more critical tone usually associated with broadsheet titles. Breadth of coverage meanwhile highlights that some titles cover the full range of news topics from politics to business, arts, entertainment, sport, etc. Other titles may take a particular focus on for example, sports or financial news. Mapping UK newpapers against these two axes produces at least three groups.

Group A contains full coverage players featuring with lengthier articles typified by titles such as the Guardian, Times or Independent. Group B contains fewer players and is populated by specialist, high quality titles such as the Financial Times. Group C comprises the main national tabloid titles since these feature reasonably comprehensive coverage of news but with a shorter, punchier writing style.

In mapping the industry, two players saw a gap represented by group D. The owners of the Daily Mail (DMG Media) faced the same challenging circumstances as all newspapers but developed an innovative offering, which exploited a strategic gap. Launched in 1999, the Metro newspaper was based on a different business model. It is free and available at commuter locations for buses, trains, subways and trams. It is short and designed to be read less than ten minutes (since this represented the optimum length of time commuters would devote to news). Most of the content is culled from sources such as the news agency Reuters but the Metro covers major news stories, sports and entertainment. Given that the product itself is free, it is based entirely on advertising revenue. The owners offer advertisers the attention of over one million consumers for five to ten minutes each weekday morning and adverts are strategically spaced amongst the articles as well as often featuring on a false front and back page feature to the paper.

The Independent newspaper was an established member of group A but faced with low circulation and questions over its viability, launched the "i" in 2010 as a shorter version of the original Independent newspaper. The i is priced competitively at 20p[4] in hard copy and for a small annual subscription on tablet or mobile devices. Offering high quality journalism but with lower word count the i now sells in higher volumes that the Independent. Both the i and the Metro occupy group D but they survive in that space using different business models. Remapping the newspaper industry using cover price as one of the two dimensions would separate these competitors into different groups and those responsible for each firm would need to decide whether to see each other as direct competitors.

One final thought on strategic group analysis merits attention. What are the consequences of being in a strategic group of one? To answer this question, it is necessary to understand whether you are an innovator moving into a new space before others have spotted it (as with the Metro newspaper example) or are the last player to leave a dying market. It is therefore worth reviewing how strategic groups have evolved over time, in say three or five year steps, and paying attention to individual organizations moving between strategic groups.

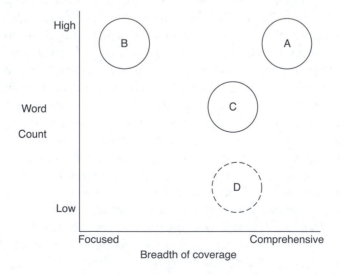

*Figure 8.5* **Strategic group analysis for UK newspaper industry**

| Core strategy statement | The challenge we face is [diagnostic statement] and our strategy is to achieve [intent] by [timeframe] by using our superior ability to [capability] to address [opportunity]. We will achieve this by... | | | |
|---|---|---|---|---|
| Aim | Retrenchment | | Consolidation | Growth |
| Tactic | Market penetration | Market development | Product development | Diversification |
| Method | Organic growth | | Acquisition | Partnership |
| Competitive stance | Cost | Differentiation | Premium | *Blue Ocean Strategy* |
| Strategic group | Within current strategic group | | In new strategic group | |

*Figure 8.6* **Option configurator**

From the analysis done in Chapters 4–7, it is possible to specify a core strategy which covers the main issues required. However, taken as a set, the five choices set out in Figure 8.6 below, enable you to generate a series of strategic options by considering different combinations of the answers to each of the areas covered.

For illustrative purposes, consider an organization which aims to grow. One option may see growth achieved through a process of gaining market share in areas where the organization already competes (market penetration), whilst another may see growth flowing from diversification. In turn, these competing choices could result from either organic growth or acquisition. Both options may see the organization persisting with a competitive stance based around differentiation, but they may differ in that option one, sees the organization sticking within its strategic group, whilst option two, envisages entering a new strategic group. These two options are summarized below:

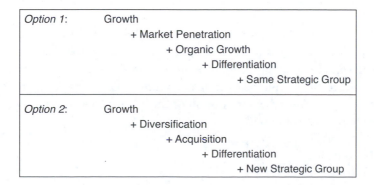

Option 1:     Growth
                    + Market Penetration
                         + Organic Growth
                              + Differentiation
                                   + Same Strategic Group

Option 2:     Growth
                    + Diversification
                         + Acquisition
                              + Differentiation
                                   + New Strategic Group

One level of checking is to look for internal consistency between the choices made for each option. For example, a *Blue Ocean Strategy* requires a strategic group of one which by definition requires that you create a new strategic group. Beyond this basic consistency test, many possible combinations emerge. It is unlikely that all will be equally attractive and most management teams quickly narrow down to a limited number of options.

## Strategists at work: Nokia

As a near 150-year-old organization, Nokia has seen dramatic changes but its recent past must surely represent one of the most turbulent periods in the organization's history. When he was appointed at Nokia's first non-Finnish Chief Executive Officer in 2010, Stephen Elop faced difficult choices. For an organization with a glittering history in the early days of the smartphone industry, Nokia had fallen behind key competitors and was in danger of becoming completely marginalized. Elop argued that the introduction of both Apple's iOS and Google's Android operating system meant that what had traditionally been a battle between individual handsets was now a war between ecosystems. Customers were at least as interested in the various apps and add-ons that were available as they were in the specifics of the handset. In crafting strategic options for the firm, there were at least two plausible choices. Nokia could either stick with the Symbian operating system that had been central to much of the firm's early successes in smartphone world or it could partner with another major player and adopt their operating system. Elop added dramatic emphasis with his "burning platform" speech which made it clear to all Nokia employees that doing nothing was *not* a viable option. Some might say that it was little surprise that Elop, a former Microsoft executive, chose to partner with Microsoft but many would argue that the choice saved Nokia. There are further details of Nokia's story in Case study 2 in Section D.

## Strategists at work in the running cases

*DMacL:* Did any of you formulate strategic options as you were developing strategy?

*Harry:* I'd answer that on two levels. On one level there are no options. We have a health service that needs to improve and a government that needs to be seen to be doing something about it. But on another level, we've really tried to devolve the options to the people that can make a difference. We're trying to encourage experimentation and a fast turnaround of the results. Anything that works, we're looking to roll out nationwide.

*RMacI:* Can you give us an example?

*Harry:* Bedtime bear.

*RMacI:* Sorry

*Harry:* The evidence is that reading bedtime stories to kids enhances intellectual capacity, enhances attachment behaviour, and so on. Its evidence based. But, how do you do it? Well, different places were trying different things and they meet every three or four months and they say, "these are the charts, we did this". They're measuring things on a day-to-day basis and what works is Bedtime Bear. He needs a story before he goes to sleep every night. So, you take Bedtime Bear to mummy and daddy and get them to read him a story. The kid gets a story. It's an aide memoir, you know, kid looks after Bedtime Bear; mum and dad read the story. So now, we've got health professionals handing out books when they go to see the kids. It's an option that works. The ones that don't work so well get dropped.

*Sandy:* We didn't have bears. What drives our thinking is that we know we have a lack of resources relative to the major IT companies moving into our world. We only have a certain amount of time; we only have a certain amount of money. We have to try to look for options that work to our best advantage. We've looked at different parts of the market and chosen on the basis of where do we have the biggest competitive advantage over many of our competitors. When we settle on that, it makes sense for us to go down that route.

*Kate:* When we launched Confused.com one of our big decisions was about whether we went for a full question set that insurers use to price a risk. I don't know whether you have ever filled out a form for car insurance but there are 105 questions in the superset if you collected everything you would end up answering 105 questions. It is absolutely massive. So, do you collect all the questions and then be able to produce an extremely accurate quote or, do you go with a subset which makes it faster but takes you down the route of an estimated quote. These were our strategic options, so we drew up a picture ... the length of time you spend on the website versus how accurate is the quote. When we launched we were the only players in the market and so started by delivering our quotes over email. The technology to do it over the web wasn't quite there yet and we made a strategic choice to launch sooner rather than later by not having the full bells and whistles. It allowed us to start learning the process of how we get people in and how the business model might work so that was a strategic choice we had to make. But we then had to change the whole business model a good few times before we settled on something that worked.

## Dos and don'ts

Before committing to a strategy, our strong advice would be to consider at least two plausible strategic options for delivering that strategy. For example, you could be fixed in your objective to grow but may wish to consider whether this is best done by acquisition or from organic growth. If the only available targets for acquisition are pursuing a different competitive orientation than your own, organic growth may seem a more attractive option. We will turn our attention to the evaluation of strategic options in the next chapter.

## Do

1　Take the time to specify at least two plausible strategic options.
2　Check the internal consistency of the choices that you are making in each strategic option.
3　Consult with key colleagues over their views.

## Don't

1　Get stuck in the middle in terms of competitive orientation.
2　Attempt to generate strategic options until you have a rudimentary strategy statement which links intent, foresight and capability.

# Who to read?

It should be clear that we have drawn on a range of key scholars to produce the options presented in this chapter. It is worth familiarising yourself with **Michael Porter's** work on competitive strategy. Not only is this the most highly cited work in the field, it contains a clear message. Whilst we may not entirely agree with the contents of that message, you should form your own judgement. A useful summary of his many contributions to the strategy field, and the ways in which his own thinking has developed since his early work, is provided in Joan Margetta's book "Understanding Michael Porter" (2012).

# CHAPTER 9

# Evaluating Strategy

O ne of the fundamental experiences for strategists is the need to make decisions. Henry Mintzberg's view of strategists is that they face complex, fragmented daily lives and often take decisions on the basis of recent interactions and partial information. The need to make decisions introduces a number of recognizable challenges such as the anchoring trap. Consider for a moment the following two questions:

Question 1: Is the population of Turkey greater than 35 million?
Question 2: What's your best estimate of the population of Turkey?

Adapted from Hammond et al. (2006)

John Hammond[1] and his colleagues argue that their arbitrarily chosen figure of 35 million in the first question tends to influence the answers given to the second question. They repeated these questions with two arbitrary guesses at Turkey's population: either 35 million or 100 million. They found that "without fail, the answers to the second question increase by many millions when the larger figure is used in the first question." Turkey's actual population is around 75 million and if you do not already happen to know this fact, the likelihood is that you would be influenced by the presence of an anchor figure. Strategists are often presented with such anchors from colleagues who may be well intentioned or who may be pursuing their own agenda. For example, a colleague may argue that your three most profitable competitors have been growing via acquisitions, then ask, should we proceed with an acquisition? Whilst, this seems transparent and obvious in isolation, it is far more difficult to spot anchors in the midst of a steady flow of information.

In this chapter we present an approach to one specific type of decision, namely decisions between the types of strategic options developed in Chapter 8. Whilst the structured process we set out is intended to be helpful, we are cognizant of the fact that such processes are open to abuse. The originator of HBO's TV series the Sopranos offers an honest insight into the ways in which decision making can be manipulated. When asked why he cast the late James Gandolfini in the lead role of Tony Soprano, he replied:

> There weren't many other candidates. We read a lot of people but in television you have to do that: troop in ten people so the network doesn't feel they're having it

pushed down their throat and then, eventually, after wasting all that time, you're convincing them to go with the one you wanted anyway.

David Chase, on the decision to cast James Gandolfini

From the Guardian (27 June 2013)

In response to the realization that making the right decision is vital, one response is to take your time. But Chase offers a salutary reminder that an apparently thorough process can, in fact, be an illusion. It is also true, that a cautious and meticulous process is open to the accusation of introducing paralysis by analysis. Indeed, Carnegie Mellon's Professor Herbert Simon coined the phrase "bounded rationality" (see Simon, 2000) to capture the part rational, part emotional way in which we tend to make decisions.

Simon suggests that we cope with complexity by simplifying situations to bound the problem. Others who study decision making suggest that we experience a strong tendency to draw on past experiences, either good or bad, as one form of boundary setting. Our ability to learn means, that we can develop shorthand or heuristics even after a single experience of a new task or decision. Former Harvard professor, Chris Argyris, championed the role of learning in a range of contexts including decision making. He defines learning as a circumstance where "the use of the programme necessary to perform the requisite action is so much under control that the control over the performance does not have to be conscious or explicit" (1977: 114). That is to say, we have truly learned something when we can execute tasks without giving it too much thought. A simple example such as learning to ride a bicycle or drive a car reinforces this sense that the activity sinks below our conscious awareness. We may drive a car, changing gears, lanes or speed without "thinking" about it. We may even be able to hold a conversation, think about our destination or admire the scenery whilst driving. However, to achieve mastery of the task such that it can be recalled in this way involves the ruthless generalization and storage of routines (Sussman, 1973). When we learn something for the first time, the experience usually involves failure, errors and disappointment. That is the essence of what is called learning by "trial and error". Argyris recognizes two different modes or models of learning, which they labelled double loop and single loop. **Double loop** learning involves learning from first principles. Imagine trying to strike a golf ball for the first time. One must conceptualize how to hold the golf club, how far away from the ball to stand, how fast to move, etc. These various "governing values" form part of our initial attempt to strike the ball. As we execute the task for the first time we may well make a mistake in one or more aspect of the problem. Perhaps we stood too close to the ball and missed altogether. Perhaps we were also trying to hit the ball too quickly and lost balance. The disappointment of missing the target would be seen as a mismatch or error.

Our learning process would take us back to reconsider the governing values of the problem, conceive a new plan for action, try this out and judge whether the results are acceptable. As we proceed we hope to reduce the mismatch or error that we experience to a point where results meet our expectations even though the outcome may not be perfect. For example, we may eventually develop a method of striking the ball which means that it travels fairly straight but perhaps not as far as we had hoped. Once, the mismatch or error reduces to a level that we can tolerate, Argyris suggests that we switch to a fundamentally different mode of learning. **Single loop** learning may continue to involve modest adjustments to the actions taken but no longer revisits the governing values of the problem. For example, our stance when striking the ball begins to become fixed and is no longer subject to revision. This is the ruthless generalization and storage process that Sussman refers to since we need standardization in order to memorize and categorize with any efficiency. A useful check is to consider how much spare mental capacity you have when executing a particular task. If the task demands all of your attention it is likely that you are engaged in double loop learning. If the task can be executed whilst you think of other things, engage in conversation or other activities, it is likely that you have transitioned from double to single loop learning. Given that most strategists have a long history of making decisions, our contention is that they will also have developed routines for making those decisions. As a means of capturing the decision making routine associated with evaluating strategic options, we suggest four criteria against which we have found useful (see Figure 9.1).

First, given the diagnosis of the organization's situation, is the strategic option in question an **appropriate** response? It is possible to imagine strategic options, which in and of themselves appear to be a good idea, but which are not appropriate to the circumstances in which the organization finds itself. When overstretched, consolidation might seem appropriate. When struggling to integrate earlier acquisitions, further growth by acquisition may not be appropriate. Further, when faced with a problematic situation, we often experience a subtle but powerful drive to try familiar solutions. These defensive routines may be comforting but they are rarely the appropriate response and are in fact, more typically one of the roots of the problem. There are now hard and fast rules but as noted in Chapter 4, an inappropriate response often further exacerbates the original problem.

Second, ask whether the strategic option in question is **achievable** within the constraints of your situation? It is not uncommon to identify strategic options which are an appropriate response to the situation but which fall foul of constraints such as the time, money or expertise required to successfully deliver against the strategy. When Steve Jobs returned to Apple his first priority was to stabilize an ailing business. Further investments in new product development would need to wait until profitability was achieved and confidence returned. The iPod, iPad and iPhone product lines could hypothetically have been winning ideas but were not achievable at that point in Apple's evolution.

A third criterion is to consider the political landscape within which the strategic option would be delivered. Some ideas are both appropriate and achievable in the technical or practical sense but there is a lack of political will to deliver a successful outcome. Hence a third question is, is it **astute** to pursue this strategic option? The stakeholder and cultural analysis from Chapter 4's diagnosis offers one means of assessing the political and cultural climate. It is not uncommon for firms to have clear norms that would be difficult to overcome. In the UK, the National Health Service has always been free at the point of delivery. Extensive involvement of private healthcare providers would not necessarily be seen as politically saleable and in circumstances where an option is seen as a bridge too far, it is likely to fail because of lack of support, buy-in and traction.

The fourth and final criterion when evaluating strategic options relates to their **sustainability**. Even in circumstances where an idea is seen as appropriate, achievable and astute there could still be reasons to set it aside. In particular, if a strategic option creates short term gain but creates long term risks or damage it is not worth pursuing unless all other options have been exhausted. The relationship between antibiotics and bacteria is a helpful means of illustrating this short term, long-term dilemma. This sense of sustainability is central to strategy since it drives home the need to link short term actions to long term consequences.

In our experience, few strategic options are uniformly good or bad. The evaluation matrix below creates a formal structure to a conversation, which would otherwise be elusive, inconclusive and overly implicit. It is not intended to suggest that a purely scientific and rational approach to evaluation is possible. Nevertheless, a rudimentary but explicit assessment of each strategic option maximizes the chances of overcoming the kinds of anchoring, framing or habitualized responses which we set out earlier.

The evaluation matrix presented below suggests a fairly detached and neutral approach to the choice of which strategic option to pursue. We would acknowledge that this overlooks the key role that emotion plays in decision making and this is an issue, which we return to in more detail in Section C. For now, we would simply observe that we all have a tendency to revise history in our retelling of events. Karl Weick describes the process by which we retrospectively account for outcomes in his book Sensemaking (1993):

> The source of coherence lies elsewhere than in intention. There is not a transition from imagination, through intention, into execution. Instead, there is an imaginative interpretation of execution that imputes sufficient coherence to the execution that it could easily be mistaken for an intention.

| | Appropriate? | Achievable? | Astute? | Sustainable? |
|---|---|---|---|---|
| Strategic option 1 | ✓ | ✓ | ✓ | ✓ |
| Strategic option 2 | ✗ | ✓ | ✓ | ✗ |
| Strategic option n | ✓ | ✓ | ✗ | ✓ |

*Figure 9.1* A³S evaluation matrix

What Weick is very eloquently drawing our attention to is the very human process of narrating events and decisions in ways, which places us in a positive light. If a story about the decisions we took is sufficiently plausible, and is told sufficiently often, it can supplant the actual set of cause and effect relationships at play. History, they say, "is told by the winners". As strategists we therefore have a tendency to claim the benefits of successful choices, whilst distancing ourselves from problematic ones. Think of controversial decisions like Coca-Cola's decision to change the recipe of its iconic product, or successful decisions like Groupon's move into online, deep-discounting. Each is told through the eyes of heroes or villains since strategic decisions are rarely neutral.

## Strategists at work: Admiral Insurance

Admiral Insurance was founded in 1993 by a small start-up team, which included Kate Buell-Armstrong from our running cases. Admiral targets those customers that other insurers are least interested in like younger drivers, owners of faster and more powerful cars, those living in inner cities or drivers with a combination of these characteristics. In an industry where many players have made losses on a regular basis, Admiral has grown rapidly and profitably. Since its creation, Admiral has lived through several major innovations including the move to internet-based sales and the creation of the aggregator business model, which occurred when it launched Confused.com. As a means of dealing with change, the founding directors introduced a simple process which they call "Champion and Challenger." Chief Executive Officer Henry Engelhardt is clear that any business needs "fresh blood, new ideas, new ways of doing things". The firm makes a virtue of low cost experimentation to generate insight into what works. When someone comes forward with a new idea, a clearly defined test is set up where the challenger (the new idea) can compete with the champion (the existing way of doing something). If the new idea is better, it is adopted and the process repeats itself next time someone comes up with a new challenger. For example, you take a 100% of the customers coming to your website; you'd say 10% of them at random will see the new version of something, the other 90% will get our champion. You look at the numbers and see what's working better. Admiral's approach represents a simple and structured approach to option evaluation.

## Strategists at work in the running cases

*RMacI:* What can you tell us about making big decisions, evaluating options? Let's start with you Sandy.

*Sandy:* It's about what are you realistically capable of doing. You might have a view which went, "If we were the best resourced organisation in the world and we had the greatest talent in the world, we could do all of this". But actually I'm not. I don't have all those resources. I might be working towards them but right here, right now, this is what I have, so this is realistically what we can do as a next step. It may be a big step, it may be a small step. At the moment we're in a discussion about the cloud and I'm in the process of collecting different views. Not being judgmental, just saying "talk to me about this, guys, tell me about it" and then we'll think about it in the context of what our business is and what are the options.

*Harry:*  In my role it was the government minister who made the big decisions. The Civil Servants are just there to advise. There's a black art in the Civil Service about advising in a way that makes it very plain what outcome you want. If they don't make the recommended decision then they're described as "very courageous".

*Kate:*  Both in the parent company, Admiral, and at Confused.com we have what I'd call a democratic spirit. People feel listened to in that they have the ability to talk about decisions and that, you know, the actual implementation can be changed as a result of that. But generally, strategic decisions are led from the top.

*RMacI:*  So big choices like should we be selling on the internet, those big step changes that have happened in your organization's story, how have those decisions been framed and taken?

*Kate:*  They've been taken by a very small coterie at the top of the organization who have maybe taken advice, who have great intellects themselves, who know about stuff, you know, they may take advice from other people. After a lot of listening, essentially it's a decision being taken by "les Grands Fromages" at the top of the organization.

*DMacL:*  But from what you're saying, Kate, they don't seem like decisions that would surprise the rest of the organization.

*Kate:*  No because we're also fairly open about where our thinking is headed.

*Donald:*  Back to that thing of trust, so they trust you.

*Kate:*  And actually, yes. I mean the management, the sort of implementation level, if you like, trust the senior management and the Board trust the management team as a whole because of their success rate. You know, nothing breeds success like success. You assume that your next thing will be a success because you've come from a track record of success.

## Dos and don'ts

Whilst we acknowledge the very human tendency to react on the spur of the moment, we also believe that planning and preparation have their place. It is therefore, a sensible first step to draw up an explicit approach which weighs the pros and cons of the various strategic options available to the organization. This is especially true since strategists often need to take people with them in order for the chosen strategy to be delivered.

### Do

1   Consider at least two plausible strategic options.
2   Use the criteria set out in the evaluation matrix but use a rudimentary scale of either yes/no or high/medium/low rather than attempting a more complex assessment.

3  Involve other key stakeholders in building a shared assessment of which option(s) to pursue.
4  Remember that options may be pursued in series or in parallel but beware of attempting to take on too much too soon. Prioritizing matters.

## Don't

1  Set up a preferred option and a straw-man option.
2  Fix the results by obscuring any negative aspects of the evaluation process.
3  Expend huge amounts of time on this evaluation process. You will typically find that you secure the majority of the available insights fairly quickly.

## Who to read?

**Chris Argyris** died in 2013 leaving a legacy of research and insights spanning half a century. His writing on learning processes is sharp, insightful and well worth reading. He has an extensive catalogue of books and articles but we would suggest starting with "Teaching Smart People How to Learn."

# CHAPTER 10

# Building a Comprehensive Strategy

s we have progressed through Section B we have been incrementally building toward the articulation of a comprehensive statement of strategy. In developing strategic options (Chapter 8) you specified ten key decision points that relate to strategy. Having evaluated at least two plausible strategic options (Chapter 9), you should now have settled on a strategy which is appropriate to the organization's circumstances, is viewed as achievable within the constraints imposed by those circumstances, is astute in the sense that key stakeholders will offer support when delivering the strategy and is sustainable in that it solves a short term problem without creating long term difficulties.

In this short chapter, we add two further dimensions to deliver what, in our view, represents a comprehensive statement of strategy. These additional items act as a link to the daily operational activities of the organization. The first addition is to make explicit what it is that the organization does to create value for customers, or in the case of public organizations, service users. We call this the **offering** of the organization. In Chapter 5 we discussed the notion that intent could either be direct or indirect. This links to the organization's offering in the wider sense. Earlier, we used Amazon as an example to suggest that it's offering could either be described as retail or trust. The former is a more direct account of how Amazon currently makes money. The latter suggests, over time, that customers engage in retail transactions with Amazon because of the extent to which they trust the firm to (a) provide product reviews from other customers and (b) handle any complaints or returns sympathetically. Both are valid views of Amazon's offering and it is a matter of preference when deciding how best to capture this. It could be that the offering is described in one sense to those inside the organization but in another when communicating to the outside world. Regardless, being explicit about the basis on which customers will value the organization is a helpful elaboration.

The second and final addition is to specify the **audience** that the organization's strategy will engage. Marketing and strategy are closely related subjects and by introducing a focus on a particular audience we begin to imply that your strategy may target particular customers, market segments or types of service user. In all likelihood, there will be an equally important but implied set of assumptions which suggest that you will not be serving other audiences. We have deliberately adopted the term audience rather than market since it applies across the full range of commercial, public and third sector organizations. Audience also permits a sense in which stakeholders in the widest sense need to be engaged by your strategy.

Combined, these two additional items link the strategy of an organization to its operational activities. For example, if the organization faces a challenge of business expansion or recovery through sales growth, the audience would comprise the customers and the offering would specify the product or service, which those customers find valuable.

Figure 10.1 Below sets out the complete list of twelve items that we see as required to build a comprehensive strategy.

Using the 12 components listed in Figure 10.1 it is possible to craft a statement of strategy that forces linkage between individual components to produce a logically coherent whole. Checking the internal consistency and comprehensiveness of your strategy then becomes straightforward. In our view, building a comprehensive strategy is not difficult. Rather, it is disarmingly simple. Adopting an almost mechanical approach to the production of strategy may seem unlikely to work but our experience suggests that structuring the key choices in this way nullifies the tendency toward a humpty-dumpty effect. All too often we see breathtakingly detailed chunks of analysis woven into an elaborate strategic plan, which nevertheless contains key

| 1. Diagnosis | An assessment of the challenge facing the organization and which the strategy needs to overcome. |
|---|---|
| 2. Intent | What the organization is trying to achieve. |
| 3. Timeframe | The period covered by the strategy. |
| 4. Capability | An active statement of core capability ... "our ability to". |
| 5. Opportunity | Trends from the operating environment. |
| 6. Aim | The outcome of the strategy specified as ... consolidation, retrenchment or growth. |
| 7. Tactic | How the aim will be delivered ... market penetration, market development, product development or diversification. |
| 8. Method | The mode of execution employed in the strategy ... organic growth, acquisition or partnership. |
| 9. Stance | The basis on which you will engage in competition ... cost, differentiation, premium or Blue Ocean. |
| 10. Strategic group | Who you will engage in competition ... within current group or in a different strategic group. |
| 11. Offering | What the organization does to create value. |
| 12. Audience | Who the organization wants to engage. |

*Figure 10.1* **The 12 key components of strategy**

omissions. Systems theorist Peter Checkland (1990) uses the analogy of a bicycle to establish what he means by an **emergent property**. He observes that a pedal, chain or wheel is incapable of producing forward motion independently. Yet when these components are assembled in a particular configuration and allowed to operate in concert, forward motion is possible.[1] In our view, strategy behaves in a similar manner. We have seen many elaborate strategies which feature the equivalent of the handlebars and seat in each other's position, three front wheels, no back wheel, a chain but no pedals. The components of strategy set out in Figure 10.1 allow a first order check to take place, namely whether all the components are in place.

---

In Checkland's terms, an **emergent property** is something which occurs at the level of the whole rather than at the level of the component parts. We return to the concepts of emergence and emergent properties in chapters 12 and 13.

---

Each of the three anonymized strategy statements below was prepared by a management team during strategy workshops that we were facilitating. They were prepared at the start of the workshop in response to a prompt question, which was "summarise your strategy in no more than 50 words".[2] None of the organizations was failing, many of strategists involved in the workshop had studied strategy in the context of MBA or similar programmes and all those concerned had long experience in leadership roles.

Example 1:  Our strategy is to keep our culture whilst growing rapidly.
Example 2:  Our strategy is to diversify.
Example 3:  Our strategy is to integrate the four operating divisions within the organization without interrupting service provision or increasing costs.

These three examples are typical of the response when we ask for a succinct statement of strategy. In our view, each is simultaneously correct in the broadest sense yet deficient in key respects. Each statement was associated with a beautifully produced strategy document that ran to several pages. Two were linked to powerpoint presentations using extensive visual images and analyses. One was used as the basis for a strategy roadshow within the organization concerned. None however, met the requirements that we suggest represent the minimum level of detail required for a strategy.

First, none of the examples specified the challenges facing the organization. Whilst these challenges were known to those working in each organization, they did not feature as an explicit recognition of the problem that the strategy was designed to address. The team responsible for the second example above knew that core markets were in terminal decline, hence the need to diversify. Second, none specified a time frame within which the strategy needed to be delivered. Members of the management teams concerned had their own individual views on timing and urgency. In some cases these aligned, but at least one member of each team held differing views on timing which they had explored with colleagues. Finally, none of the examples given specifies ends (intent), means (capabilities) or conditions (opportunities in the operating environment) with sufficient clarity.

When presented out of context, these responses to our "say your strategy in 50 words or less" challenge seem vague. Having repeated this process with many management teams, we would suggest that strategists often operate with implicit, and in some cases transient, views on the key components of strategy. This is understandable given the busy lives that strategists lead but it is often compounded by a lack of consensus amongst their peer group. With limited additional effort, the checklist approach we are proposing forces ambiguities to be clarified and oversights or omissions to be rectified.

Assuming that the basic components of strategy are specified, the next challenge is to assemble them in such a way that they operate in concert. We tend to work with three different versions of strategy statements, which vary in the level of specificity that they require. The first of these represents a minimal, but robust strategy which acknowledges a particular challenge, which the organization faces then links a statement of intent to an assessment of the operating environment and the resources available to the organization. It first appeared in Chapter 7 and it links ends, means and conditions but does so in relation to a specific timeframe which bounds the strategy and increases the likelihood of focused activity to deliver that strategy.

If any of the five components set out in the minimal strategy (see Figure 10.2) are missing or ambiguous, we would consider it as an inadequate statement of strategy. Many organizations find it helpful to use this template as a checklist. A further elaboration of strategy forms the basis of what we describe as an intermediate strategy, which specifies nine of the 12 components. Finally, a fully specified strategy contains defined responses to all 12 component parts of the strategy statement.

Figure 10.2 Sets out these three variants of strategy statements.

| Minimal robust strategy | The challenge we face is [DIAGNOSTIC STATEMENT]. We will develop and exploit our superior [CAPABILITY] to capitalize on [OPPORTUNITY] and achieve [INTENT] by [TIMEFRAME]. |
|---|---|
| Intermediate strategy | The challenge we face is [DIAGNOSTIC STATEMENT]. Our strategy is therefore one of [AIM] delivered through [METHOD]. We will develop and exploit our superior [CAPABILITY] as the provider of [OFFERING] to [AUDIENCE]. This will allow us to capitalize on [OPPORTUNITY] and achieve [INTENT] by [TIMEFRAME]. |
| Fully specified strategy | The challenge we face is [DIAGNOSTIC STATEMENT]. Our strategy is therefore one of [AIM] delivered through a combination of [TACTIC] and [METHOD] competing on the basis of [STANCE] within [STRATEGIC GROUP]. We will develop and exploit our superior [CAPABILITY] as the provider of [OFFERING] to [AUDIENCE]. This will allow us to capitalize on [OPPORTUNITY] and achieve [INTENT] by [TIMEFRAME]. |

*Figure 10.2* **Strategy statements**

The linguistic form of the three strategy statements in Figure 10.2 is intended as a guide and starting point rather than a restrictive and formulaic requirement. The main purpose of these guides is that they allow the assembly of progressively more detailed accounts of strategy. Whilst we would encourage flexibility and creativity in terms of sequencing and wording we would strongly suggest that the basic components set out above should always apply in building a robust strategy.

We close by offering one illustrative example of a fully specified strategy. When working with an independent food manufacturer we developed a strategy statement in collaboration with the management team. The eventual output (which has been anonymized) read:

> The challenge we face is that our core market is not growing and our strategy is therefore to become the leading player in our sector. This strategy will be delivered through a combination of market development and the acquisition of competitors to achieve economies of scale allowing us to exploit our superior ability to manage costs in the production process. We will therefore compete on the basis of cost, offering consistently high standard goods at low production costs. We are seeking to become the dominant player within our strategic group by 2015. In so doing we will achieve growth in turnover to at least £25million and be seen as the preferred provider of our products to our target customers.

Using the checklist from Figure 10.2 we can see that all 12 components are in place in this sample strategy statement, even though the ordering and wording has changed slightly to improve readability. This was not the first version of the strategy articulated by the management team concerned but over the course a few short and structured conversations it became a shared and clear view of the firm's strategy.

As we will see in Chapter 11, once assembled, a strategy statement such as the one shown above represents the beginning not the end of the strategist's journey. Key decisions flow from the articulation of strategy. For example, how much managerial attention, financial resource and time will be spent on each individual component of the statement? It is possible to see how the specification of a strategy in this way can generate action plans that begin to deliver the strategy. In the final chapter of this section we put this carefully conceived strategy into the wider context of our strategy cycle.

## Strategists at work: Oticon

Few organizations become more famous for the way in which they are managed than for their products or services. Danish hearing aid specialists Oticon were founded in 1904 and now have sales offices in over 20 countries. When Lars Kolind was appointed as Chief Executive Officer in 1988, Oticon was facing grave difficulties. The firm had lost its way just as the digital revolution was affecting its industry. Surprisingly for an internal candidate, Kolind eventually settled on a revolutionary approach based around a new strategy. Rather than focus on cost cutting, Kolind and his fellow directors initiated a new strategy which he set out in a six-page memo encouraging staff to "think the unthinkable" (see Foss, 2003 for further details). The new strategy placed a clear emphasis on competing through innovation and rapid product development. To deliver step changes in performance in these key areas, Kolind coined the term "spaghetti organization" to capture the far reaching implications of an approach which saw individuals designing their own working day. Everything hinged around a short project approval process. Once a new idea was approved, the project leader selected their own team from amongst the staff. This meant that people worked on multiple teams, often performing different roles in each team. Indeed, there was even a requirement that everyone worked on at least one project that took them out of their normal sphere of activities. To make this management revolution work, Kolind knew he needed to change the physical infrastructure of Oticon's offices, the IT and support systems, the incentive system and the very nature of what it meant to have a job. American management writer Tom Peters observed that such dramatic change would either have to happen over a weekend or take forever (1994). After careful planning and consultation, Kolind's plan was implemented quickly and effected significant performance gains.

## Strategists at work in the running cases

**RMacI:** Did you write your strategy down in order to be explicit about the decisions you were making?

**Kate:** We did in the early days of Confused.com where we documented things quite carefully. We actually used Porter's material extensively, starting with Five Forces and working through other things too like strategic options and mutual reinforcement. In part we did that because, with the exception of me, the management team was actually quite inexperienced and I was trying to teach them a way of thinking about these sorts of strategy issues. But as time has gone on, and they've gained more experience, I think we probably write less down now than we used to. I would take the view that actually it is quite time consuming and often you don't have the time to be formal even though it helps to crystallize your thinking about some things. Maybe it also depends on the type of person you are, sometimes you don't need that. I think the more experience you get the more you find yourself saying "well actually I don't need to write that down I just do that in my head". Saying that, at Admiral we documented the strategy as a rolling five-year plan which was an enormous spreadsheet – the size would blow up a lesser computer. But you could run simulations through it to help you decide if a change was helpful or not in the scheme of the overall plan to be profitable.

**Sandy:** For us, writing it all out in the form of a strategic plan was a big thing. It pushed the management team to make some agreements and to stick to them. I'd say one of the benefits of the work we did on strategy was to formalize what some of the thinking was and to get people to buy into that. It helped to go through the thought processes and we arrived at not dissimilar conclusions as to the best way for the business to develop. A lot of it came down not being able to compete with certain people in certain areas of the market because that's not where our strengths lie. Writing it all out helped focus our minds on where do our strengths lie and where are the opportunities?

*Harry:* Personally I'm not a big fan of strategy documents. I'd rather focus on enabling the people who can make difference to take responsibility for getting on with it. That said, the political side of my job meant that we did see action plans, manifesto pledges and the like being turned into strategy documents. Like Kate said, maybe its personality related. Whatever works for you I guess.

## Dos and don'ts

As indicated by our three strategists, a written strategy is not a prerequisite for organizational success. Many strategists survive without a written account of their strategy. Some may inherit organizational circumstances where the strategy has been in place for some time and it is largely a question of continuity, others actively choose to operate with a tacit and implicit sense of strategy. Why then, should you take the time to write your strategy down We suggest several reasons for the disciplined practice of writing strategy as explicitly as possible. First, **strategic drift** suggests that at some point a reorientation will become necessary. This may be easier when both the existing and the new strategy are explicit. Second, most strategists work in circumstances where they cannot deliver outcomes alone. The need to involve, engage and inspire others offers a powerful motivation for making sure that they have a shared understanding of strategy. Third, by engaging others in crafting a strategy you expose your own thinking, assumptions and biases to scrutiny and, in dialogue with others, you may spot weaknesses or omissions. Fourth, it is not nearly as difficult as it is sometimes portrayed. Using the approach suggested here, strategy writing becomes a simple task that is quick, efficient and produces logically robust outcomes.

---

Organizations experience **strategic drift** when they gradually focus on the delivery of an agreed strategy to the exclusion of an awareness of what is going on around them. As a result, most organizations experience the need for periodic adjustments in their strategy to bring them back into alignment with trends in their operating environment.

---

## Do

1  Adopt the logically articulated format set out here in sentence form. The structure forces coherence and its intelligibility is the best gauge of this coherence.

2  Allow yourself and others permission to develop strategy statements iteratively and collaboratively. Whiteboards and flip charts are powerful tools in the early stages of strategy writing.

3  Test drive your strategy to assess how others react. Does it appeal, is it clear, do they interpret it in the same way that you expected?

4  Consider developing a shorthand, strapline or soundbite version of the strategy after you have defined each of the key components but not before. Amazon's "get big, fast" strategy is a good example of a soundbite **but** this needs to be linked to a fully articulated strategy.

## Don'ts

1  Don't make it too long. We have purposely restricted the strategy to around 100 words, one paragraph and only a few sentences. A much longer strategy document may eventually follow, setting out supporting data, competitor analysis, etc. The aim here is to specify a complete strategy as succinctly as possible.

2  Don't imagine that you should have only one strategy – unless you only face one challenge.

3  Don't be afraid to tear up your strategy and start again. By making the process of strategy writing quick and easy, we are minimizing the sense in which you become wedded to something that has been painstakingly crafted over many weeks and months. If the strategy doesn't feel right, it should only take minutes to identify the source of the problem and effect a redraft around those components.

# Who to read?

**Peter Checkland's** work on soft systems methodology is very influential amongst researchers studying systems theory. Whilst, he does not directly discuss strategy he offers one of the clearest articulations we have found on emergent properties, which helps reframe Mintzberg's notion of emergent strategy.

# CHAPTER 11

# The Strategy Cycle

**H**aving established the process by which strategists can produce carefully conceived plans, covering the 12 key decision points which in our estimation represent a comprehensive strategy, we now return to the strategy cycle model which we introduced briefly in Chapter 1. In so doing, we present our own distinctive approach to strategic management, which blends strategic logic with the dynamics of bringing strategy to life in organizational settings. In Section C we will offer a more theoretically grounded justification for this approach and discuss the theoretical developments, which led us to create the strategy cycle. For the time being we will maintain a clear focus on how to address the practical problem of doing strategy. We have used the strategy cycle in a wide range of commercial, charitable and public organizations. It draws on two distinct but complementary dimensions of leadership. The first of these deals with functional and performance related operational issues, whilst the second is concerned with what the strategy means for those involved.

The symbolic activities and inspirational prowess of leaders is something we can all recognize when we think of famous leaders, yet most accounts of strategic management neglect these concerns. In Chapter 2, we highlighted recent interests in the strategy literature where the so-called strategy-as-practice movement has sought to draw attention to what strategists actually do. In our experience, what they actually do is talk. Not idly or without purpose; rather, strategists talk to themselves and to other stakeholders about what is happening around them. They interpret events and compare these with their aspirations and fears using two specific types of talk. One relates to the organization as a business and talk here tends to feature diagnoses, analysis, benchmarking, measures, targets, etc. Meanwhile, a second and parallel stream of talk is going on focused on the organization as a social phenomenon. Here the talk tends to focus on anecdotes, images, rumours, gossip, speculation and storylines (either real or imagined).

When we focus on strategy as something that organizations have, our attention is drawn to logical and control-oriented tasks. In Chapter 4 we highlighted the fact that this can mean that we focus on problem-solving rather than problem framing. When we focus on the strategy as something which organizational members talk about, we expand our view of what is happening. There is, of course, an important place for business related issues but our tendency to place these issues in the foreground often pushes other social, organizational and cultural issues to the periphery. Our solution is to recreate the historic role of the Bard as a means of blending logic with the need to maintain and develop social order, engage others and build cohesion through creative acts such as storytelling and other forms of "meaning-making". This process sits alongside the more traditional concerns with making sure that everything is "working" or functioning. So, for us, strategic management involves the familiar tasks involved production of rational plans on the one hand, and the creative development of an engaging and shared sense of meaning on the other.

To begin our explanation of the strategy cycle, we focus on the familiar path set out in Figure 11.1 below. In highlighting the need to produce a carefully conceived plan we are in complete agreement with the strategic management orthodoxy. In Chapters 4–10 we have provided a structured approach to the development of such plans by moving from a diagnosis of the challenge that the plan is intended to address, to the creation of a comprehensive strategy statement. Yet, already the strategy cycle is moving beyond a traditional view of planning in key ways.

First, strategic plans are not born in a vacuum. They develop from our ability to imagine a future state for the organization. When John F Kennedy suggested that NASA would place a man on the moon and return him safely to earth, he was stretching beyond what was seen as achievable. Similarly, Jeff Bezos, Bill Gates, Steve Jobs and others are attributed with anticipating a future state which was, in some cases, dramatically different than the prevailing circumstances. Second, plans rarely make a seamless transition from idea to action. Rather, we acknowledge that strategists are confronted with the need to improvise when the reality of the lived situation does not map precisely to the predicted circumstances of the carefully conceived plan. This is a truism, which is recognized in many spheres. Professional boxers use the phrase "everyone has a plan, until they get punched in the face".[1] Within the strategy cycle, strategists engage do not engage in improvisation randomly but in a way, which is informed by the planning process which preceded the need for improvisation. Planning is therefore an essential pre-condition which equips those involved with a repertoire of responses and, equally importantly, with a finely tuned sense of who and what to pay attention to (and how) when encountering unexpected departures from the plan. Third, as improvisation in occurring, the strategy cycle acknowledges that strategists will attempt to craft a story that generates meaning from what is happening in order to explain why it is happening. Making sense of what is happening around us is a quintessentially human tendency. Using leadership to engage others in this process is the real craft of strategic management. The gap between what we thought would happen and what actually appears to be happening demands our attention and requires us to seek a new version of social cohesion, shared purpose and collective action. As the original plan runs into difficulties we are challenged to move forward, somehow.

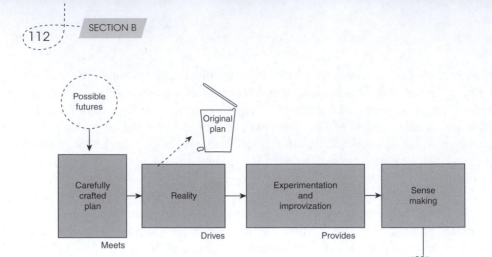

*Figure 11.1* **Moving beyond strategy as plans**

Having set out three distinctive features of the strategy cycle, we need one further addition to complete our explanation of how strategists and strategy interact. Everyday life is busy and to cope we each use simple heuristics or **rules of thumb**.

> **Rules of thumb** offer a shorthand way of guiding decisions. Less precise but also much less time-consuming than a full analysis, rules of thumb allow us to be roughly right most of the time.

A common mistake when attempting to change strategy is to believe that sufficient careful planning will allow you to anticipate all eventualities and to design detailed contingencies from the outset. Our advice is to avoid this impossible task. Instead, we advocate spending time identifying and reframing the rules of thumb, which underpin the organization's current form. These rules of thumb, rather like the rules of a game or grammar, provide structure within and through which emergent order arises from interactions. By engaging colleagues in a conversation about the organization it is possible to negotiate a shorthand account of the organization's practice. For example, Apple's insistence that it controls both hardware and software is one example of a rule of thumb.

Rules of thumb occur in at least two different types. One set governs how and where we conduct business. One example would be General Electric's (GE) dictum that every GE business should be number one or two in its sector. Others may dictate issues such as profit margins, risk appetite or relationships to other members of your supply chain. These **rules of thumb for business** do not necessarily hold true for every circumstance but they allow broad coherence to decision making processes. A second type governs the way we interact with colleagues. The UK high street firm, Pret a Manger, insists that all managers spend time in-store making and serving sandwiches on a regular basis to reinforce a particular culture which promotes close communication between management and employees as well as a passion for the quality of the food served. This is an example of a **rule of thumb for organization** since it suggests particular patterns of behaviour, which will be seen as acceptable and by implication, behaviours which would be seen as inappropriate. In any organization, these two sets of rules of thumb are inter-related, helping to sustain and generate each other as depicted in Figure 11.2.

Woven together like strands of organizational DNA, these two sets of rules of thumb interact each time a decision has to be made. A commercial opportunity may present itself and, in deciding whether it is worth pursuing, strategists must ask whether it fits with the rules of thumb. Where something conforms to both the business and organizational rules of thumb, it will be taken forward. However, there will be occasions where opportunities highlight tensions between the organizational and business rules of thumb. Perhaps something is commercially lucrative enough to satisfy the business rules of thumb but involves behaviours that are seen as unacceptable. Or, the opposite situation may arise if something which feels like a good thing to do, is financially marginal or incurs more costs than it recovers. In circumstances where such tensions are encountered, strategists must work to find an accommodation or resolution of the situation. Perhaps it is necessary to revise one or other set

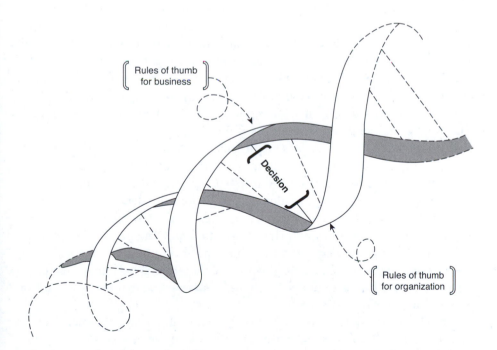

*Figure 11.2* **Rules of thumb for business and organization**

of rules. Perhaps a more nuanced understanding becomes apparent for example, we should do the right thing so long as it incurs a loss of no more than 5%. Surfacing, reassessing and stewarding these rules of thumb are essential parts of the strategist's job. Another of their job's is setting in place a climate that fosters confidence in those who find themselves making tradeoffs between rules of thumb when situations, such as those described above, arise. Indeed, since rules of thumb are simplified and idealized structures, they can only ever act as a rough guide. In actual situations, sets of rules will operate in unique ways in that they will be "functionalised" differently each time they are invoked. Perhaps this is the true source of diversity and creativity in strategy and is the basis of the kind of structured improvisations that give rise to a form of emergent strategy. Later in Chapter 13 we will suggest that these rules of thumb act, at least partially, to condition what emerges during periods of improvisation.

How then, does one identify rules of thumb? Based on the work presented in Chapters 4–10, one obvious source of desired or ideal rules of thumb is the comprehensive strategy statement which each template builds cumulatively into a set of 12 key decision points. Each key term could be expressed as a rule of thumb. Indeed, our view is that this is the real value of crafting a plan. Rather than focusing on the production of a detailed script, our use of planning focuses on establishing the broad principles which will underpin subsequent improvisation.

Armed with an idealized set of rules of thumb from an agreed strategy statement you may feel prepared for the journey ahead but it is worth noting that there alongside these newly articulated rules of thumb, there are likely to be an extant set in operation. Many of these will have become established in the organization precisely because they have been helpful and appropriate. However, the fact that you are countenancing the introduction of a new strategy suggests that at least some of your rules of thumb may need to be reassessed. It is often observed that culture eats strategy for breakfast[2] and it is for this reason that the strategy cycle focuses on talk in both business and organizational terms. Many good strategic intentions have withered in the face of organizational resistance from within.

A key stage in the strategy cycle is the surfacing existing rules of thumb. Our own approach is to instigate a reflexive conversation amongst members of the organization, typically in a workshop setting. A first step may simply be to ask people to tell a striking story about their organization and, in so doing, to detail key moves, decisions and other distinctive features of the narrative. It is then possible to replay these stories in terms of rules of thumb. The stories told may feature recurring themes around the importance of external partnerships and acquisitions (see the ABB case) or conversely, may focus on organic growth (see the Admiral Insurance example in Chapter 9). Figure 11.3 sets out key questions, which we tend to use when establishing an existing set of rules of thumb.

As an interesting aside, we would note that these rules of thumb emerge in the very conversations they are said to generate. This recursive process however, does not affect the fact that, whatever the philosophical or ontological status of rules of

Q1.  Can you describe the organization through a story which exemplifies either positive or negative aspects of its current state?

Q2.  What, if any, are the recurring patterns or themes in the organization?

Q3.  What are the rules of the game in the organization?

Q4.  Does the organization have any bad habits…and can these be expressed as rules of thumb?

Q5.  Who breaks the rules of thumb? under what circumstances? and what are the consequences for the rule breaker(s)?

*Figure 11.3* **Prompt questions for existing rules of thumb**

thumb, we can usefully talk about them *as if* they are real since they are real in their effects. Therefore, the strategy cycle needs elaborated to show how conversations about both categories of rules of thumb interact with the more formal process of planning (we return to this theme shortly). As individuals attempt to make sense of what is going on around them, they iterate between the unexpected events which they encounter and how these experiences chime or clash with existing and/or aspired rules of thumb.

Pioneering researchers Chris Argyris and Donald Schön (1974) highlight a further complexity, which many strategists encounter. They suggest people often say one thing whilst doing another. They describe this distinction as a gap between espoused theory (how we say we will behave) and theory-in-use (how someone else would describe what is actually being done). In the context of the strategy cycle, this is important since it implies that simply espousing new rules of thumb may not equate to those rules being operationalized in day-to-day life. For example, saying that you're a people person doesn't necessarily mean that you behave in ways which are consistent with that claim. In our experience, people have a surprising capacity to say "yes" but to do "no". In one case, a stated objective to increase creativity, entrepreneurship and risk taking was delivered through an assessment process, which required multiple levels of authorization and a risk assessment based on projected five year cash flows. In another, the oft heard claim that "our people are our most valuable asset" was wryly observed to contrast with the multiple rounds of redundancy in a business that was making substantial profits. There may be many causes of this gap between our aspirations and our actual behaviours. These might include the reassuring familiarity of old habits and a fear of perceived uncertainties. Regardless, strategists must recognize the need to support warm words with firm actions.

Alongside an honest appraisal of existing rules of thumb, we advocate the importance of identifying areas where new rules of thumb will underpin and enable the delivery of a new strategy. In crafting a strategy statement, we purposely avoid the development of vision or mission statements. However, we approach the same end game by identifying an aspired set of rules of thumb. Our experience suggests that wholesale change to all rules of thumb is both unwise and unworkable. Rather, attention should focus on a limited number of adjustments that are judged to be of significant consequence.

One of our recurring messages is that strategies "belong" to challenges (based on diagnoses of situations). It therefore follows that an organization may have multiple strategies, each linked to a (separate) challenge. For us, mission only then makes sense at an organizational level as an aggregated reflection of all of the challenges faced by the organization. Or indeed as a more fluid phenomenon that shifts as one challenge is met and another starts to be tackled. Our treatment of vision is also slightly different than that which you might encounter elsewhere. Mission might be about what you intend *to do* in overall terms, whereas vision, for us, is more meaningful as an aspirational view of how the organization might look and feel in an ideal world and this theme therefore does feature in the strategy cycle. Hence, whilst we are not fundamentally opposed to the ideas of mission or vision, we have seen many that are top-down wish lists or fantasies. These often fail to connect with the lived reality of the organization and as such can erode the credibility of the strategy with which they are associated. The mission-vision variant of strategy tends to be all wishbone and no backbone. Good visions and missions, like good jokes and stories are the kind that people want to hear or (re)tell again and again. Also, like jokes, if a vision or mission statement needs explanation it has likely missed the mark.

As an alternative to the traditional form of mission or vision statements, our approach encourages strategists to articulate the rules of thumb that, if applied, would generate an idealized future version of the organization. Figure 11.4 offers a list of prompt questions which we would use to provoke a conversation about the organization's future.

By now, you will have crafted a plan and reviewed current/future rules of thumb. At this juncture, two further tasks fall under the remit of strategists. First, is that they must take some responsibility for creating conditions in which change may occur. Change is most problematic in circumstances where nothing is changing. The deliberate act of introducing instability may be viewed as an act of vandalism and we are not suggesting that this is done casually or unthinkingly. However, our experience is that new strategies tend to flourish when there is sufficient fluidity to create the opportunity for new rules of thumb to take hold. The onset of a crisis, either real or precipitated, is often helpful in these circumstances. Changing the structure, the people, the roles, the processes or some combination of these create a sense of organizational fluidity in much the same way that a plough turns the soil in preparation for new growth. As noted by Argyris and Schön, strategists may happily proclaim old rules of thumb to be outlawed, yet may revert to them under pressure

Q1. Can you describe a version of your organization as you would ideally like it to be?
Q2. In terms of decision making …
 a. What rules of thumb would underpin business decisions?
 b. What rules of thumb would underpin the ways in which people were treated and behaved in the organization?
Q3. What are the key differences between your aspirational rule set and those describing current norms and patterns?

*Figure 11.4* **Prompt questions for new rules of thumb**

in much the same way that an ex-smoker might reach for a cigarette during times of stress. Sometimes deliberate and disruptive measures help to disable or disrupt these habitualized responses. In one manufacturing setting, the management team removed all horizontal surfaces to prevent the build-up of inventory. In another, the managing director had "tell me I shouldn't be here" emblazoned on the overalls he had to wear on the shopfloor to try and break the habit of spending time micromanaging. In the past we have used simulations and outdoor exercises to groups see and feel their own tendencies to resort to habitualized practices such as deferring to particular individuals (see MacLean et al., 2002 for other examples). However, fluidity tends to invoke anxiety and therefore this requires close attention and on-going effort to avoid settling back into more stable circumstances too quickly.

Having created the circumstances in which change may occur, the final task which strategists must take responsibility for is the application of feedback. In particular, there is a distinction between positive and negative feedback. The former is a form of amplifying feedback whilst the latter is controlling, restorative and focuses on control. Strategists should pay particular attention to the transformative effects of positive feedback[3]. The key managerial task is to look for small signals, expected or unexpected, that are consistent with the new rules of thumb. Anything, which reinforces these new rules of thumb is encouraged in order that the effects may be amplified and a new organizational form begins to emerge. For example, if the new rule of thumb required faster responses to customers, any accidental, incidental or lucky interaction that led to a faster response should be reinforced. This reinforcement may take the form of praise, publicity or attention but it may equally involve unpacking what happened and systematizing new ways of doing those things that appear to have worked.

In the strategy cycle, the most sensitive period is that which occurs when the carefully conceived plan meets everyday reality. The mismatches that occur drive improvisation and experimentation and during this critical period one of two things will occur. Unattended, the most likely outcome is that organizational members will experience significant pressure to revert to tried and tested ways of operating. The strategist's job is therefore actively to search for opportunities to reinforce the new rules of thumb. The unexpected events are typically the result of the carefully conceived plan not working out in practice, or more specifically, not working as had originally been envisaged. The process of spotting, and indeed creating, patterns (real and perceived) involves a form of behaviour that is simultaneously, culturally rooted, personal, expressive, artistic, political, negotiated, and many other things besides. Whilst it would be an over simplification to say that negative feedback corresponds to the traditional "functional" concerns of command and control, and positive feedback to a more Bardic form of leadership, there is nevertheless something in the distinction. "Managing" positive feedback is more concerned with meaning than with function.

Earlier we noted that the strategy cycle model would need expanding to incorporate the other theoretical elements discussed above. We can now add the various forms of talk and stories, some of which can be managed, some of which is formal, some of which just happens and some of which is shaped by influential stakeholders at all levels of the organization. The strategy cycle shows talk, both rational/business-oriented and organizational/culturally oriented interacts over time both shaping and shaped by the emerging strategy (Figure 11.5).

Within the strategy cycle, the traditional distinction between formulation and implementation is much less meaningful since each is an aspect of the same cycle of conversation and action. It follows then, that *who* participates is perhaps the most important strategic decision of all since there is no handover process.

## Bards: the art of strategic leadership

In Chapter 1 we promised to draw attention to a new form of strategic leadership which highlighted the role of Bards in weaving the cultural fabric of the organization and an engaging view of that organization's potential future together using creative, aesthetic faculties that are all too often consigned to the margins on the basis that they are emotional, subjective or, perhaps worst of all, irrational. Our approach suggests that emergent strategy in an organization is synonymous with the ways in which we fully describe it; that is, the stories we tell about the strategy in turn, feed back into what is emerging. The art of spotting and telling stories is

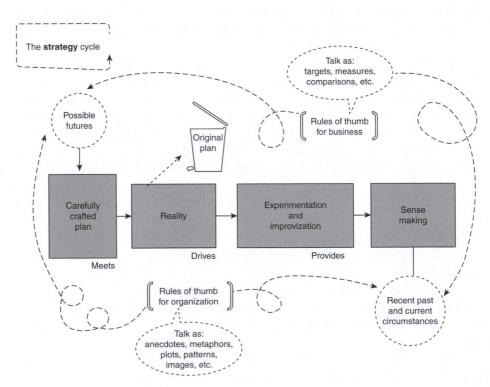

*Figure 11.5*  The strategy cycle

fundamental to the very process of producing the experiences that end up embedded in those stories.

The narrative backdrop in play during periods of instability determines whether those involved experience change as anxiety or an adrenaline high. Above and before anything else, the narrative must be worthy of our attention. It may rely on multiple media: words, imagery, soundbites, performances or oration. The key point here is that the construction of the living breathing strategy involves processes and faculties, which are artistic and aesthetic as much as they are scientific and rational. The strategist effects leadership by being both ruler and bard.

The crafting of an agreed or, perhaps even, contested, narrative is the key act of leadership in the strategy cycle, yet we feel it almost goes unnoticed in the strategy literature. It relies on someone with the ability to turn real events and fragments of accounts into coherent and compelling narratives that sustain a sense of belonging and engagement whilst simultaneously helping to heighten and sharpen intent. This coherent account is then expressed as rules of thumb, which capture and reinforce the way in which the organization behaves. This is the strategist as bard, the poetic counterpart to the hard logic of strategic choices and positioning. Imagining a future twist in the ongoing narrative, sharing this and compelling others to engage with that imagined future is the sign of a master storyteller.

Of course, organizations are complex. Most of us are intentional; we adopt an intentional stance when we do things purposefully. Yet when we act, we remain open to the fact that the responses we get in any situation might influence both what we intend and what might happen. Intention thus evolves. The strategy cycle reflects this key observation and thus moves beyond a rational view of mechanically realising a preformulated plan, no matter how carefully conceived. We believe that strategists can be intentional without necessarily subscribing to a rational planning view of strategy. Likewise, we can give a place to our desires, to willpower or even simply to surrender. For us, emergence is a both a **negotiated** process and one which can be **governed** in at least some bounded sense through intentional action on the part of those involved.

The strategy cycle then is the summation of more than two decades spent working with organizations on their strategic management processes. It contains many recognisable ideas (which we hope we have acknowledged) and one or two less familiar ideas. In the final section of the book we will offer a more academically grounded view of the key theoretical distinctions between our own approach and the work of our peers and predecessors. In the meantime, we would simply note that the bard sits on the right hand side of many of our familiar educational dichotomies – science and art, matter and meaning, function and form to name but a few. The strategy cycle seeks to bring the bard back into the limelight and to celebrate a more integrated and complete form of organization.

Figure 11.6 below offers a final template to complete the strategy cycle. It captures and structures the various tasks that we have suggested strategist's need to perform if they are to successfully navigate the transition from carefully conceived plan to a living breathing strategy.

| Desired Rules of Thumb | |
|---|---|
| Business:<br>1.<br>2.<br>n. | Organizational:<br>1.<br>2.<br>n. |
| **Habits to Break** | |
| Business: | Organizational: |
| **Turning the Soil** | |
| To create conditions for change we will:<br><br>Change processes ☐<br>Change roles and remits ☐<br>Relocate people / resources ☐<br>Alter measures / incentives ☐<br>Change the structure(s) ☐<br>Change our infrastructure ☐<br>etc. | |
| **Managing Feedback** | |
| We'll deliver positive feedback by: | We'll deliver negative feedback by: |

*Figure 11.6* The strategy cycle template

# Strategists at work: Honda

Today, Honda is a major player in the global motorcycle industry. In the 1950s, the Japanese firm decided to enter the American market where it would have to compete with incumbent players such as Harley Davidson as well as other international manufacturers such as Triumph and Norton (both UK) or Moto Guzzi (Italy). Kihachiro Kawshima arrived in the US in 1958 to develop a plan for conquering the market. Japan and America have always been very different countries but the contrasts were perhaps more stark than ever in the immediate aftermath of the second world war. Looking around, he saw that most American's motorcyclists rode large, powerful bikes and decided that Honda should launch with its own equivalents of these products. Two problems emerged. First, with no brand heritage at their disposal, Honda struggled and customers stuck with existing brands such as Harley Davidson. Second, Honda's larger bikes suffered reliability problems in the US perhaps because of the longer journeys they were being used for, or because of differences in riding styles, or a mixture of both. Whilst these difficulties were unfolding around them, Honda staff worked hard to build relationships and spent time commuting between meetings on smaller, lightweight bikes just as they would have done back in Japan. These Honda Supercub bikes drew attention from locals and became a hit with a different type of customer who had no desire to ride a large, noisy Harley Davidson and did not see themselves as a "biker" with all of the cultural baggage which that entailed. Initially Kawshima was reluctant because selling the Supercub had not been his original intention. Honda eventually adopted a slogan "you meet the nicest people on a Honda" to exploit the differences rather than the similarities of their product offering. Richard Pascale, the American academic, argues that Honda's eventual success was down to the willingness of Kawshima and other senior Honda executives not to take their initial strategic positions too seriously. Pascale argues that the Japanese don't use the term "strategy" to describe a competitive master plan but rather that it connotes something closer to "adaptive persistence." In our own terminology, Kawshima developed a carefully crafted plan, realized that it wasn't working and improvised. By applying positive feedback and being willing to revisit some of their rules of thumb, Honda was able to capitalize on the popularity of the Supercub. Sometimes, the unexpected failure of one plan carries within it the opportunity for a far better one to emerge.

## Strategists at work in the running cases

*RMacI:* So we've arrived at the end game. How did you put it all together. What role did stories and narratives play in your organization?

*Harry:* When I took on the job of Chief Medical Officer, I sought out Sir Michael Marmot. He is the guru on health inequality has written reports for the UK, Europe and the world at the request of the World Health Organisation. He has a 30 year history of research in this area and I said "look, I'm going to try and do something about this; I want you to be my sounding board". We've stayed in touch and he's been very helpful to me. A couple of weeks ago I went down to give him a sign off report and he said "you know, up until a few years ago I would have said you really should be doing randomized controlled trials of this but the stories you're telling me are really important; and if the stories tell you something works why shouldn't you just go out and do it?" I'll give you one example; the data we're collecting shows that mortality is declining in Scotland as we're making all these changes. Our hospital mortality, over the 10 years up until 2010 was falling at about 1.3% per annum. Since we introduced these changes it's been falling at the rate of 4.2% per annum, a threefold increase, the equivalent of about 10,000 fewer than predicted deaths. I tell colleagues that it is like the UK cycling team. You know, Sir Chris Hoy said that they made big gains through the addition of lots of little gains. 0.1% here; 0.5% improvement there, added up to a 5% improvement which is enough to win the gold medals. And changes to the way we treat people in hospitals, run charts of the impact of reading to children, all these little things make the difference.

*DMacL:* In part it's about the data but in part, it's about the story that you're weaving Harry. The optimism and hope that it creates and conveys.

*Harry:* I don't know about that. I'm just trying to get people to do the right thing.

*Kate:* At Admiral [parent company of Confused.com] we've got some simple rules that we're guided by. One is hire the best and brightest people, you can always train them in the insurance side of things but you can't train for attitude. Another, is that people should be happy at work. If they're not, there's a serious problem. A third would be "if it moves, measure it". We capture data on everything and we're very analytical about those things but very loose and entrepreneurial about others. I suppose a fourth would be that we're big on the champion and challenger thing. There are no sacred cows. Everything is up for grabs if you've got a better idea, we'll trial it. It keeps us fluid and nimble. When we launched Confused.com we were first to market and it had a real feel of being pioneers. Since then others have come into the market and we've had to retell our story as one of fighting back against some solid competitors.

*Sandy:* At Pointer, we have a strong belief in training; in bringing through our own people and teaching them from the ground up. We are a family business but family extends to a whole set of people who have worked with us most of their lives. There's a commitment there but it's not entirely without downsides. Sometimes, we're a little too informal with each other. Meetings and things can rumble along and we've had to sharpen up on following actions through to make sure stuff happens. We're incredibly good with clients and will do everything and anything to get projects done properly for them. We're having to work at doing some of that "extra mile" stuff inside the organization in terms of managing, following up and delivering the strategy.

*Harry:* And folk will say "well, which changes made the difference?" The truth is that they all made the difference, it's a complex system. There is no one lever.

*DMacL:* And on that bombshell, we'll stop.

## Do's and don'ts

Whilst it may be tempting to develop a strategic plan and believe that the hard work is done, this is rarely the case. Think of the plan as the "end of the beginning" of your job as a strategist.

### Do

1 Listen carefully to the stories that you hear about your organization, both from colleagues and from those outwith the organization. Such stories are a bountiful resource from which you can learn much.
2 Translate the stories and recurring patterns that you see into rules of thumb.
3 Be honest in your assessment of why the organization is the way it is. Bear in mind the delusional tendency to say what you would like to hear rather than what you need to hear.

### Don't

1 Panic. Remember that your carefully conceived plan was always likely to go astray. Your attitude as this happens will have a huge bearing on whether you see the opportunities to influence the emergence of a new way of being, or become locked in fruitless efforts to force the world to fit your expectations.

2 Overstretch yourself. First, you are unlikely to change all of your organization's rules of thumb simultaneously. Rather, target your attention to one or two important changes which you think you can deliver. Second, change usually brings an initial loss of efficiency and it is important to think about the amount of slack available during the change process.

## Who to read

**Kathy Eisenhardt** (Stanford) and **Donald Sull** (London Business School) have written two articles in the Harvard Business Review, which discuss strategy in terms of simple rules. Of the work we've come across that applies complexity thinking (in the form of simple rules) to strategy and organization, theirs is amongst the most accessible and practical. Both articles are packed with examples drawn from well-known firms and both are worth reading since they drive home the benefits of thinking of strategy in these terms.

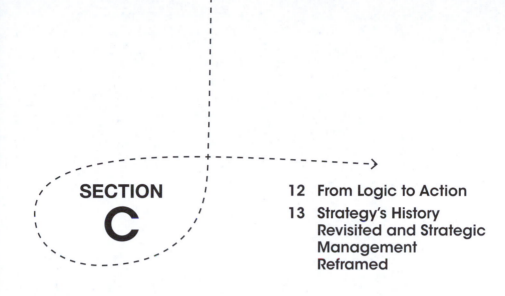

**SECTION**

**C**

12  From Logic to Action
13  Strategy's History
    Revisited and Strategic
    Management
    Reframed

## Introduction

In the Section B we addressed the challenge of translating a set of aspirations into significant outcomes. Having thus far set out our own views of how strategists work, in this section we change tack and tone. There are two motivations for this: first, given that our "prescriptive" stance laid out in Section B may seem somewhat simple, singular and perhaps lacking in self-criticism, we seek to reassure readers that the simplicity of our approach is the result of what has been a complicated and occasionally fraught journey spanning more than two decades of research and co-experimentation with a myriad of strategists; second, since our overall approach in Section B might be summed up somewhat paradoxically as *"invest significant time and effort in the rigorous and disciplined process of articulating a focused and carefully conceived plan – which you should then be open to abandoning"* we hope to explain why we would say such a thing. In so doing, we will place our own work into the broader context of the extant literature on strategy.

Hence, we move from the more instructional messages of earlier chapters and begin making more explicit reference to both our own theory and key contributions from others. In Chapter 12, we discuss the issue of action, and in particular, the idea of "creative action" which underpins our own view of the process of improvisation. Whilst planning is important, a focus on planning can inadvertently lead to the marginalizing of aesthetic, poetic, political and embodied, intuitive aspects of our behaviour. Our strategy cycle therefore places an emphasis on these Bardic aspects of the strategist's role. In Chapter 13 we turn our attention to the wider body of work on complexity theory and present our own ideas on "conditioned emergence" to deepen our explanation of emergent strategy as the collective expression of creative action.

# From Logic to Action

The process we have set out in this book is designed to generate a carefully crafted strategy. Yet a strategy in written form has no capacity to make a difference in the world unless it achieves the transition from logic to action. After all, what's the point in all that intellectual work if nothing more tangible flows from it?

Most of the time, we make the unspoken assumption that strategy is geared towards action. Yet a significant body of academic work suggests that many managers experience the sense that their own individual actions are poorly connected to the intellectual logic of the organization's official strategy. One particular experience exemplifies the view that organizations often have a momentum and pattern of their own which seems impervious to logically driven pronouncements of strategy. We were asked to work with the directors of a large public organization as a new strategy was developed. One director seemed particularly disengaged and the following exchange took place in an interview:

*RMacI:* How do you think the new strategy will play out in your part of the organization?

*Director:* [long sigh] You see, the thing is [long pause] ... you'll go away eventually. In a couple of years you'll be replaced by someone else asking what I think about some other "big idea". In the meantime, I'll go on doing what I do. And things, well, they'll rumble along. When you've been here long enough, you realize that that's all that matters.

This exchange captures the sense in which established organizations tend to persist with a particular way of being, even in situations where a new strategy has been intellectually agreed by senior management. In other settings we have heard similar sentiments expressed. One is a so-called "stern ignoring" which captures the sense of deliberate avoidance of new strategic ideas, imperatives or processes. The other was "a pent up reservoir of resignation"[1] which beautifully conveys the passivity engendered by some attempts to launch new strategy.

These very human reactions brings to life one of the dichotomies we identified in Chapter 2, that is strategic action "deliberate" and in line with a grand blueprint, or is it "emergent" arising from deep within the cultural fabric of the organization? In our own research we addressed this question by examining our underlying assumptions about human action.

## Action in strategy

The term "action" is often used by people in organizations to denote the translation of a strategic plan or blueprint into a coherent stream of individual activities. Often, one grouping formulates the strategy before it is handed over to others to implement. In Chapter 2 we traced the roots of this separation between formulation and implementation to the early contributions of Chandler, Sloan and Ansoff. In extreme cases, formulation is reserved to a single individual. One explanation for Chandler, Sloan and Ansoff's views was that they were forged in a time where hierarchies were more fixed and social mobility was lower. Yet even today, the single dominant strategist can still be found, as indicated by the quote from the Chief Executive of a UK FTSE-100 business:

> I've never been a fan of strategy by committee. I do the strategy. It takes me a year or two to think it all through and then I'll come and present it to the board and I'll listen to their views and I'll knock the rough edges off. Once we're happy, we set to implementing it and I'll start thinking about the next version for another couple of years.

Whether this view of strategy appeals to you or not, we would simply note the extent to which it implies a particular view of action which is separate from, and usually subsequent to, thinking. There are other ways to conceptualize action. Some see action as kind of triggered reflex, often intellectualized or post-rationalized after the event. Others see action as a messier process where thoughts, intentions and interpretations seem to grow out of one another. Our research suggests that when strategists talk about action they often draw on a range of ideas and assumptions about how action occurs, why and when it happens, and even who takes action. We would summarize these differences in three distinct views of action: rational, cultural and creative (see Table 12.1 below).

We suggest that the CEO quoted above is working with a **rational view of action**. This view tends to dominate in organizational life and suggests that strategy is simply the manifestation in a business context of the familiar schema "ends, means and conditions" which underpins much of Chapters 4–11 in Section B of this book. Equating ends with strategic intent; means with capabilities; and conditions with environmental foresight, as we have done thus far, suggests that strategists are seen as rational. In fact, the locus of action in a rational view is actually the organization which is envisaged as a problem-solving monolith working to effect optimal results. The individual is absent in this presentation of rationality which foregrounds the quality of the ideas and logic deployed rather than details about those deploying them. Heavily informed by classical economics, the rational view accepts that maximizing profit through the creation of sustainable competitive advantage is the only account of strategy worthy of attention. Beyond, or perhaps behind, economics, the real roots of the rational view lie in the natural sciences. Specifically, Newtonian mechanics. As strategy seeks to match capability with foresight in pursuit of intent, we see the underlying driver of matching supply and demand. This in itself is an expression of the root assumption that the universe naturally tends towards equilibrium as a stable, balanced mechanism. With rational action, the organization is a machine.

A **cultural view of action** offers a second perspective. Here, ends, means and conditions are replaced by hidden collective structures such as values, assumptions, norms and beliefs. In operation, these give rise to routinized and recurring forms of practice which bind us together socially. The primary drive to action is no longer rational but the felt need to belong. Belonging occurs in clubs, families, professions and many other organizational groups. This cultural view of action is not rational in the strict "optimising" sense described above, yet it is certainly not irrational. We act in order to belong and, ultimately to survive. Rather than being viewed in rational or irrational terms, a cultural view of action holds that behaviours are not necessarily driven by conscious or intellectual processes. Much of the time action is the expression of unconscious, learned or socialized behaviours. With a cultural view of action the conservation of cultural implies that occasional threats to the survival of an organization, or its collective identity, are seen as disruptive. Hence, changing strategy is no longer a purely rational process of choosing then implementing. Rather, it becomes a process which focuses on interpretation and sustainability.

The **creative view of action** represents a third more recent and less obvious explanation than either its rational or cultural counterparts. This creative action perspective draws attention to the micro and fine-grained details of specific individuals in particular situations. In this much more situated sense, action emerges from a cocktail of interacting personalities, chance, aesthetic expression and evolving intentions. These are shaped through logical structures, embodied in urges and the kinds of ongoing social process through which we all try to advance agendas (public and private) whilst constructing and reconstructing our sense of who we are in the world. Importantly, this view teases out a temporal dimension which sees individuals as intentional rather than necessarily rational, and as active creators of, rather than creations of culture.

Returning for a moment to the distinction between formulation and implementation, it is now clear that what is a neat demarcation for a rational view of action becomes somewhat blurred or even counterproductive when viewed from cultural or creative perspectives. Those seeking a fuller treatment of these different views of action might refer to the work of social theorist Hans Joas (1996). Our own research with teams of strategists leads us to believe that a rounded explanation of strategy can only come from an attempt to span the three different views of action presented above. Elsewhere we have used a boxing match to represent the simplest form of competitive engagement (see MacLean and MacIntosh, 2012). When Muhammad Ali fought George Foreman for the world heavyweight championship in 1974, the two contestants had very different boxing styles and physical attributes. Both Ali and his

*Table 12.1* Three views of action

|  | Rational | Cultural | Creative |
|---|---|---|---|
| Key concerns | Optimality, problem-solving | Belonging, sustainability and survival | Creativity novelty, innovation and transformation |
| Focal units | The organization | The collective | Situated individuals |
| Key process | Control | Co-ordination | Negotiation |
| Process style | Scientific-logical | Cultural-cohesive | Political-interactive |
| Key concepts | Ends, means and conditions | Norms, rules, routines, structures | Interaction, emergence, identity |
| Key influences | Economics, natural sciences | Anthropology, cognitive psychology | Politics, social theory |
| Implications for strategy | The organization is a rational actor seeking to maximize competitive advantage; strategy becomes a cohesive, systematic mechanical process of enacting intellectually derived tasks | Strategy centres on repeated patterning of resources and activities. The objective becomes stability, sustainability, legitimacy, belonging and survival | Strategy flows from creative, entrepreneurial and politically oriented actors operating in co-evolving networks. Individuals engage in situated instances of accepted practice and innovative improvisation |

trainer, Angelo Dundee, stated before the fight that their strategy would be to combat Foreman's greater strength with Ali's speed and agility. We would argue that this is a rational response and it generated detailed planning and preparations. In fact what transpired was rather different. Following months of training for a strategy in which he would outmanoeuvre his opponent, Ali made a subtle but significant alteration in the moment. Deviating from the planned strategy, Ali elected to utilize his speed and agility offensively rather than defensively. He attempted to throw knockout punches with a "right hand lead," a highly unorthodox tactic for a right-handed fighter. Throwing a punch with "the wrong hand" is a high-risk strategy since opponents can see the punch coming from a greater distance and, in throwing such a punch, the boxer leaves himself dangerously exposed to a counter-attack. Such punches are therefore rarely seen in professional boxing and regarded as something of an insult when they are used. We believe this demonstrates what Hans Joas would call *emergent intention* in the remark of one commentator "I don't think he had discussed this [throwing a right hand lead] with his trainer, I don't think he had even decided that he would definitely try it until the first bell sounded". (Mailer, 2000). Whilst rational action was involved in the preparatory phase, once situated, the strategist improvised based on interactions with the crowd, his opponent and his own sense of self.

## Rethinking implementation

The rational view of action, depicted in Table 12.1 is probably still the dominant view in strategy and in many other fields. Rationality suggests a particular view of implementation where intellectually derived goals are brought about through coordinated and planned actions throughout the organization. Resources, people, timsecales and budgets are made to fit with the plan. Operating conditions are read defensively in order to ensure that the plan remains feasible. As with any mechanical system, communication conveys what is required to each part of the organization to produce orchestrated movements. Feedback on any deviations allows corrections to be managed accordingly. Implementation then, is reduced to a familiar command and control sense of project management. Figure 12.1 depicts the logical and linear set of consequences that flow from a rational view of strategic action. This begins with the Chandlerian sense that structure follows strategy and elaborates this to detail a set of consequent and subsequent decisions. Once set, strategy leads to an appropriate choice of structure, key processes, resources to operationalize these processes, systems to support them and incentives to ensure their effectiveness. The logical consequence of this overlapping set of rational decisions is that appropriate outcomes follow the setting of strategy.

This presentation of strategy has remained largely unchanged since Igor Ansoff introduced the idea of corporate strategy in 1965. In the intervening four decades, the conceptualization of implementation has been modified slightly to acknowledge the limits to rational processes. For example the idea of limited or "bounded" rationality (Cyert and March, 1963) represents an attempt to factor in cognitive limitations such as the shortage of information or difficulties with information processing so that more real-time adjustment and risk-management might be required; but the process of implementation is still regarded as a somehwhat mechanical process of translating intellectual structures into observable action – albeit imperfectly.

In a rational view of strategic action, implementation becomes an operational issue and strategic management itself is restricted to the process of prioritization in terms of time, resource and attention relating to the choices set out in Chapters 8 and 10. Given the different predispositions of individual strategists to concentrate on intent, capability or foresight (see Chapter 1), we would argue that the reality is often that a board or team can talk past each other. Thus, implementation rarely proceeds in the rational, linear, mechanical fashion implied by a purely rational view of action.

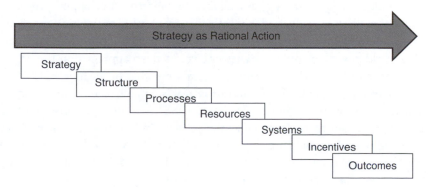

*Figure 12.1* **Strategy as rational action**

Implementation failure has been a recurring theme in the strategy literature (see Pettigrew, 1992) . Henry Mintzberg's notes that "when a strategy fails, those at the top of the heirarchy blame it on implementation lower down. 'If only you dumbbells appreciated the brilliance of the strategy we created' ... those down below might respond 'If you're so smart, why didn't you take into account the fact that we are dumbbells ?'". (1994:25).

## Emergent strategy and culture

The rational view of formulating then implementing strategy has been under serious and sustained attack since the late 1970s. Chief amongst the critics was Henry Mintzberg, (see his book "The Rise and Fall of Strategic Planning" quoted above and written in 1994). Mintzberg challenged the idea that workers were following any kind of plan. Instead, he claimed, they were responding to a myriad of factors. Whether juggling a raft of commands and demands from various superiors, subordinates and colleagues, or responding to unanticipated requests from customers and suppliers, few people find that their day runs to schedule. Mintzberg invokes two fallacies to substantiate his claim that the rational perspective was flawed: first, the "fallacy of prediction" reminded us that in today's turbulent environments it was neither sensible nor possible to predict what might happen with any accuracy – so plans have weaknesses from the word go; second, "the fallacy of detachment" alerts us to a more philosophical standpoint that says it is simply not viable to have a meaningful and unproblematic handover of ideas from the "head" of the organization (in the form of its leaders) to the "the body" (in the form of the majority of employees charged with operationalizing the strategy). Generating meaning and understanding requires participation. If the majority of colleagues didn't participate in the creation of the strategy, it seems strange to imagine that they will share a common understanding of that strategy regardless of how many times it is communicated to them. In Chapter 7, in the discussion of the running cases, Harry Burns makes precisely this point when he says "you can't expect people to be committed to something that they've no hand in designing".

Mintzberg's work has been influential in pointing out some difficulties with the dominant rational view of strategy as a deliberate collective mechanical process. Yet, one might argue that initially it offered little by way of value to practical managers. If strategy is an emergent pattern, where does it come from and how does one manage in such a worldview? For some, the answer lies in a deep appreciation the organization's context and the myriad of political interactions that occur therein (Pettigrew, 1973). For others, organizational culture is not so much a product of strategy; rather it is the other way around (Johnson, 1988). Culture gives rise to strategy and any strategy, which is developed intellectually by an elite group in isolation from the bedrock of organizational culture is likely to fall victim to it. This gave rise to a major interest, from the late 1980s onwards, in the idea of strategic change as culture change with a consequent managerial focus on "programmes" which sought to change culture, values or both as means of enabling strategic change. The "culture change" approach to strategy involves a somewhat uncomfortable combination of cultural and rational views of human action since it suggests that before trying to introduce any new strategy, the organization should engage in some cultural adjustment with a view to increasing the likelihood of the new strategy taking root. Consequently such approaches are characterized by efforts to intervene in the cultural and symbolic fabric of the organization.

It is essential to note that culture is primarily conservative (see Table 12.1), the main purpose of which is to ensure continuity, identity and belonging. Culture therefore tends to change slowly, incorporating and internalizing incremental changes as they occur. If more radical culture change occurs it is typically a last resort in the interests of survival. In our experience, observable culture change usually happens hesitantly and gradually, often as a consequence of major structural reconfigurations such as a new top team or CEO, a merger, relocation or crisis[2]. Moreover, some attribute culture as the primary cause of strategic failure through strategic drift (Hensmans et al., 2013). This happens when organizations become so culturally inward looking, or so lacking in internal diversity that behaviour verges on the unquestioning. Small signals from the external environment are overlooked and by the time the need for change is fully recognized a dramatic adjustment is needed. This sense of losing touch with customers, competitors and technologies is a familiar tale and is evident in most organizations at some point in their evolution.

Perhaps the most commonly cited definition of organizational culture is "the way we do things round here" (Drennan, 1992) and the latest manifestation of a cultural view of strategy is the "Strategy as Practice" movement (see e.g., Johnson et al., 2003; Golsorkhi et al., 2010). In this view, strategy focuses on practice at a fine-grained level rather than the grand conceptual abstractions of the rational view. Nevertheless, we tend to become socialized into our organizational settings such that we lose our ability to read cultural signals. Hall argues that "culture hides much more than it reveals, and strangely enough what it hides, it hides most effectively from its own participants" (1959: 53). Those inside the organization become steeped in the culture to the point that rational judgements on whether things are normal, acceptable, helpful or limiting become difficult. For this reason, Cohen describes cultures as "collections of solutions 'looking for' problems" (1968) in that the most comfortable, reassuring thing to do is to repeat tried, tested and familiar processes.

## The creativity of action

The third column of Table 12.1 introduces a third view of action in which the fundamental concerns are creativity and novelty. This is more consistent with a view of strategic action geared towards continual evolution and innovation punctuated by periodic episodes of more radical transformation during which the entire organization may change both radically and quickly. Globalization and the deregulation of many markets mean that the key to success is often to be able to innovate faster and more effectively than your competitors. Strategic innovation might mean producing new things, producing the same things in different ways or a combination of these. Innovation can, and should, take many forms.

Perhaps because this is a more recent concern, there is less agreement on how to proceed with a view of strategy that prioritizes learning and ongoing innovation. As suggested in Table 12.1, there are a broad range of influences on the view of action as inherently creative (MacIntosh and MacLean, 1999 or MacLean and MacIntosh, 2012 for a review). There is however, some agreement that the focus switches away from the behaviour of large corporate bodies, or even the common norms and structures of culture down. Instead, a creative perspective on action points towards the messy diversity of everyday life at the level of human interaction.

German social theorist Hans Joas (1996) has sharply criticized the rational and cultural concepts of action outlined above, instead developing a theory of creative action based on a combination of insights from the traditions of American Pragmatism and German philosophical anthropology. He questions the validity of approaches which assume a teleologically rational (ends, means and conditions) view of action, instrumental control of the body (by the intellect) and either autonomy of individuals or complete herd-like nature of social groups. In so doing, Joas aims to move action theory onto a new philosophical footing.

As an alternative to rational and normative views, Joas devised a theoretical framework which holds that:

1  Intention is a continually emerging (and evolving) facet of an ongoing dialogue between means, ends and context
2  The body is the "source" of personal expression (e.g., intuition and emotional urges) – and is not necessarily an instrument of the intellect and,
3  The development of identity is seen as one of the key issues in ongoing processes of social interactions.

Overall then, our focus on the embodied strategist chimes with a growing recognition in social theory of the creative and expressive role of the intentional human body in processes of interaction with others in equally unique situations. For this reason, our strategy cycle incorporates the critical transition from planning to improvising, suggesting that such improvisation occurs within a context of strategic talk about the organization in both cultural and business terms. The acknowledgement that action is informed by a (partial) understanding of ourselves as situated in unique, creative situations which are replete with personality, experience, thought, sensitivity, emotion, intuition, health, biography and aesthetic awareness remains simultaneously the most radical, and most challenging offering of a theory of creative action.

Given the challenge of conceptualizing action from a creative perspective, it is perhaps understandable that so many textbooks and academic debates seem to linger in the disputed and somewhat divided territory of action as explained by rational and cultural theories and models. In our view, creative action, in its attempt to overcome and transcend a prevailing and dichotomized view of action, offers a "post-Cartesian" alternative more suited to the demands of today's social economy. The creative view of action also fits more comfortably with other growing interests in the wider strategy literature such as the source(s) of dynamism, innovation and learning.

Nevertheless, with such an array of factors to consider, and indeed a focus on diversity, one might assume that this highly situated perspective means that the very idea of management becomes something of a fantasy. We would counter this view with insights from two bodies of work which offer guidance: learning and complexity theory (the latter of which we cover in the final chapter). There are other promising approaches to innovation and learning in strategy – such as those being developed in the micro-foundations theme of resource-based thinking (see e.g., Barney et al., 2011) and dynamic managerial capabilities literature (see e.g., Helfat et al., 2007); however, we will concentrate here on what we have found to work in our own practice. In the final chapter we will set out our own approach to strategic management and say a little more about complexity theory in so doing. Here, we will complete our overview of the transition from strategic logic to strategic action by talking about learning.

In order to innovate, organizations (or least those individuals and groups that constitute the organization), must learn. Many organizations now place heavy emphasis on developing their learning capabilities. Our argument is that the ability to learn a new strategy is perhaps the most important learning process an organization can cultivate. To understand how individuals and organizations learn we turn to the work of American psychologist, David Kolb (1971).

When faced with any new or unfamiliar task, Kolb argues that we learn in four distinct stages (see Figure 12.2). First, we spend time planning the task ahead. When the planning reaches a conclusion, it is time to act. Inevitably, we begin to reflect on the actions we have taken and finally, we begin to theorize about cause and effect relationships in what occurred. When learning to drive a car, we may stall the engine.

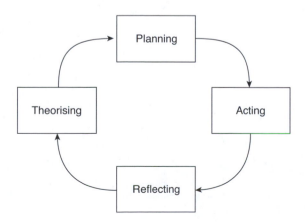

*Figure 12.2* **Kolb's learning cycle for individuals**

We might begin to understand the relationship between the position of the clutch, the gear lever and the amount of throttle required. This leads to a refined plan, further action and further reflection. Kolb argues that learning is essentially our navigation around these four component parts of the learning cycle.

Peter Honey and Alan Mumford refined Kolb's work by suggesting that different people learn in different ways. Kolb's cycle represents an idealized model but people invest time and energy across the four stages in the model dependent upon their learning style. There is no such thing as a good or a bad learning style, simply what is right for you. Some prefer to learn by doing, others by reading, others still by observing. Differences in learning style, or the propensity to dwell in (or omit) certain stages of the cycle become particularly important when it comes to working in teams. It's vital that teams work their way round the learning cycle effectively. An amended version of Kolb's individual learning cycle is shown in Figure 12.3 (see Kim, 1993).

By navigating the team learning cycle effectively it should be possible to help groups learn more effectively. However, left to their own devices however, most teams fail to live up to this ideal. We've all been involved in teams which, despite containing talented individuals, underperform. Obviously the team's capacity to learn and innovate should be greater than the sum of its parts. Without some conscious efforts on the part of those in the team, this usually isn't the case. Most strategists and strategy teams are familiar with co-ordinated action and joint planning. Indeed for many organizations these two activities are commonplace. Joint planning is the stuff of both regular meetings and more infrequent away-days. The intention of such meetings is to produce a list of actions which will then drive co-ordinated action. This is often synonymous with the strategy being handed over to others further down the chain of command during implementation. The next meeting typically begins with a review of the action list and minutes of the previous meeting. However, public reflection and developing a shared understanding of events are often overlooked or performed in a

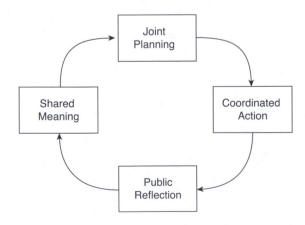

*Figure 12.3* **Team learning cycle**

perfunctory manner. To engage in public reflection is to be open about unexpressed assumptions and habitual behaviours. Neither is particularly comfortable territory in most management teams. Similarly, developing shared meaning requires us to think aloud in the company of our peers. This too is dangerous and uncomfortable. The net result is that most management teams that we have worked with tend to short-circuit these potential difficulties by covering these aspects of the Team Learning Cycle privately. Perhaps this is the real reason why some strategists default to a position of individual responsibility for strategy (such as the FTSE-100 CEO quoted earlier in this chapter). Whilst this may be more comfortable, we do end up substituting in assumptions, private judgments and/or guesses for their socially agreed counterparts. Our experience suggests that management teams that avoid public reflection and building shared meaning spend a disproportionate amount of time "managing" the incoherence that this produces when it comes to supposedly coordinated action.

We have found a focus on learning processes invaluable in dealing with a more individual and team-based view of what actually happens during what might otherwise be called the implementation phase of strategic management. It aligns with the ideas of creative action and experiential strategy as outlined earlier, yet it also connects with a rational and cultural design approach to implementation if one adopts a reflective practice perspective on the creation of meaning. The learning cycles set out above show the process of learning and in our final chapter we will show how this relates to the lived reality of emergent strategy.

# CHAPTER 13

## Strategy's History Revisited and Strategic Management Reframed

In the first section of the book, we gave a brief overview of the history and evolution of the strategy literature (see Chapter 2). Here we revisit some of the major contributions to strategy research and set our own particular take on strategy in this broader context. Thus far, we have laboured the importance of developing a robust set of strategy statements using the cumulative process set out in Chapters 4–10. We laboured the importance of adopting a highly disciplined process and developing a robust, comprehensive strategy statement. Then in Chapter 11, we placed this *plan-centric* activity in the context of our strategy cycle. This experiential and cyclical model indicates that, somewhat paradoxically, "the carefully conceived plan" gives way to an improvised and emergent form of strategy-as-creative action. In Chapter 12 we elaborated three views of action and set out in some detail what the theory of creative action entails. Now, in this final chapter, we complete our journey through the strategy literature by returning to the historical development of strategy, in terms of organization and management. We draw on complexity theory to try to locate our own work – and this book in particular – in that wider context.

In previous chapters we introduced the notion of the strategist as Bard because of the important role that narrative plays in placing current events, both planned and unplanned, as well as future aspirations into the context of the organization's history. When we reflect on our own experiences of organizational life, we know the importance of storytelling as a means of communication. In crafting, telling and retelling the story of what the organization is trying to achieve, we see clear connections between the role of bards in historical times and the less obvious responsibilities of strategists in modern organizations.

In what follows we will attempt to show how strategists might engage with their responsibility for the cultural fabric of the organization through a specific set of practices, which are often neglected to the expense of both the organization and the individual. In organizational terms such neglect may reduce both engagement and innovation, and for the individual the danger is that they spend much of their lives in activities, which offer an impoverished sense of fulfilment. Indeed, as we have written elsewhere, sometimes organizational life can seem dominated with concerns for function and efficiency to the point that experiences in organizations, though never meaningless, can seem corrosive to the preferred forms of meaning and ways of being held by many of their members; in some ways such organizations might be thought of as pathological or "diseased" (MacIntosh et al., 2007).

Our review of strategy in Chapter 2 makes clear that there is a long tradition of strategy research. However, consideration of the practices which create and sustain culture; which involve our artistic or aesthetic faculties and are central to our appreciation of qualities such as beauty, desirability, empathy (and their opposites) have been, by and large, relegated to the sidelines.

Of course some strategy relates to rational, quasi-scientific decision-making. We would describe this subset of strategy as the domain of rules and rulers. We are concerned however, that there has been a tendency to over generalize from those limited circumstances amenable to rational decision-making to the extent that situations which are simply too complex, urgent and emotionally rich for rational processing are not considered.

In his review of narrative in strategy, Freedman (2013) introduces the distinction between system 1 and system 2 decision-making from the field of cognitive science. System 2 decisions are described as "conscious, explicit, analytical, deliberative, more intellectual and inherently sequential" and "just what was expected of strategic reasoning". Such decisions are often slowed because they generate excessive complexity, the demand that they place on decision makers "could be depleting and unpleasant, leading to a loss of motivation" (op cit: 603). Freedman is arguing that logic has its limits. System 1 processes, on the other hand, he relates to a quote by philosopher Isaiah Berlin (p. 613).

> A capacity for integrating a vast amalgam of constantly changing, multi-coloured, evanescent, perpetually overlapping data, too many, too swift, too intermingled to be caught and pinned down and labelled like so many individual butterflies. To integrate in this sense is to see the data (those identified by scientific knowledge as well as by direct perception) as elements in a single pattern, with their implications, to see them as symptoms of past and future possibilities, to see them pragmatically – that is, in terms of what you and others can or will do to them, and what they can or will do to others and to you.

Of course decisions based purely on this system 1 reasoning could also be problematic. They are open to the accusation that they are overly subjective, biased and unappealing to others. Nevertheless, Berlin's "capacity for integrating a vast amalgam" seems a fitting description of the processes that might have been used by poets and bards as they sought to make sense of complex social phenomena in order to create reassurance, hope and social cohesion. Bards operated in a highly uncertain world of tribal conflicts and turbulent conditions much as modern strategists face a fast-moving, even hypercompetitive landscape.

In the words of Brendan Lehane, "... *bards kept alive the ancient stories of a race, dramatized new events, and entertained the courts with their long, stylised narratives*" (2005: 28–29). Becoming a bard involved training that was "long and hard" (Chadwick 2002) so this class of work was neither informal nor on the sidelines. Bards helped to sustain social order and the cultural life of their clan. Lehane's term "stylised narrative" is interesting. Freedman (2013: 615) notes that narratives can sometimes oversimplify the nuances complexity of real life in perhaps because of a desire to create heroic, deliberate, successful and memorable adventures. The "stylised narrative" form with which we most often associate bards is of course poetry. In her book on the Celts, Chadwick (2002: 255) quotes Kuno Meyer's description of Gaelic and Welsh poetry

> It is a characteristic of these poems that in none of them do we get an elaborate or sustained description of any scene or scenery, but rather a succession of pictures and images which the poet, like the impressionist, calls up before us by light and skilful touches. Like the Japanese, the Celts were always quick to take an artistic hint; they avoid the obvious and the commonplace; the half-said thing to them is dearest.

Again we see parallels with the modern strategist's need and desire to assimilate details emerging in a potentially overwhelming flow of information, then to present these back to colleagues with flair and style. One of the key skills in doing so is to avoid spelling anything out in final coherent form since in Mintzbergian terms, the final form is likely to emerge over time. The skilful strategist thus spots possibilities, scatters them as seeds, then has the patience to let them germinate in a myriad of situations which, in turn, give rise to further elaboration of the emerging narrative. Storytelling is in this sense an iterative process; part retrospective sensemaking in the Weickian sense (1995) and part aspirational in the context of the strategy statements crafted at the outset.

Holding this tension between was has passed and what has still to come, Alastair McIntosh (2004: 121) suggests that the bard is continually required to

> Step outside of the consensus trance reality, observe the psychodynamics of individual or social disease, and then step back in to protest for change.

For many years the leadership literature has been fascinated by the role of transformational leaders (see Burns, 1978) who inspire those around them to "do more than they originally expected to do" (Fu et al., 2010). We are struck by the similarities from a more ancient tradition where bards engage in purposeful action, glimpse emerging patterns and engender collective responses acting as a midwife to the (re)birth of the organization. Using stories, they spread awareness and engagement through commanding oratory, compelling visions and imagery and, above all, as McIntosh suggests "stepping back in" to agitate for change. Nothing persuades like the conviction of someone practising what they preach and sticking to their vision. Perhaps the most powerful demonstration of this in our lifetime has been the late Nelson Mandela.

Others have recognized the importance of narrative (see e.g., Mitroff and Mitroff, 2012). Our own views on the importance of narrative for strategists were arrived at indirectly from our on the use of complexity theory (see MacIntosh et al., 2006 for a thorough review of complexity theory in organizational settings). Our conditioned emergence framework (MacIntosh and MacLean, 1999) helped us to understand the practices involved in first identifying and then engaging with emergent properties. Our thinking led us to focus on the role of both positive and negative feedback processes in shaping the emergence of strategic patterns. Before looking at emergence in relation to strategy, we first offer a summary of some of the ideas from complexity theory that inform our approach.

## Complexity theory

The development of complexity theory, as it has been popularly titled, is regarded by some as signaling the arrival of a "new scientific paradigm". Classical science describes a universe where events are determined by a combination of initial conditions and mechanistic laws, which play out as the cogs of a huge machine roll forward. You may recall from high school science lessons the mantra that every action is met by an equal and opposite reaction. The second law of thermodynamics adds a further twist, stating that as it does that mechanisms run down over time, losing both energy and internal organization. Hence, when studying the organization as a machine, managers in large hierarchical structures constantly need to *re*-organize otherwise *dis*organizing systems.

Some aspects of everyday life seem to contradict this classical view. Evolution points to a world where the level of order seems inexorably to increase, not decrease. Nobel-prize winner Ilya Prigogine and colleagues, in the field of non-equilibrium thermodynamics and phase transitions, began to explain the generation and development of order in the world in dramatically different terms (Prigogine and Stengers, 1984). Essentially, their work indicates that change, development and transformation take place in open systems (not mechanisms) which exist in far-from-equilibrium conditions (not equilibrium) and that such open systems constantly exchange energy with their environment. In a review of complexity theory, Plesk and Greenhalgh (2001) suggest that it offers "new conceptual frameworks that incorporate a dynamic, emergent, creative and intuitive view of the world [to] replace 'reduce and resolve' approaches". Our work with strategists has convinced us that this view of open (or complex) systems is better suited to today's organizations than the machine metaphor.

According to complexity theory,[1] systems behave in a stable manner until they reach a critical threshold, often termed a bifurcation point. As this bifurcation point is approached, the system becomes stressed and unstable. The system moves from equilibrium to so-called far-from-equilibrium conditions, opening up the possibility of radical, rapid and qualitative change. In far-from-equilibrium conditions, systems become open to their environment – importing energy and exporting entropy (which is a measure of disorder). It is during periods of such disequilibrium that systems become susceptible to tiny signals and random perturbations which would have had little impact were it still at equilibrium. Positive feedback can turn these tiny changes into "gigantic structure breaking waves". (Prigogine and Stengers, 1984, xvii), or as Lorenz more poetically terms it "the butterfly effect" (1963). Coveney and Highfield (1996) provide a good historical account of complexity theory and our own summary offers a review of complexity theory in organizational settings (see MacIntosh et al., 2006).

Complexity theory is organized around a number of central concepts. First, complex systems are **densely interconnected** such that one part of the system can influence many others. Second, as indicated above, complex systems tend to exist in **non-equilibrium** states. Third, **feedback** processes are central to the relationship between stability and change and in particular the balance of negative (i.e., restorative or damping) and positive (i.e., amplifying) feedback influences the extent to which system-wide effects occurs. Fourth, **simple rules** or deep structure (Drazin and Sandelands, 1992), offer a means of explaining complex systems since order is seen to emerge through the repeated enactment or application of simple rules. For instance, Reynolds managed to simulate the flocking behaviour of birds using only three rules.[2] In concert, these concepts suggest that in complex systems, order emerges from within a system through a process called **self-organization** (Kauffman, 1993). Whilst the detailed form of such emergent order cannot be predicted, the range of broad possibilities is, to some extent, determined by the simple rules and the connections which were applied to generate the order.

## Conditioned emergence

In our own research on strategy, we have drawn on complexity theory and learning to produce an integrative framework: Conditioned Emergence (see MacIntosh and MacLean, 1999 and 2001). We argue that if the structures, processes and procedures of an organization can be thought of as being generated by a simple set of order-generating rules, then the negotiation of these rules is a central task for strategists. This explains why, in Chapter 12, we focus on the articulation of business and cultural rules-of-thumb as a key feature of our experiential view of strategy. The emerging patterns that we call strategy, whilst unique and unpredictable in detail, can be thought of as being generated and governed by a set of simple rules of thumb. Further, we suggest that strategists need to pay close attention to feedback processes during the emergent enactment of a strategic plan since complexity theory indicates that positive feedback[3] can drive an organization from one state to another. In working with organizations we are struck by the organizational dominance of negative feedback mechanisms (e.g., budgets, forecasts, progress reports and corrective action plans) and the comparative lack of any formal positive feedback mechanisms.

The strategy cycle, which we describe in Chapter 11 identifies two distinct forms of talk about what is happening, in strategic terms, to the organization. On the one hand we have formal measures (sales orders, employee turnover, advertising spend, market share, profit, benchmarking and the like); on the other we have more personal, partial and informal talk (stories, anecdotes, accounts of patterns, gossip about who did what, what might be about to happen next, hopes, fears, etc.). Whilst it would be far too simple to connote the formal analytic talk as regards expectations and reality with negative feedback and the less formal, less predictable narrative talk with positive feedback, there is nevertheless something in this relationship. In our experience of working with strategists, informal talk is often associated with the unexpected, both good and bad, and critically, with what it all means for the individuals, the organization and the original plan. This is a central assumption in our approach. Meaning, as distinct from data and information, is always emerging; always on the move. Whilst negative feedback processes are of course part of the way in which meaning is woven and created in organizations, change, novelty, creativity and innovation are more likely to be bound up with the operation of what are called positive feedback processes. As such they are unpredictable, non-linear, possibly **paradoxical** and often suggest new possibilities. Oddly perhaps, these are terms that one might use to describe poetry. Hence our desire to draw attention to bardic roles and processes. Whilst unfamiliar and beyond our control, the development of narrative, for example what strategy means and whether it should be embraced or otherwise, is as much influenced by a form of social poetry as it is by business logic. We will return to this claim shortly.

> **Paradox:** From the earliest philosophers we have a fascination with circumstances where two incommensurable truths appear to co-exist. In organization theory, Lewis describes paradox as related elements which "seem logical in isolation but absurd and irrational when appearing simultaneously"(2000:760). In the context of our discussions here we might conclude that strategy is both deliberate _and_ emergent. We have published elsewhere on the theme of paradox (see Beech et al., 2004).

Finally as regards conditioned emergence, if system-wide transformation occurs in far-from-equilibrium conditions, then the adoption of a new strategy is likely to require that the organization becomes open enough to its environment to trigger change and in Chapter 11 we laid out some practical ways in which this can be done.

We were (and are) conscious of potential criticism of conditioned emergence as being reductionist, over-simplistic, or too mechanistic in its stance. We are also mindful of connectionist arguments such as those put forward by Cilliers (1998), which dispute the existence of order-generating rules. Nevertheless, the approach offers an opportunity to tackle issues surrounding the role of human agency and system dynamics in a direct and theoretically consistent fashion. Perhaps more importantly, as a guide when working on strategic development, we and others have found it useful.

Conditioned emergence combines our understanding of emergence and emergent properties with the insight that in human settings (as opposed to the natural sciences where much of complexity theory originated) issues such as willpower, politics, aesthetics, poetics and design afford us some influence over the broad shape of what emerges. In this particular case, that influence relates to the emergence of a strategic pattern.

To help visualize Conditioned Emergence we adapted a more traditional bifurcation diagram (see Figure 13.1).

This amended bifurcation diagram depicts the journey of an organization undergoing change to some or all of its strategy. The journey toward a new strategy typically begins with the realization that performance is deteriorating. As we suggest in Chapter 4, most organizations monitor performance but typically in different ways, paying particular attention to some indicators whilst remaining less concerned with others. As decline sets in, the organization is replete with well adapted processes and has become so adapted to one strategy that it has little or no spare capacity for further change. This is why organizations experience strategic drift (Hensman et al., 2013). Finally, the effects of ongoing environmental changes put mounting pressure on the organization and it begins, as a last resort and for reasons of survival, to explore new ways of working and being. As performance levels slide toward some critical level, members of the organization resolve to address the situation. In defining a new strategy, organizations enter a bifurcation zone where instability and disequilibrium are encountered. During this time, the new and existing versions of the organization's strategy compete with each other. This produces further instability and continues until a symmetry breaking event occurs, locking in either the old strategy or its replacement.

Hence, two possible trajectories emerge from the bifurcation zone. If a new strategy is adopted, it starts off somewhat shakily as the organization learns and adapts. In the short term this incurs a loss of performance until such time as new routines are established and performance recovers. One of the ways in which the existing strategy can defend itself against change is "trying harder" which generally yields short term improvements without addressing the underlying cause of the decline. The other trajectory in Figure 13.1, labelled trying different, suggests that the organization is following a qualitatively different strategy.

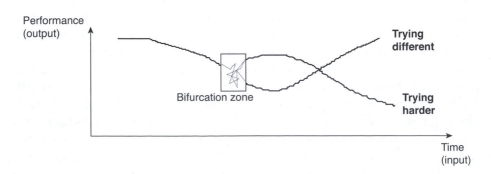

*Figure 13.1* **Amended bifurcation diagram**

In one organization we worked with, cash flow was the most talked about perform-ance measure, which was declining. The CEO demanded that he sign every purchase order over £500. In the short term, this close attention did improve cash flow as colleagues deferred any unnecessary expenditure. In the longer term however, the decline continued as the underlying cause of poor cash flow (in this case a dated product range and inefficient production processes) remained unchanged. During the period when both the old and new strategy are co-present, the organization experiences strong switching pressures because short term measures such as the close management of cash flow described above can effect short term gains. Ulti-mately, and after a few false starts, the business in question did transform. It is now the premier business of its kind in national terms and continues to grow – but only after the three aspects of conditioned emergence described above were simultane-ously present – new rules of thumb, organizational fluidity and processes of positive as well as negative feedback. What it became was in some ways what was envisaged (market leader) but in other ways surprising (directorial changes, a new location, and a product/market offering different from that embedded in the strategists' care-fully crafted plan). The business made the most of unexpected events. In the midst of improvisation, a new format emerged.

## Emergence, strategy and strategic management

We have already drawn attention to two views of emergent properties. In Chapter 2 we noted Henry Mintzberg's view that strategy emerged over time rather than being conceived then delivered in a rational and deliberate sense. This **emergent strat-egy** (see Figure 13.2) occurs as the originally planned or intended strategy, when translated into deliberate actions, falls victim to a form of "the death of a thousand cuts". As the intended strategy becomes an unrealized strategy, it is overtaken by a myriad of apparently independent local events that nevertheless seem to cohere

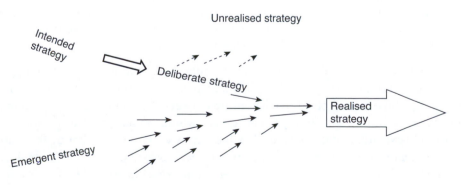

*Figure 13.2* **Mintzberg's emergent strategy**

into a recognizable and recurring pattern, almost as if the organization had its own sense of momentum, independent of any rational plan. At a particular point in time it becomes possible to discern a patterning of these small, independent events and to retrospectively recognize them as part of an emergent strategy.

The second view of emergence was introduced in Chapter 10 from Peter Checkland's observation of emergent properties as those properties that appear at the level of the whole.

In complexity theory, emergence is a central concept (see Goldstein, 1999) denoting the appearance of macroscopic patterns in collections of elements amongst which non-linear interactions are taking place. We would suggest that this definition of emergence draws out two distinctions which move beyond both Mintzberg (see Mintzberg and Waters, 2006) and Checkland (1990). First, a complexity theory view of emergence concentrates analytical attention on the process by which emergence occurs through time, whilst Mintzberg tends to suggest the gradual realization that a strategy *has* emerged. Second, the central importance of non-linearity in complexity theory introduces a tendency toward unpredictability in ways that mechanical systems, such as Checkland's bicycle, do not. In a complex system patterns cannot be understood in terms of simple sums or differences of interactions between the elements because they arise out from the interconnectivity of the system in a way which makes cause and effect relationships difficult to characterize. In organizational terms then, emergent properties are the very strategic and cultural patterns that we have discussed earlier in the book. The process of stewarding emergent properties into being requires both traditional management practice and more Bardic processes – where the very act of narrating a possibly emerging pattern becomes part of the very feedback processes that constitute its development.

Emergence, and the role of human action in the creation of emergence, is perhaps best illustrated by a familiar example, quoted here from the contemporary philosopher Roger Scruton (1997):

> When a painter applies paint to a canvas, he creates a physical object, by purely physical means. This object is composed of areas and lines and paint arranged on a two-dimensional surface. When we look at the painting, we see those areas and lines of paint and also the surface which contains them. But that is not all we see. We also see a face that looks out at us with smiling eyes.

Scruton's example successfully conveys the inherently social nature of emergent properties in human as opposed to physiochemical or microbiological settings. For example, whilst there is clearly a relationship between the configuration of elements in a painting and the qualities of the image as a whole, we have a relatively impoverished understanding of that relationship. Intuitively we know that altering the shape of the mouth, or the proximity of the eyes to each other, alters not only the local geometry of these features, but also the general impression created by the face. Yet we cannot fully understand the relationships between the components until we see them as a whole. Emergent properties are thus said to be ostensive in nature (Goldstein, 1999).

Painting also raises the question of the relationship between subject and object – the extent to which what we see is a creation of observation, relying on the observer for the particular form of its existence. If subject and object interact in this way, then emergent properties may be considered as causative phenomena in their own right. Consider the way in which the emerging appearance of a face on the canvas can influence the artist's behaviour in real time, shaping both the appearance of the face and artist's technique and practice. In a very real sense, both the face and the artist are developed out of the process of interaction – each is both created by and creator of the other.[4]

Our contention is thus that a similar creative dynamic is at play *during* the process by which a Mintzbergian emergent strategy comes to be recognized, yet little mention is made of emergence in this more processually nuanced sense within the strategy literature. The late and highly influential complexity theorist Brian Goodwin claimed that to understand the dynamic of emergence we needed to develop a new science of qualities (1999). Such a science would require open recognition of the role of participation in understanding emergent phenomena. Further, this process of participative enquiry would make explicit use of phenomena such as intuition and feeling. A less radical starting point would simply be to acknowledge the role of emotion, intuition and art more openly in our organizations, and indeed to cultivate and celebrate them. So here we have a direct link with the theory of creative action introduced in the previous chapter – *the participation and influence of the strategist in the creation of emergent strategy is a fully embodied process that lies beyond the reach of purely rational or cultural explanations.*

Creative, narrative and artistic processes at one time played a vital role in the life and development of social systems. Recent research in strategy suggests that these processes still matter (Fenton and Langley, 2011; Freedman, 2013; Kupers et al., 2012) highlighting the critical role of the narrator as storyteller and interpreter (Tsoukas and Hatch, 2001). Casting the strategist as bard expands their responsibilities beyond the production of a compelling and logically robust analysis and draws in the aesthetic and emotive importance of narrative and meaning. Ann Cunliffe's view of managers (and in our particular case, strategists) as practical authors highlights the reflexive and interpretive role that we each play in narrating our own situation (2001). A social constructionist perspective (Berger and Luckman, 1967) on strategy suggests that our fantasized view of the situation is at least as important as any other (see MacIntosh and Beech, 2011).

Our argument in this book is that the strategy cycle requires the incorporation of a Bardic process, which reconnects us with a fuller and more human sense of purposive endeavour (Chia and Holt, 2006). This in turn produces more enriching, fulfilling and healthier individuals and organizations.

In Section B we argued that a robust strategic logic was imperative. In isolation, this claim would place our work within a very traditional view of strategy. Yet we have also claimed that plans never really come to fruition. Indeed we opened this book with the observation from Robert Burns that plans often go astray. Therefore, we are simultaneously occupying a space in the literature which acknowledges that strategy is an emergent phenomenon. We would therefore describe our own contribution to the wider strategy literature as neo-Mintzbergian.

There are no singular or simplistic answers to questions such as: Are strategists planners or observers of an emergent process?

Neither description on its own is sufficient. Paradoxically strategy is planned in some ways and emergent too. In stricter terms, the distinction has been oversimplified and misunderstood. Plans, of course, emerge. That is to say, they arise out of meetings of people engaged in creative interaction who eventually, and perhaps temporarily, cement their agreement in a plan. Likewise, given that they all know that in reality something different is likely to happen, they are in a way planning for emergence.

This is not simply antics with semantics. It is an accurate account of what actually happens. A more interesting question is why is this what happens? In many ways the answer remains something of a mystery, which in our view, is perhaps to the good. The careful, robust and coherent planning process that produces the strategy statement derived in Chapter 10 serves more than one purpose. On one level, the logical plan is an artefact in its own right. On another, the process of planning enables the formation of connections and principles that hold good during the lived reality of whatever actually happens. Both end up being central to the shape of what eventually emerges.

In our view, the debate on emergent versus deliberate strategy is simply a debate between rational and cultural concepts of action. To some extent, the incorporation of insights from complexity theory, learning and creative action allow the debate to fade away, but in its place, a new challenge arises. Here we have placed our own emphasis on the creative and interpretive process by which strategic actions are woven into a narrative by strategists as they try to deliver the intended strategy. Paradoxically, they try to deliver the strategy knowing full well that this will never happen in the shape they first envisaged. Yet still they try – and the art of balancing persistence with a dream (or fear) on the one hand, and openness to novelty and not-knowing on the other, is the real craft of the strategist. This craft calls for an elusive process, embodied in a rare individual or group – part art, part science; part plan, part poetry; part chieftain, part bard.

Revealed at last then, this for us is the true nature of strategists at work.

# SECTION
# D

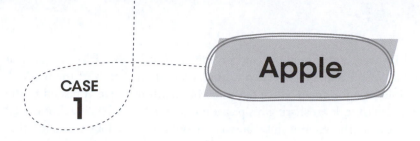

# Apple

## The Architects of Apple's Success
## Tim Cook, Jonathan Ive, Steve Jobs, Angeliki
## Papachroni and Robert MacIntosh

### Introduction

When Tim Cook took the reins at Apple investors, customers and colleagues were unsure what would happen. By the end of 2013 Apple Inc. had continued its stellar performance under the leadership their new CEO. During his first two years of Tim's Cook leadership, Apple maintained its position in a number of markets and strengthened its capabilities in others. Many had thought that the company would lose its way without its remarkable co-founder and leader Steve Jobs, yet Apple is still holding strong. Cook has overseen the introduction of the iPad mini, the new iPhone series with the 5S and 5C series and released the iOS7, Apple's most significant change to its operating system in years. Despite fierce competition Apple topped Fortune magazine's list of the world's most admired companies for sixth year in a row and for the first time in 13 years surpassed Coca-Cola to become the world's best global brand according to Interbrand.

This case will shed some light on the role of three distinctive strategists who have helped shape Apple's remarkable growth: the "design guru" behind all Apple's recent innovations Jonathan Ive, the "operations wizard" and now CEO, Tim Cook and of course the visionary Steve Jobs. Jobs had founded Apple, led the firm to early successes then been ousted from his own firm in a boardroom coup. Upon his return in 1997, Jobs set about returning Apple's competitive advantage to a focus on design and innovation. As demand for their products grew, the importance of an efficient global supply chain began to play an equally important role.[1] These two key aspects of the company are embodied in two strategists who could not be more different yet who both add incredible value to the business. Tim Cook, eventually became COO and was responsible for Apple's streamlining of operations. Jonathan Ive is a British designer who is often credited as the guru behind the look and feel of Apple's products. During the time of Jobs' leadership, these three men combined to lead the company through the digital music revolution of the iPod and the iTunes, redefined the future of mobile media and computing devices with the iPad and revolutionized the mobile phone with the iPhone. All this, while strengthening Apple's position in personal computers with the Macs, iLife, iWork and professional software.

Cook and Ive were not brought in and promoted through Apple's management structure by accident. Steve Jobs shared a unique bond with each of them. Cook appealed to Jobs' eye for detail, efficiency and cold hard logic. Ive appealed to the designer and idealist in Jobs, sharing his passion for iconic products that combined form with function. The relationships between Cook, Ive and Jobs was such that after Job's passing many commentators refuted the picture of the future of Apple that so many painted. Walter Isaacson, biographer of Steve Jobs, gave his own answer to the question of who is going to make key product decisions post-Jobs. The answer, Isaccson said, is that Cook – a cool, rational and operational wizard – is "joined at the hip" with chief designer Jony Ive – a sensitive, artistic type whom Jobs described as his "spiritual partner." Cook is the decider-in-chief, Isaacson said, but the working partnership between Cook and Ive has the same effect as "joining the two halves of Steve's personality".[2]

These three very different men shared common values in relation to Apple's core intent which aimed to see the company *"making the best products in the world"*. In what follows we will demonstrate how each of Apple's three key strategists embraced these values and contributed to the company's stellar performance.

## Steve Jobs: bringing the inspiration back

When Steve Jobs returned to Apple in 1997 he found his company on the edge of bankruptcy. His intent was clear, to make Apple a great company once more by re-establishing its basic values. "Apple had forgotten who Apple was", he said and he began a series of strategic changes that would mark the company's impressive turna-round in the years that followed. He combined a ferocious attempt at cost cutting with an unwavering demand that Apple kept making better products, a philosophy that is engrained in Apple's DNA to this day. His approach to strategic change was fundamentally different from past attempts to turnaround the company as its focus was not solely on cost cuttings for short term financial gain but rather because short term survival would enable a second wave of innovation that would bring customer value.[3]

Through a series of strategic decisions during his second stint as CEO, Jobs (re) set the basis of Apple's DNA: focus on a limited number of products that would get unlimited support from the company, enter markets were the company would own both the software and the hardware, have total control a customer experience and focus on design that was so good that customers would notice. Building on the product's innovative features and distinct design, Apple's product line included a limited number of products placed at the premium end of the market. Jobs' early acts as a returning CEO saw him axe 70% of new products in development, revamp the marketing message to reconnect to the maverick and creative values of the brand and put reaffirm design at the heart of Apple. The launch of the iMac in 1998 was the first signature product that reflected Apple's renewed design ethos; user friendly and technologically innovative it became the fastest selling Macintosh model ever. The iMac, promoted as "the computer for the rest of us" combined unique design features (a translucent case that would support all peripherals designed for Windows based computers) with a compelling price of $1,299. iMac's wide audience acceptance, with 70% of sales coming from Apple converts, helped Apple double its worldwide market share to 6% by the end of 1998.[4]

A few years later Apple revolutionized the music industry with the introduction of the first iPod in 2001 and the iTunes music store in 2003, which formed a digital hub for seamless operation between software and hardware, just as Jobs had envisioned. The company's strategic moves at that time saw Apple building products that offered a specific type of user experience and retaining total control of both hardware and software to deliver that experience. Notably, this approach that was the antithesis of what was happening elsewhere in the industry, which tended to focus on open industry standards. Apple carefully preserves its ownership of software and hardware despite criticism from peers, third party developers and some customers. Apple's strategy of tight integration between software and hardware permeated all of its product categories. As Steve Jobs described:

> One of our biggest insights [years ago] was that we didn't want to get into any business where we didn't own or control the primary technology because you'll get your head handed to you.

This tight Apple ecosystem was further reinforced with the iPhone launch in 2007. Initially priced at US $599 and US $499 for the 8GB and 4GB models respectively, the launch of the iPhone was yet another highly anticipated event from Apple as customers lined up days in advance to get their hands on the new product. In less than a decade, the iPhone's stellar success threatened NOKIA's 50-year-old mobile business, which once enjoyed a near monopoly in the handset market particularly for what would today be termed smartphones. In the first quarter of 2014 Nokia's mobile phone shipments dropped by 14.9 million units to just 47 million, while Apple shipped 6.3 million more iPhones than it did the year before to end its own fiscal quarter with sales of 43.7 million devices.[5] For his part Tim Cook noted: "I think [Nokia] is a reminder to everyone in business that you have to keep innovating and that to not innovate is to die."[6]

The launch of the iPad in 2010, was yet another Apple success, revitalizing a niche and up to then risky product category. Despite early claims that the tablet market was destined to fail and posturing that this was an uninteresting market, Apple sold 14.8 million iPads[7] within its first year of release and with the launch of the iPad 2 sales rose further to 32 million in 2011 giving Apple two-thirds of the tablet computer market. Following the iPad's success, the tablet computer market grew to approximately $35bn in 2012.[8] The iPad was priced at $499 for the basic version and $829 for models with larger memory and a 3G wireless connection. Apple's pricing strategy was therefore consistent with products being more expensive than most competitors but still attainable to a mass market.[9]

Whereas Jobs was repeatedly voted one of the best CEO's and greatest entrepreneurs of all time, his was well known for his flamboyant personality and strictness. Employees described working for him as both a daunting and exciting experience. When asked about his demanding reputation he replied:

> My job is to not be easy on people. My job is to make them better. My job is to pull things together from different parts of the company and clear the ways and get the resources for the key projects. And to take these great people we have and to push them and make them even better, coming up with more aggressive visions of how it could be.[10]

Despite his demanding character and often criticized harsh leadership style, Jobs was also known to be an inspiring leader, setting the bar high not only for Apple's employees but first and foremost for himself. *"We don't get a chance to do that many things, so everyone should be really excellent,"* he said in one of his interviews. *"Life is brief and then you die, you know? This is what we've chosen to do with our life. So it better be damn good. It better be worth it."*[11]

He held huge influence within the company; no decision would be made without him taking the lead, and for that reason many analysts highlighted that no other company was so tightly linked to its founder and CEO as Apple was with Steve Jobs. A tremendous advantage whilst he was fit and healthy, his dominance and centrality to every decision became a source of worry as his health began to deteriorate. There was growing skepticism about the viability of Apple under a different CEO. Ever the architect, Jobs made the necessary arrangements to provide a smooth transition and guarantee the future of the firm. Tim Cook, then COO of the company, replaced Job's on a temporary basis during periodic absences for medical treatment. In effect, he was trusted by Jobs before he was trusted by commentators and investors.

As for Jonathan Ive, Jobs told his biographer Walter Isaacson that the designer was his "spiritual partner" and that he gave Ive more operational power than anybody else at the company.

## Jonathan Ive: the design guru

Ive joined Apple in 1992 and ever since has been a key part of shaping Apple's culture, brand and products. The iconic status of products like the iMac (1998), the iPod (2001), iPhone (2007) and iPad (2010) are testament to his influence. His work has earned him not only the reputation of a design guru but also a Royal title from Queen Elizabeth: Sir Jonathan Ive is considered today Apple's most valuable employee.[12] Despite his worldwide fame, little is known of the British designer. Following the company's infamous culture of secrecy, his laboratory is argued to remain sealed from the rest of Apple's campus in San Francisco.[13] Guiding all his breakthrough ideas was his relationship with Steve Jobs: "It's an amazing synergy. It's about the leader of a company valuing design and the leader of design valuing the company," says Thomas Meyerhoffer, who worked in Ive's design team for three years.[14] Ive and

Jobs worked together on all of Apple's iconic products and they contributed to each other's success: Don Norman, who worked at Apple in the `90s as vice president of the company's advanced technology group, said that while Ive had good design ideas "sitting on the shelves," he needed Jobs to get those designs off the shelves. "Jony has always been Jony – brilliant," Norman said. "What he needed was a Steve Jobs to say, 'Make this happen'.[15] Jobs's himself was only too aware of the influence and creativity that Ive provided, close contemporaries often referred to them as Jives and the duo were often spotted taking long walks across the Apple campus.[16]

Their working relationship started when Steve Jobs returned to Apple in 1997: he was touring the company's labs and stumbled upon Ive's work. At that point, Jobs had been intent on hiring a designer from outside Apple to revamp the company's product line. Seeing Ive's work convinced him that the answer was already within the firm.[17] Jobs decision to entrust Ive with key product decisions and he subsequently considered this one of his best strategic decisions. The introduction of the iMac, the first fruit of their collaboration, is an indicative example of Job's forward thinking and Ive's creative potential. The iMac was an all-in-one translucent, colorful computer with a handle on its top. Ive explains the importance of this in a way which reveals much about his personality and design philosophy:

> Back then, people weren't comfortable with technology. If you're scared of something, then you won't touch it .... I thought, if there's this handle on it, it makes a relationship possible. It's approachable. It's intuitive. It gives a sense of its deference to you.[18]

As the years passed by, the relationship between Jobs and Ive became stronger. In one of his last interviews Jobs said: "The difference that Jony has made, not only at Apple, but in the world, is huge. He is a wickedly intelligent person in all ways. He understands business concepts, marketing concepts. He picks stuff up just like that, click. He understands what we do at our core better than anyone" And perhaps hinting at the managerial structure that would eventually replace him, Jobs said, "He has more operational power than anyone else at Apple except me. There's no one who can tell him what to do, or to butt out. That's the way I set it up".[19]

Ive endlessly seeks new sources of information and inspiration outside Apple's campus. Whilst working on ideas for the iMac Ive spent hours in a sweet factory looking for colours that would suggest a product which was for fun as well as work.[20] More recently he travelled to Japan to meet one of the country's leading makers of "katana" a material that would help him in his search for the thinnest computing devices. The second generation iPad was one result of Ive's continuing search for perfection through the process of making a product over and over again. The iPad2 was one third thinner than its predecessor and the recently launched iPad air is thinner still.[21]

Asked about Apple's design philosophy Ive noted: "It's very easy to make something that is new, but it won't be new the day after tomorrow. So we are trying to make things that are *better*".[22] Making the best products in the world is an idea well established within Apple's culture; "its raison d'être" as Ive has mentioned, which drives the actions and decisions of every Apple employee. As he explains

> Apple's goal isn't to make money. Our goal is to design and develop and bring to market good products. We trust as a consequence of that, people will like them, and as another consequence we'll make some money. But we're really clear about what our goals are.[23]

This indirect attention to financial goals is important in explaining Apple's strategy. Make great products that people will want. The money will follow. As a result, Apple focuses on a limited amount of products refreshing these annually as compared to the rapid-fire product introduction favoured by many of its competitors. Each product receives a significant amount of investment, a recipe that was well established under Job's leadership. This way Ive noted "We say no to a lot of things that we want to do and are intrigued by so that we only work on a manageable amount of products and can invest an incredible amount of care in each of them".[24] As competition intensifies, the focus on quality over quantity is a point the company is continuously emphasizing. In a joint interview with Ive, Craig Federighi (Apple's Vice President of Software engineering) explained "Look at the camera space, companies are chasing megapixels but the pictures often look horrible because of their tiny sensors...My family cares about taking a good picture, not a megapixel count. We carry that through to all the decisions we make about our phone. What experience is it going to deliver? Not what number will it allow us to put on a spec sheet".[25] In order to reach this level of design competency and product perfection, every aspect of hardware or software component is thoroughly examined and reworked until the design team feels that there is no other way to go. This involves a long and painstaking process of reducing complexity and ending up with products that appear to be simple and intuitive to use. Ive emphasizes this point:

> I feel that it's lovely when as a user you're not aware of the complexity. I think we feel our job is to try to solve tough, difficult problems, but we don't make the complexity of the problem apparent in its resolution. I mean, there are so many examples of objects or solutions or software where they solve difficult problems, but goodness, it's really clear how difficult the problem was they've solved.[26]

Ive's ability to translate Apple's vision of sophisticated yet intuitive products into sales led to his promotion in 2013 to the role of lead designer for both software and hardware, making him the driving force behind all Apple's product decisions.[27] His promotion marks an important shift in the company's structure. Previously, Steve Jobs held those same responsibilities

## Tim Cook: the efficiency guy

"In the 26 years that Fortune has been ranking America's Most Admired Companies never has the corporation at the head of the list so closely resembled a one-man show".[28] This inextricable link between Apple and its visionary founder Steve Jobs was one of the main reasons analysts thought that the future of Apple under a new leader would never recreate past glories. While Steve Jobs was a visionary entrepreneur, Apple is much more than a vision driven company; it excels in cost leadership, operations and service.[29] During Cook's first 16 months as CEO, Apple introduced the next generation iPhones and iPads and has seen its stock price rise 43%.[30]

Cook has a long and well-established career as the man behind Apple's operational excellence. During his time as the Senior Vice President of Worldwide Operations in early 1998, he was responsible for Apple's streamlining of operations. Recognized for his discipline and focus on efficiency, Cook made some difficult decisions about Apple's operations including closing most of its manufacturing plants and streamlining logistics. During his tenure he pushed Apple component suppliers to relocate next to assembly plants, leading to suppliers keeping parts in their inventory. In one fiscal year 1998–1999 the company held six days of inventory valued at $78 million, down from 31 days, or $437 million, the year earlier; by the end of 1999 inventory levels dropped further to two days' worth, or about $20 million.[31]

Cook was groomed to succeed Jobs as Apple's CEO. It was Cook who handled day-to-day operations during Jobs' leave of absence due on health grounds in 2003, 2004 and 2009. Another medical leave followed in 2011, and in August 2011 Jobs resigned from his position as CEO. Before his death, Steve Jobs made sure that the leadership transition would be as smooth as possible and that Cook would have all the necessary support to carry on this difficult task. Cook recalls the moment when Jobs shared with him his plans of succession:

> "I still remember how he started this discussion. He said, "There has never been a professional transition at the CEO level in Apple." He said, "I want to make this clear. I saw what happened when Walt Disney passed away. People looked around, and they kept asking what Walt would have done." He goes, "The business was paralyzed, and people just sat around in meetings and talked about what Walt would have done." He goes, "I never want you to ask what I would have done. Just do what's right." He was very clear.[32]

In stark contrast to his predecessor flamboyant personality, Cook is known as a low key and soft-spoken workaholic, who guards his privacy closely. At the same time he is known to have a tough side: in meetings although calm and almost unreadable he is said to sit silently rocking his chair; any change in the pace of his rocking is thought to signal discomfort. "He could skewer you with a sentence," a colleague has reported.[33] In a recent interview Cook gave his own view on how he is described by the media:

> The person you read about is robotic. There are some good things about that, perhaps. (Laughs.) Discipline comes to mind. But it sounds like there is just no emotion. People that know me, I don't think they would say that. I certainly am not a fist-pounder. That isn't my style. But that and emotion are two different things.[34]

His slower and more thoughtful leadership approach is characterized by more delegation and collaboration. During Apple's product presentations, he is not the one dominating the stage and within everyday operations he seeks the advice and opinions of others.

> I'll tell you what I do, "Whether there's something that I think I know really well or I don't know at all – and there's a huge range there – I always enlist other people, because the people around the table are phenomenal people. I've never felt that I had to know it all, do it all, any of those things. I think you could have an S on your chest and a cape on your back and not be able to do all those things. I know of no one that can do all that. Maybe there are, but I'm not. So I rely on a lot of people for a lot of different things".[35] His mentality is demonstrated when asked about Apple's stock performance: "I don't feel euphoric on the up, and I don't slit my wrists when it goes down," he says. "I have ridden the roller coaster too many times for that".[36]

Yet Cook makes it clear that he intends to build upon Apple's fundamental values and ensure that Jobs' vision of the firm would persist. On his first day as CEO he sent the following email to Apple employees to reassure them that he would remain faithful to Apple's DNA: "I want you to be confident that Apple is not going to change. I cherish and celebrate Apple's unique principles and values. Steve built a company and culture that is unlike any other in the world and we are going to stay true to that – it is in our DNA. We are going to continue to make the best products in the world that delight our customers and make our employees incredibly proud of what they do".[37]

In one of his recent and rare interviews he underlined his belief that Apple should remain focused on having a small number of products that integrate software, hardware and services. A strategy that as he points out, has been criticized in the past, is now followed by Apple's most important competitors (like Microsoft's and Nokia's synergy).[38] He underlined the importance of a flexible organizational structure that leaves no room for the distractions caused by politics and bureaucracy.[39] Instead of a large siloed organization Cook aims to continue Jobs legacy of running Apple as the "biggest startup there is". Weekly executive team meeting and product meetings ensure that everyone is on the same page in terms of all that is happening in the company, a company process that is inherited from Job's days as CEO:

> We go through every product that's shipping, how it's doing. We go through every new product that's on the road map – what's going on, how the teams are doing, and any key issues there are ... By keeping that cadence and being religious about it – people don't travel during that time; everyone is there, and they're not delegating – it makes the company run a lot smoother. You don't get out of sync because you're constantly coming together.[40]

Whereas the main elements of Apple's corporate philosophy are well maintained, in his first full year as Apple's chief executive, Tim Cook took several steps to make

Apple his own. His first bold move was removing Scott Forstall from Apple, an executive who run iOS and was supposedly one of Job's wunderkinds. Cook's decision on his removal was supposedly based on Forstall's "political" stance within the organization and bad collaboration with the other top executives.[41] Cook then put Apple's top designer, Ive, in charge of software and hardware "human interface", a role that puts the designer in the forefront of all product decisions. Analyst's explained this decision in view of intensifying competition by Samsung and Google; "Tim is a supply-chain expert and he needs to rely on people like Jony to be able to make the right decisions," said David Yoffie, a professor at Harvard Business School in Boston,[42] while others underline that by letting Ive lead Apple's design Cook has mitigated speculations that Apple is falling short on innovation.[43]

Other Cook changes included instituting a charity match policy at Apple, giving Apple investors a stock dividend for the first time in the company's history and instituting more transparency into the supply chain.[44] He said:

> "We want to be as innovative with supply responsibility as we are with our products. That's a high bar. The more transparent we are, the more it's in the public space. The more it's in the public space, the more other companies will decide to do something similar. And the more everybody does it, the better everything gets. It's a recognition that we need to be super secretive in one part about our products and our road maps. But there are other areas where we will be completely transparent so we can make the biggest difference. That's kind of the way we look at it."[45]

In another instance, during a rare outbreak of public criticism regarding Apple's problems with the company's Maps program, he did not hesitate to publicly apologize and even name competing mapping programs customers might use until the problem was resolved.[46]

By the end of 2013, two mobile trends were working against Apple, lower prices and the continuing rise of Android software.[47] Six years after the release of the original iPhone, which dominates the smartphone market, Apple was competing fiercely with both new and old players: Samsung Electronics; Motorola and Nokia which were respectively part of Google as well as Xiaomi of China and Micromax of India who compete on the lower end of the market.[48] In the midst of intense skepticism about whether Apple's impressive innovation pipeline would be maintained, the company added an iPad mini to its lineup and introduced two new iPhones models (the iPhone 5C and iPhone 5S). Whereas the market was expecting a lower priced iPhone that could compete in emerging markets, against competition from Samsung, the 5C came at a price of only $100 less (costing $550 unsubsidized) than the top-of-the-line 5S (costing $650 unsubsidized). At the same time, since 2012 the average unsubsidized price for a smartphone (the phone's full price, without any discount that comes with a multiyear contract) fell from $450 to $375.[49] Cook said that the intention of the company was never to sell a low cost iPhone:

> There's a segment of the market that really wants a product that does a lot for them, and I want to compete like crazy for those customers," he says. "I'm not going to

lose sleep over that other market, because it's just not who we are. Fortunately, both of these markets are so big, and there's so many people that care and want a great experience from their phone or their tablet, that Apple can have a really good business.[50]

Despite criticisms regarding the high price and the lack of a fundamentally breakthrough innovation, Apple sold a record breaking nine million new iPhone 5s and iPhone 5c models, within three days of their launch on 30 September 2013. The signs are that Apple's fanatic customer base is keeping faith with the brand.

## Conclusion

By the end of 2013, Apple Inc. was facing significant challenges: would the newly appointed CEO, a soft spoken operations wizard, be able to replace the charismatic leadership of Steve Jobs? Would the company be able to keep up with its reputation as market disrupter at a time when competitors are imitating Apple's strategy?

Tim Cook may not be an inspirational leader in the same mould as his predecessor but it is clear that he is making careful steps to maintain Apple's stellar performance (see Table C.1). Of his former colleague he said in a tribute: "*He [Steve] left behind a company that only he could have built and his spirit will forever be the foundation of Apple. We will continue to honor his memory by dedicating ourselves to the work he loved so much*".[51] Only time will tell how long the recipe of fewer but greater products with integrated software and hardware can cast a spell over customers.

## Discussion questions:

Q1.   The Apple case describes the three key individuals in the firm's history (Steve Jobs, Jonathan Ives and Tim Cook). How would you describe their strategy styles?

Q2.   Choosing the period when either Steve Jobs or Tim Cook came into office as CEO, how would you diagnose the challenge facing Apple at that point?

Q3.   In the case study, can you see any rules of thumb which appear to guide/ explain Apple's operation?

Q4.   Does anyone appear to change or challenge any of these rules of thumb? If so, do they encounter any difficulties?

Q5.   What unexpected events does Apple encounter and how does the firm respond?

Q6.   What capabilities does Apple appear to have?

Q7.   What should Apple's strategy be for the next five years?

*Table C.1*  **Apple Inc. selected financial data***

| | Year ending September 2013 | Year ending September 2012 | Year ending September 2011 |
|---|---|---|---|
| **Total net sales** | $170,910 | $156,508 | $108,249 |
| **Net sales by product** | | | |
| *iPhone* | $91,279 | $78,692 | $45,998 |
| *iPad* | $31,980 | $30,945 | $19,168 |
| *Mac* | $21,483 | $23,221 | $21,783 |
| *iPod* | $4411 | $5615 | $7453 |
| *iTunes, software & services* | $16,051 | $12,890 | $9373 |
| *Accessories* | $5706 | $5145 | $4474 |
| **Unit sales by product** | | | |
| *iPhone* | 150,257 | 125,046 | 72,293 |
| *iPad* | 71,033 | 58,310 | 32,394 |
| *Mac* | 16,341 | 18,158 | 16,735 |
| *iPod* | 26,379 | 35,165 | 42,620 |
| **Cost of sales** | $106,606 | $87,846 | $64,431 |
| **Gross margin** | $64,304 | $68,662 | $43,818 |
| **Total operating expenses** | $15,305 | $13,421 | $10,028 |
| **Net income** | $37,037 | $41,773 | $25,992 |

*Source:* Apple Inc.
* Dollars appear in millions and units in thousands.

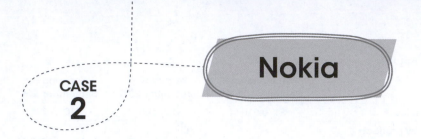

## Leading in Turbulent Times
## Angeliki Papachroni and Robert MacIntosh

### Introduction

**Nokia Corporation** has a long history evolving as it did from a riverside paper mill in Finland in 1865 to a global telecommunications leader responsible for the connectivity of over 1.3 billion people by early 2000. During that time, the company has produced rubber boots, car tyres, electricity and TVs. The firm clearly has a remarkable capacity for adaptation.[1] Having reached the new millennium as the biggest mobile phone company in the world with a market value of $250 billion. Few foresaw what happened next. Within a few years Nokia lost market share to Apple, Research in Motion and later Samsung, putting the company's value at about 12% of its peak.[2] In 2002, Nokia was Britain's number two super-brand; by 2010 it was 89th.[3] Faced with such rapid deterioration of its competitive position, how did the company respond? This case focuses on Nokia's restructuring efforts during 2010–2013, under a newly appointed CEO: Stephen Elop. The first non-Finish executive to ever lead Nokia, Elop, assumed control at a turbulent time and he concluded that drastic action was necessary. With his "burning platform" memo openly addressed to all Nokia employees, the new CEO aimed to instill a sense of urgency and vision. Using emotive language, he compared Nokia to someone standing on a burning platform[4] whose only option is to jump into the water to save himself. Nokia, partly defined by the Finnish concept of "sisu" or "fighting spirit" needed to undergo another episode of reinvention to transform itself.[5] Despite massive restructuring efforts, Nokia's once flagship device division was sold to Microsoft in 2013 for about $7.2 billion.[6] In what follows we review the strategic moves made by Elop during one of the most turbulent periods in the company's history.

### Searching for a new leader

A few months before the telecom crisis in 2000, Finland based Nokia's stock price peaked at $60 and market capitalization exceeded $250 billion. Soon after the crisis hit, Nokia's stock was crumbling at $16.[7] By 2010 Nokia was facing intense competitive pressures on two fronts: in the low-cost segment Nokia faced producers from emerging economies competing on the basis of price whilst simultaneously, at the higher-end of the market, Apple's iPhone had changed consumer expectations and Samsung followed with the launch on a number of successful smartphones.[8] A subtle shift was taking place from an emphasis on "volume" where Nokia had a clear historical lead to "value" as represented by Apple's iPhone. Consumers were beginning to expect different things from their mobile devices and previously separate technologies (diary, music, gaming, telephony, e-mail and web-browsing) were beginning to converge. In contrast to Apple, Nokia had a big product range with significant profits coming from products at the lower end of the spectrum and beyond the US market where Apple was expanding rapidly. The net effect of these trends was a period where Nokia remained the clear leader in terms of market volumes, whilst Apple quickly became the most profitable handset maker.[9] According to analysts, it took Nokia three years from the introduction of the first iPhone to recognize what was happening to the market and to adjust its strategy accordingly.[10] Without a premium product, Nokia's operating margin for devices in 2010 had collapsed to 12.5% (from 21.7% in 2008). In the same time period, Apple's operating margin was 29% and RIM's 24%.[11] According to analysts, Nokia missed the onset of the smartphone revolution due to a mix of poor leadership, complacency caused by earlier successes and an overly consensual organizational culture.[12] Despite its mantra of being customer focused, Nokia was also said to have grown less responsive to customer needs especially in the US market, where consumers turned towards the user-friendliness and innovativeness of Apple. Unlike its rivals, Samsung and LG, Nokia failed to invest adequately in the US, leading to the company's decline in this key market.[13]

Nokia's financial position was also tightly linked to its home country Finland. According to figures from the Research Institute of the Finnish Economy (ETLA), in the decade 1998–2007 the company contributed a quarter of Finish growth and sometimes paid as much as 23% of all Finnish corporation tax. Over the same period, the mobile-phone manufacturer's spending on research and development made up 30% of the country's total, and it generated nearly a fifth of Finland's exports.[14]

By 2010 Nokia was looking to replace its CEO Olli-PekkaKallasvuo who was accused of failing to meet the challenges posed by Apple's iPhone, Google's Android operating system and Samsung's rapid product introduction.[15] Nokia's market share remained respectable but this may have masked a failure to win the hearts and minds of a new generation of smartphone consumers. Analysts were suggesting that Nokia's new CEO appointment needed to be a "dreamer" rather than a "bean counter".[16] In September 2010, Nokia announced that Stephen Elop, would take the position of CEO. This was a notable break from tradition since Elop was the first non-Finnish CEO in Nokia's history. He lacked experience in the mobile handset market but had been leading Microsoft's Business Division (mainly the Office software suite) and was responsible half of Microsoft's profits.[17] Before joining Nokia, Elop was a member of Microsoft's senior leadership team responsible for the company's overall strategy. In this position, he oversaw the Microsoft Office systems and other communications tools and applications for consumers, small and mid-size businesses, as well as large organizations and enterprises.[18]

His software background was considered a valuable asset by Nokia at the time despite criticisms that highlighted Elop's more pragmatic rather than visionary leadership style.[19] On the other hand Elop's low-key style was considered compatible with Nokia's culture of seriousness.[20] On the morning of his first appearance as CEO he reportedly blended in with the Finnish executives and was more concerned in being accepted than being different. His love for ice-hockey, a shared passion for both Canadians and Finns[21] offered one way of connecting with colleagues. On that day he said his role was to "lead this team through this period of change, take the organization through this period of disruption".[22] Elop's appointment at CEO was one part of a wider change at Nokia, as Chairman Jorma Ollila, the architect of Nokia's cell phone success, and smartphone chief Anssi Vanjoki had both announced that they would leave the company with ex CEO Olli-Pekka Kallasvuo.[23]

The new CEO therefore faced many challenges. He needed to stop the downward spiral at Nokia and bring back its innovative edge. He had to decide on a software strategy that would clearly mark the company's position in relation to Apple's and Google's ecosystems. Nokia's own software at the time was performing poorly as the company operated different software platforms (Symbian and Meego) and Ovi story (Nokia's own application store) had about 13,000 items comparing to Apple's almost a quarter of a million at the App Store).[24] George Linardos, Product Manager for Ovi at the time explained the challenge of innovating whilst trying to ensure backwards compatibility with a large user base.

> In Nokia's case, we're in an existing business shipping hundreds of millions of phones a year, with obligations to keep certain revenue levels. So what we did was more like having to remodel an old Victorian house while we were living in it ... Nokia needs to Americanize while simultaneously protecting its assets in the rest of the world. An injection of Silicon Valley attitude will play well in the United States, but the company must take care not to unsettle staff in Europe and elsewhere.[25]

## The burning platform

In response to these challenges Elop announced a series of strategic decisions aimed at increasing openness, accountability and speed in the organization. The first day as a CEO he is said to have sent an email to all Nokia employees asking them three questions: *"what do you think I need to change? What do you think I should not change? What are you afraid I'm going to miss?"* He received thousands of replies that underlined management indecision and staff frustration mostly because of a perceived lack of accountability.[26] Elop's view was that energy was being wasted: *"When you have a large organization where accountability is unclear, many people make decisions and some of them cancel each other out"*. He saw his role as *"playing back to employees what it was I was hearing"*, through blogs, responses to individual e-mails and direct meetings.[27] Juha Äkräs, Nokia's head of human resources at the time added that *"This dialogue was broken in our company ... When you have a high-tech company you think that technology solves all your problems and you forget that good face-to-face communication is important.*[28] Three weeks into his tenure as CEO, Elop launched a comprehensive review of the company, code-named Sea Eagle. *"Stephen forced us to look in the mirror and to really be real about what had happened,"* said human resources head J. Akras.[29]

Having consulted with employees, Elop sent a memo to all Nokia staff setting out the severity of the firm's condition and the need for urgent action. Using the metaphor of a worker standing on a burning platform, his memo was leaked to the press and became one of the most popular incoming-CEO announcements. According to Elop, the "burning platform" memo was the "point of consolidation" and his decisiveness was perceived at the time as a clear sign of leadership and direction for the company.[30] In a recent interview he noted said of his first few days as CEO:

> When I started I found pockets of brilliance, plus numerous unpolished gems, that together were clear proof of why, and how, Nokia had been able to lead the mobile industry for the past 12-odd years. But I also found many, many frustrated people who had seen Nokia get bogged down by layers and layers of management, committees, and supervisory committees, plus all the other potentially fatal diseases that can beset successful companies. Most critically, however, the world – the context for our industry – had undergone a remarkable shift from a battle of devices to a war of ecosystems, and it became clear that big changes were needed to compete more effectively in the future.[31]

Elop's burning platform memo suggested that Nokia had to consider carefully and bravely its next steps; Nokia had to change its "behavior" as the "battle of devices" was now a "war of ecosystems".

> There is a pertinent story about a man who was working on an oil platform in the North Sea. He woke up one night from a loud explosion, which suddenly set his entire oil platform on fire. In mere moments, he was surrounded by flames. Through the smoke and heat, he barely made his way out of the chaos to the platform's edge. When he looked down over the edge, all he could see were the dark, cold, foreboding Atlantic waters. As the fire approached him, the man had mere seconds to react. He could stand on the platform, and inevitably be consumed by the burning flames. Or, he could plunge 30 meters in to the freezing waters. The man was standing upon a "burning platform," and he needed to make a choice. He decided to jump. It was unexpected. In ordinary circumstances, the man would never consider plunging into icy waters. But these were not ordinary times – his platform was on fire. The man survived the fall and the waters. After he was rescued, he noted that a "burning platform" caused a radical change in his behavior. We too, are standing on a "burning platform," and we must decide how we are going to change our behavior.[32]

Elop continued by describing the competitive environment and what it meant for the future of Nokia, and specifically its software strategy. Some read his intention as linking Nokia with a software platform like Microsoft's.

> The battle of devices has now become a war of ecosystems, where ecosystems include not only the hardware and software of the device, but developers, applications, e-commerce, advertising, search, social applications, location-based services, unified

communications and many other things. Our competitors aren't taking our market share with devices; they are taking our market share with an entire ecosystem. This means we're going to have to decide how we either build, catalyse or join an ecosystem. This is one of the decisions we need to make. In the meantime, we've lost market share, we've lost mind share and we've lost time.[33]

## Creating the third mobile ecosystem

Shortly after the burning platform memo, in February 2011, Nokia announced that it would adopt Microsoft's Windows Phone as its primary smartphone strategy, in order to compete with Apple's iPhone and Google's Android. The two companies would also partner in mobile ads and mapping whilst Nokia's application and content store and Microsoft's Marketplace would be integrated. Before the official announcement Elop briefed 200 senior managers on this transition, who were given Windows running handsets in order to familiarize with the new platform.[34] This was a bold move and ended Nokia's sense of independence.

The new partnership ended speculation about Elop's next move which he had raised when talking about deciding whether to "build, catalyze or join an ecosystem".[35] With Microsoft, Nokia set about creating a new "global mobile ecosystem" capitalizing on Microsoft's software and Nokia's hardware expertise to bring the Windows Phone to a wider cross section of price ranges, geographies and market segments.[36] The decision also signaled the demise Nokia's own operating system, Symbian, which was used by almost 400million users worldwide. In contrast, at the point of the announcement, Microsoft's Windows Phone 7 software was used by four million users. This engendered skepticism from many commentators and sparked rumors of a possible takeover of Nokia by Microsoft.[37] The rumors were denied. Another point of contention was the number of Nokia employees who would lose their job with the end of the Symbian platform: *"It was a huge shock, followed by lots of denial, and some people are full of anger"* said a former Nokia employee.[38] Addressing this point Elop said: *"I know this is the most difficult time in this journey. The shareholders don't like ambiguity, humans don't like ambiguity either".*[39]

This generalized skepticism and ambiguity towards the Nokia-Microsoft partnership was reflected in investor's reaction: Nokia's stock price dropped by 12% on the day of the announcement with analysts regarding it as an acknowledgement that Nokia's Symbian-based strategy had failed.[40] Executing the partnership effectively was considered key at this point in order for Nokia to regain ground lost to Google and Apple; however the challenges of innovating together with a partner with a completely different organizational culture were highlighted.[41] The consensus was that Nokia's efforts to create a third pole in the mobile ecosystem had very slim chances of success:

> Windows Phone 7 isn't going to make Nokia better than Apple. It may make Nokia better than it is today, but there are few reasons for high-end buyers to choose Nokia-Windows devices over today's iPhones. Android has done really well mostly

because of carriers, and less because of hardware makers making magical phones. So unless Nokia can talk a bunch of big carriers into favoring Nokia's Windows phones over Android in its marketing strategy, not much is going to happen.[42]

## Organizational restructuring

A few months into the partnership Elop said in an interview: "Part of that change is not just what we do with products or organization, but it's very much about shifting our mindset to a challenger mindset, to reflect on the fact that we have significant competition, we have to fight hard, we have to show intellectual curiosity, make sure we understand the competition. ... We have to go faster, and harder, and more aggressively now than we've ever gone before because of the competition.[43]

In order to achieve this "challenger mindset" and restore Nokia's former agility, Elop restructured Nokia to strip out bureaucracy, accelerate decision making and increase both transparency and accountability within the company. *"What has been crucial in 2011 is the growing change in Nokia's internal culture. We have focused on three significant changes of attitude, [emphasizing] urgency, accountability, and empathy – ensuring that we are better connected to consumer, supplier and operator requirements and able to anticipate what they might need in the future"* Elop said in an interview after his first year as CEO.[44]

The "burning platform memo" highlighted repeatedly that Nokia had lost time and was failing to match the dynamic pace of its competitors. To make his argument even more forceful he often quoted a Nokia employee who half-joked that Chinese manufacturers were "cracking a device" much faster than it took Nokia to "polish up a PowerPoint presentation". Mary McDowell, Head of the mobile phones division said that Nokia was suffering from bureaucracy: *"Somewhere along the way, the process became the product.*[45]" A number of committees and boards were responsible for different parts of the product process, stalling decision making: a "brand board" discussed branding decisions, a "capability board" looked at information technology investments and a "sustainability and environment board" monitored Nokia's green credentials.[46] Elop himself noted:

> Part of the reason I have confidence in our ability to change gears, is because when you look at the things that slow you down – like length of decision-making, confused missions between teams – those are problems we can solve ... We were in a leadership team meeting and someone said "OK, we've got this issue to deal with: what's the expected date?" And someone else said, "Well, that's probably going to take three or four weeks". It's like "Hey, guys, we can't take three or four weeks on this one. We need to be looking at it in seven days" – so that's what we're going to do.[47]

One of Elop's first steps was to remove most of these committees to speed up decision making. The Group Executive Board, was renamed the Nokia Leadership Team in an attempt to emphasize the importance of leadership. Key decisions were directed to the appropriate leadership team or team member: *"Too many things were coming through headquarters before they were going back out,"* said Elop, adding that employees e-mailed him to say: "*Look, I'm right here in the region. I can make this simple little decision, [but] I'm waiting for someone who is 10 time zones away and has three bosses of their own*".[48]

Increasing accountability and transparency was key for Elop: "We're shifting to a model where accountability really matters," he said. "It should be clear who gets to make a decision. It should be clear that that person is celebrated when good things happen. It should be clear that, if someone's not living up to their role, then we need to help them".[49] McDowel, a senior executive who was under this new structure directly accountable for strategic decisions that would traditionally had been debated in committees compared this newly acquired autonomy with driving a canoe; "There are rocks and white water, but you're a little bit more in control".[50] Another senior executive, Steven Robson vice-president for Finance and Control team described the change: "Always, someone in the room turns round and asks 'Who's accountable for this?' Before it was 'Let's discuss this', 'Who's going to decide this?' and then it would be passed to the next level up".[51] The goals and incentives of the leadership team were also made more transparent; top executives were informed on specific targets they should aim for. According to Juha Akras, head of human resources "People aren't doing contradictory things ... With this transparency, we are more aligned".[52]

Nokia's internal structure was streamlined to increase efficiencies: in the years 2011–2013, the company reduced headcount by more than 20,000 and consolidated or closed 40% of its sites worldwide. Product launches were reduced to 25 per year compared to more than 50 in earlier years and even the company's Espoo headquarters in Helsinki were sold and leased back.[53] Whereas some analysts interpreted this move as a sign of Nokia's deepening problems, corporate controller Kristian Pullola said the decision signaled "nothing is sacred when it comes to driving the focus on cash".[54]

Along with these restructuring efforts attention was paid to market intelligence. Nokia had been slow in accessing fast-growing markets such as China and India, allowing Samsung and HTC to steal share. In order to address this Elop brought in new talent. Juha Putkiranta was charged with factories, supplies and logistics, and Chris Weber, new head of sales and marketing, both joined the senior leadership team. Both would now report directly to the chief executive. "We really ratcheted up the degree to which the senior leadership and layers below were involved in what was going on", Elop said. A "change task force", put in place in 2011 became a "turnaround leadership group" last year as it became clear, Mr Pullola says, that Nokia needed to become "even more disciplined and focused" on cash control.[55]

## Aftermath

Despite the restructuring efforts described above, Nokia's share price dropped 83% in three years, Samsung was now the world's biggest handset maker and in January 2013 Nokia cancelled its dividend for the first time in its 148-year history.[56] The company swung from $5.1 billion in profit in 2008 to losing $4.5 billion in 2012 (see Figure C.1) and it's $4 billion in debt has been downgraded to junk status by S&P,

Moody's and Fitch.[57] Two years of Elop's leadership, the resulting partnership with Microsoft, the Lumia series had failed to revive the company.[58] In an effort to attract audience attention Nokia decided to launch its new Lumia handsets (Lumia 920 and a lower-price version called the Lumia 820) a few weeks before Apple announced the iPhone5. Nokia's share price plunged 15% on that day as the Lumia 920 proved to be an upgrade of a previous model and Nokia did not provide with pricing and carrier partner details.[59] Meanwhile Apple sold 5 million iPhone5 handsets in its first weekend. By the end of 2012, Windows phones had 2.7% global handset share behind Android, Apple, Symbian, Blackberry and Samsung's proprietary Bada OS and just 4.1 million Windows phones were sold in the second quarter, compared to 98.5 million Android and 28.9 million Apple devices.[60]

In Q2 2013, Nokia reported revenues of 5.7 billion euros, down 24% from the year before and its Asian market plunged from 64% in 2010 to just 1%.[61] In view of this poor performance by the end of 2013, Nokia agreed to sell its Devices & Services business to Microsoft for $7.2 billion. In a move towards greater synergies, Microsoft's chief executive Steve Ballmer announced that the company was in the process of transforming itself from one that "was known for software and PCs, to a company that focuses on devices and services".[62] The acquisition also included a 10-year licensing arrangement with Nokia so that Microsoft can use the Nokia brand on current mobile phone products.[63] The purchase was said to have been completed in 2014, when about 32,000 Nokia employees would be transferred to Microsoft. As the combined company will be supplying both hardware and software, Microsoft aimed for a gross margin of $40 per phone sold, which would in turn be invested in marketing and innovation that would further promote Microsoft's customer base.[64] Following the announcement, Elop stayed in place as Nokia's Executive Vice President, Devices & Services and a member of the Nokia Leadership Team.[65] For Finland Nokia's demise marked the end of an era where Nokia was an indisputable leader in telecommunications.

## Conclusion

This case has focused on Nokia's turbulent journey during the leadership of Stephen Elop (2010–2013). Despite initial hopes that the company would be revitalized under a new leader, Elop's restructuring efforts and strategic decisions failed to restore Nokia's competitiveness and innovation. In the end, Microsoft bought Nokia's once flagship Device and Services business in September 2013. Elop's "burning platform memo" was based on a story of survival against the odds but the reality for Nokia was a form of survival that few would see as palatable.

## Discussion questions

Q1. The Nokia case describes the period when Stephen Elop became Nokia's CEO. How would you describe his strategy style?

Q2.  What was Elop's diagnosis of the challenge facing Nokia at that point, and do you agree with this diagnosis?

Q3.  In the case study, can you see any rules of thumb which appear to guide/ explain Nokia's operation?

Q4.  Does Elop appear to change any of these rules of thumb? If so, did he encounter any difficulties?

Q5.  Did he encounter any unexpected event and how did he respond?

Q6.  How would you describe the narrative that Elop develops in his burning platform memo?

Q7.  What should Nokia's strategy be for the next 5–10 years?

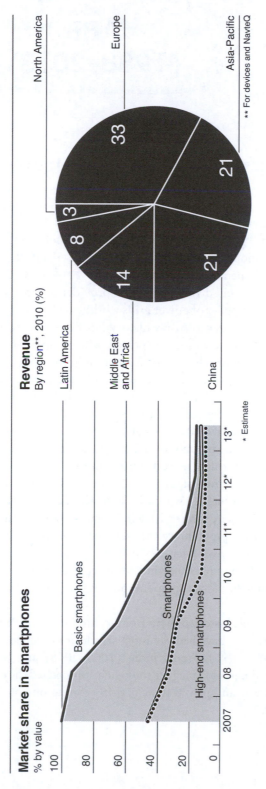

*Figure C.1* Nokia's declining share in smartphones and revenue by region[66]

*Source:* Hill, A. (2011) 'Inside Nokia: trying to revive a giant', FT.com, 11th April 2011.

# ABB
# (1988–2013)

## Robert MacIntosh and Angeliki Papachroni

### Introduction

Formed by the 1988 merger between ASEA of Sweden and Brown Boveri of Switzerland, ABB is now one of the world's largest engineering companies. A global leader in power and automation technologies based in Switzerland, the company employs 150,000 people and operates in 100 countries. By 2014 ABB was the largest supplier of industrial motors and drives, the largest provider of generators to the wind industry, and the largest supplier of power grids worldwide.[1]

Despite its current position however, ABB's history has been marked by turbulence with periods of significant success interspersed with periods of significant difficulty (see Table C3.2). Immediately after its formation in the early 1990's ABB experienced significant expansion fueled by a series of bold acquisitions under the leadership of founding Chief Executive, Percy Barnevik. Praised at the time for his role in one of the largest cross-border mergers ever seen, Barnevik's tenure as CEO also saw a series of decisions which would eventually bring the company to the brink of collapse. In mid-2002 the company reported a huge quarterly loss and market capitalization plunged by 25% overnight. Faced with mounting debt, the then chairman Jürgen Dormann assumed the role of CEO and launched a multi-year program to re-focus ABB.[2] By 2005, ABB had its 5th CEO, Fred Kindle (for a detailed list of ABB's CEOs see Table C3.1). A former McKinsey consultant, Kindle led the company throughout its return to profitability and stability through cost-cutting and restructuring, only to resign a few years later due to "irreconcilable differences" with the board in terms of ABB's strategy. In 2008 Kindle was replaced by Joe Hogan who followed a strategy that combined a focus on operational efficiencies, organic growth and targeted acquisitions.

This case will review the whole history of ABB from its formation in 1988 to 2014, focusing on the three leaders that have had the most significant influence on ABB's story: Percy Barnevik (1987–1996), Fred Kindle (2005–2008) and Joe Hogan (2008–2013). As three very different strategists they each approached the challenges faced by ABB in their own way and played their part in creating one of the largest conglomerates in the world.

ABB (1988–2013) 173

# Percy Barnevik: Pursuing aggressive growth

In August 1987 Percy Barnevik announced the merger of ASEA with Brown Boveri, creating a new force in the European market for electrical systems and equipment. At the time the newly formed ABB became a metaphor for the changing economic map of Europe[3] and was systematically voted within the world's most admired companies[4] mainly because of its then CEO Percy Barnevik whose charismatic leadership was compared to GE's Jack Welsh. Associates said Barnevik wanted nothing more than to be as admired as Welch, and that he checked GE's share price several times a day: "Jack Welch was an obsession," says Jean-Pierre During, a former ABB controller who was part of Mr Barnevik's inner circle. Mr Barnevik says he had no "hang-up" about Mr Welch but was "fascinated by Jack's ability to squeeze profits."[5] At the time, Barnevik was described as a corporate pioneer: "He is moving more aggressively than any CEO in Europe, perhaps in the world, to build the new model of competitive enterprise—an organization that combines global scale and world-class technology with deep roots in local markets".[6] His vision for ABB was to build a new type of organization which brought the maxim think global, act local to life.[7]

In order to realize this vision, Barnevik followed a strategy of aggressive growth through acquisitions. One of the biggest acquisitions was the $700 million purchase of Westinghouse Electric Corp's power-transmission and distribution business in 1989, which gave the company a strong position in the US and turned ABB into a leading supplier of power equipment.[8] The same year Barnevik spent $1.6 billion to acquire Combustion Engineering, the manufacturer of power-generation and process-automation equipment.[9] Bearing in mind that these major acquisitions occurred whilst the organization was still handling the merger of Asea and Brown Boveri, it is clear that Barnevik was moving forward at pace. Combustion Engineering, of Stamford, Conn., insulated its boilers with asbestos and had been hit by a series of lawsuits from individuals who claimed the asbestos had caused respiratory damage. Despite warnings from ABB lawyers of the litigation risk Barnevik proceeded with the acquisition,[10] a decision that would cost ABB millions of dollars in the future in asbestos lawsuits.

Overall it was estimated that in the course of five years Percy Barnevik spent nearly $5 billion on 200 purchases. Barnevik's acquisition strategy gave him the nickname "Percyfal," a reference to the knight Parsifal who went on the quest for the Holy Grail by colleagues: "Percy was addicted to acquiring companies," said Tom Sjokvist, a 20-year veteran of ABB and head of its low-voltage-products division.[11] However, this acquisition spree was said to have led to the company's record debt of $5.2 billion by 2002.[12,13]

By 1991 ABB was growing fast. The company generated annual revenues of more than $25 billion and employed 215,000 people around the world, while its business was split equally between Europe and non-EU countries.[14] Barnevik described

ABB's challenges in being a truly global organization: "ABB is an organization with three internal contradictions. We want to be global and local, big and small, radically decentralized with centralized reporting and control".[15] In order to address these contradictions Barnevik developed a management structure, dubbed the matrix, which was based on two main axes. On the one hand the company was structured as a distributed global network, where executives around the world made strategic decisions which straddled national boundaries. On the other hand the matrix comprised of a collection of traditionally organized national companies, each serving its home market. "ABB is a company with no geographic center, he said in an interview. Are we a Swiss company? Our headquarters is in Zurich, but only 100 professionals work at headquarters and we will not increase that number. Are we a Swedish company? I'm the CEO, and I was born and educated in Sweden. But our headquarters is not in Sweden, and only two of the eight members of our board of directors are Swedes. Perhaps we are an American company. We report our financial results in U.S. dollars, and English is ABB's official language".[16]

Barnevik described ABB's matrix system, as a structure designed to leverage core technologies and global economies of scale without eroding local market presence and responsiveness. ABB's operations in the developed world were organized as national enterprises with presidents, balance sheets, income statements, and career ladders.[17] For example, ABB did not simply sell industrial robots in Norway; instead Norway had an ABB robotics company charged with manufacturing robots, selling to and servicing domestic customers, and exporting to markets allocated by the Business Area leader. Similarly, there were 1100 such local companies around the world whose presidents reported to the Business Area leader, usually located outside the country, and the president of the national company of which the local company was a subsidiary.[18]

> The vast majority of our businesses fall somewhere between the superlocal and the superglobal. You want to be able to optimize a business globally—to specialize in the production of components, to drive economies of scale as far as you can, to rotate managers and technologists around the world to share expertise and solve problems. But you also want to have deep local roots everywhere you operate—building products in the countries where you sell them, recruiting the best local talent from the universities, working with the local government to increase exports. If you build such an organization, you create a business advantage that's damn difficult to copy.[19]

A top management team including Barnevik and 12 other executives from around the world oversaw ABB's strategy and performance.[20] At the time the matrix won praise for its decentralized hierarchy that gave power to local managers.[21] Barnevik himself had experienced the combination of an Anglo-Saxon education and a Swedish upbringing. He stressed the need for global managers to have respect and deep knowledge of the local market: " ... We can't have managers who are "un-French" managing in France because 95% of them are dealing every day with French customers, French colleagues, French suppliers. That's why global managers also need humility. A global manager respects a formal German manager—Herr Doktor and

ABB (1988–2013)  175

all that—because that manager may be an outstanding performer in the German context".[22]

During most of his tenure, Barnevik was praised for his leadership and management innovations and was highly supported by both the board and the markets. Under his leadership ABB revenue nearly doubled to $34.6 billion while net income grew by nearly 70% to $1.2 billion.[23] However several of these acquisitions would turn out to be questionable, eventually losing the business money.

By 1997 Barnevik changed roles within ABB. The founding CEO had combined the roles of Chairman of the Board, President and CEO giving him almost unpredecented power in a firm of ABB's size. In 1997 Barnevik became ABB's chairman and Goran Lindahl assumed the role of CEO but it was far from easy to step into Barnevik's shoes. Aggressive expansion in Asia and Eastern Europe combined with ABB's liabilities from earlier acquisitions relating to asbestos exposure created circumstances where the firm began to encounter serious operational difficulties for the first time since its formation.[24] Additionally, ABB's heavily decentralized organizational structure was producing conflicts and serious communications problems within the different divisions of the company.[25] It was reported that some country directors wouldn't publish their plans for contract bids for fear of internal competition from other divisions, while the freedom of each division to use their own spreadsheet software resulted in 600 different programs being used around the organization.[26]

Lindahl's promotion to CEO followed a period as a Vice President in ABB and he took over the company at a time when ABB was hit by the Asian financial crisis. Despite restructuring efforts Lindahl was replaced in 2001 by Jörgen Centreman, then head of ABB's automation business. During his tenure, Centreman faced major liabilities from asbestos claims associated with acquisitions made early in Barnevik's tenure as CEO. These liabilities and other trading challenges meant that ABB reported its first ever loss of $691M in 2001. Eventually, Barnevik himself was forced out of office leaving ABB mired in debt, its stock performance plunging and with a number of pending lawsuits[27] (see Figure 1).

A few months later, it was revealed in the press that Barnevik along with Goran Lindahl had left ABB with $136m of pension and retirement benefits between them; posing serious questions about ABB's management structure and governance.[28] At the time many reports criticized Barnevik's organizational model for giving too much power to the CEO.[29] In 2002, after two CEO changes with the company in deep crisis ABB's board convinced its chairman, Jürgen Dormann a low-key, turn-around specialist, to step into the CEO role and rebuild ABB.[30] Dormann's focus at that point was to simplify ABB's organizational structure and restore its culture of discipline and accountability, while facing huge liabilities from asbestos lawsuits. Asked about Bernevik's leadership, he commented: "We had a lack of focus as Percy went on an acquisition spree ... the company wasn't disciplined enough ... And the management structure lasted as long as it did because "no one wanted to undo the Percy stuff. Mr Barnevik did an admirable job in the early 1990s but you have to ask what a company looks like in the years after a chief executive steps down".[31] By 2003,

ABB, once a \$40 billion company, was valued at about \$3.91 billion.[32] After spending two years stabilizing the company, Dormann replaced himself as CEO with Fred Kindle.[33]

# Fred Kindle: a return to profitability

Before joining ABB in 2005 Fred Kindle, an ETH engineer with consultancy experience in McKinsey, was CEO of Sulzer AG, where he had led a successful turnaround in that firm's fortunes. When he assumed duties as ABB's CEO, the company was still facing major operational and strategic issues; the organization had halved in size and profit margins were lagging behind industry averages. The company's stock performance was down 6% compared to the previous year. "Recommending ABB these days is like convincing someone to remarry the wife he just divorced,"[34] commented Ben Uglow, an analyst at Morgan Stanley in London.

Kindle committed to improving margins to 7.7%, up from 5.2% in 2004 (excluding asbestos costs) and pushed managers to focus more on profits than on growing revenues. At the time the US market, ABB's largest market was still lagging behind in profitability mainly due to execution problems.[35] Another of Kindle's priorities was to control internal spending as overheads had reached \$507 million in 2004; his goal was to reduce that to \$350 million in 2005. "ABB has spent too much on discretionary out-of-pocket items," he said.[36]

Part of ABB's five-year strategy from 2005 to 2009 was a significant organizational restructuring aimed at restoring ABB's operational focus. As a result one layer of management was removed, and two core divisions (power and automation) were replaced by five business areas (power products, power systems, automation products, process automation, and robotics). Kindle referred to this restructuring as an evolution of ABB's strategy: "We remain focused on our core power and automation businesses. The strategy involves a balanced approach to value creation by widening our focus beyond growth to higher margins, greater return on capital and cash generation". CFO Michel Demare, added: "Our new targets for net income and cash flow are intended to put more emphasis on our bottom line and our ability to convert profit into cash".[37] Apart from boosting ABB's profitability Kindle's efforts were focused on streamlining the organization rather than pursuing growth through acquisitions: "At the end of the day", Kindle said, "our aspiration—my aspiration—must be to generate profitable growth, and not growth for growth's sake".[38]

Kindle's first success came when ABB reached an agreement for ending the decade long legal battle over asbestos liabilities. The \$1.4 billion settlement was \$232 million more than a previous rejected offer but less than investors had feared.[39] At the end of July 2007 ABB sold its oil and gas production plant Lummus Global to the Chicago Bridge and Iron Company for \$950 million, in an attempt to focus on its largest businesses (power and automation technology). In June of the same year ABB reported that profits for the second-quarter of 2007 nearly doubled to \$729 million, compared to \$367 million for the same period the year before.[40]

ABB (1988–2013)    177

Kindle however was perceived as being conservative in terms of how ABB would invest its money and he reportedly rejected acquisitions he regarded as being too expensive.[41] In 2008 ABB released its fourth-quarter earnings reporting a rise in net income to $1.8 billion, from $422 million, a year earlier, while margins rose to 13.1%, from 11.1%. The company also said it would be buying back up to 2.2 billion Swiss francs ($2.0 billion) in shares. Analysts estimated at that time that ABB had cash reserves of around $5 billion, but rumors had it that Kindle was favored smaller acquisitions worth up to $2 billion as he told Germany's *Handelsblatt* newspaper in late January that there would be no "mega-deals" in the coming months, or at least as long as market conditions remained uncertain.[42]

Eventually, after overseeing a period of strong organic growth and profitability Fred Kindle left ABB in 2008 in an abrupt move, which was described as being "due to irreconcilable differences about how to lead the company."[43] The Board of Directors named Chief Financial Officer Michel Demaré as interim-CEO. During a press conference, Michel Demare and the company's chairman, Hubertus von Grünberg, did not elaborate on what "irreconcilable differences" amounted to, but media speculation persisted that Kindle's departure was related to the company's acquisition strategy.[44]

## Joe Hogan: balancing growth and operational efficiency

Following three months of interim management, Joe Hogan assumed control of ABB, joining the company from rival General Electric Co in 2008. Hogan had a distinguished career in GE for 23 years and during his last years as director of GE Healthcare he oversaw the company growing by $11 billion.[45] His track record in buying and integrating companies was said to have played a key role in his selection in as ABB's CEO. Hogan viewed his appointment in the following terms: "What I think they were looking for was a balance of growth and operational experience in running a big company. Of course, growth is very important. But there's also a huge emphasis at ABB on operational skills. Hailing from GE didn't hurt me in that respect".[46]

Joe Hogan was also the first American to ever lead ABB, a fact that kept him in his toes regarding his first months in the company: "Usually, companies only turn to an external candidate when they're in trouble. Coming from the US in particular, I expected to meet some resistance and not to be accepted easily. It's what you'd expect in an American company". [47] His low-key style and resistance to introduce immediate changes in the organization, however, was said to have helped towards a smooth transition: "Chief executives should never make any immediate decisions based on their first impressions. There were some things I wasn't comfortable with – for example some organization structures that were different to what I grew up with at GE. But I've taken my time. You've got to understand first why something is done that way. I've seen some big mistakes by business leaders because they want to change things to suit their comfort zones" he said.[48]

By the time he assumed the role however ABB's performance was deteriorating as clients were cutting back on investments amid the global economic crisis. In order to protect profit margins, Hogan set an efficiency program to cut costs by $1.3bn a year and soon upped the goal to $2bn to meet a sustained drop in orders. Hogan realized this cost-cutting strategy in a period of downturn could possibly endanger ABB's ability to grow when conditions improved, however he believed that ABB had at that point sufficient margin to achieve those goals.[49]

In contrast to his predecessor whose efforts were largely focused on restructuring, cost cutting, and organic growth, Hogan paid equal attention to shielding ABB's R&D through investments and acquisitions. Hogan said in an interview: "Yes, suddenly restructuring moves up the agenda. But you don't drop all growth initiatives as a result. I've been through cycles before and what you have to do around that... Of course there's a risk. It would be naive to think otherwise. But our goal has been to shield sales and shield research and development. These are the two components you want to protect in a downturn".[50]

In announcing his first mid-term strategy paper since taking the helm in 2008, Hogan said acquisitions could give a 3% to 4% annual sales boost, securing ABB against an economic slowdown.[51] During his tenure he spent $20 billion on investments and acquisitions to broaden ABB's reach and portfolio including the purchase of drives maker Baldor Electric Co., low-voltage products maker Thomas & Betts Corp[52] and Power-One Inc., a California-based maker of solar inverters. The acquisition of Power-One Inc. gave ABB, a foothold in a market that was expected to grow by more than 10% annually and was considered an example of how Hogan was bringing new technology to the company's portfolio.[53]

Hogan also focused on reducing geographical gaps in ABB's portfolio, particularly in the US, where he believed the company was under-represented in comparison with rivals such as GE and Siemens.[54] His attention also turned towards growing Asian competition for infrastructure projects. "What happens at ABB in the next few years is not more of the same," Hogan said in a presentation. "We have to really start to expand ourselves more broadly and more balanced across the globe and go deeper into specific markets, such as renewables, data centers or services".[55] This focus towards a more balanced global portfolio was key in a context of continued economic uncertainty: "Most of markets will go sideways over a period of time," he said. "This required ABB to invest in markets where it saw growth and shift costs and resources from areas that aren't going to grow as strongly. ABB's broad geographic, industry and product spread helped protect it against some of the uncertainty".[56]

After five years at the helm, Hogan unexpectedly decided to step down "for private reasons" in 2013. Overall, Hogan's track record of cutting costs and protecting margins was considered "exemplary in the industry". According to analysts "Several larger acquisitions to fill technology white spots and expand the company's presence in North America were highly successful".[57] ABB's spokesman Antonio Ligi said Hogan didn't resign because of ill health and there was no conflict with the board or

ABB (1988–2013)    179

chairman, declining to give further details.[58] In response ABB named one of its top managers Ulrich Spiesshofer as the new company CEO in September 2013.

## Conclusion

ABB one of the biggest conglomerates in the world has had a turbulent history of leadership transitions and deep organizational changes in order to meet external demands and internal pressures. This case focuses on the leadership style and strategic decisions of three key ABB leaders: it's first CEO Percy Barnevik who led the company into a period of aggressive growth and acquisitions; Fred Kindle who took the helm of ABB at a time when the organization was facing the threat of bankruptcy and focused on rationalization and return to profitability through organic growth and finally Joe Hogan who followed a mix of organic growth strategies and selective acquisitions to reinforce ABB's return to profitability.

## Discussion questions

Q1.   The ABB case describes the three longest serving CEOs in the firm's history (Percy Barnevik, Fred Kindle and Joe Hogan). How would you describe their strategy styles?

Q2.   Choosing the period when one of these CEOs came into office, how would you diagnose the challenge facing ABB at that point?

Q3.   In the case study, can you see any rules of thumb which appear to guide/explain ABB's operation?

Q4.   Do Fred Kindle or Joe Hogan appear to change any of these rules of thumb? If so, do they encounter any difficulties?

Q5.   What unexpected events to these CEOs encounter and how do they respond?

Q6.   What narrative(s) do the three CEOs appear to foster and how did they approach the job of crafting these narratives?

Q7.   On what should the next CEO of ABB focus their attention?

Table C3.1  List of ABB's CEOs

| 1. Percy Barnevik | 1987–1996 |
| --- | --- |
| 2. Göran Lindahl | January 1997–December 2000 |
| 3. Jörgen Centerman | January 2001–September 2002 |
| 4. Jürgen Dormann | September 2002–December 2004 |
| 5. Fred Kindle | January 2005–February 2008 |
| 6. Michel Demaré – interim | February 2008–September 2008 |
| 7. Joe Hogan | September 2008–May 2013 |
| 8. Ulrich Spiesshofer | June 2013 |

Table C3.2 Selected ABB financial data[59] (1988–2012)

| | 1988 | 1989 | 1990 | 1991 | 1992 | 1993 | 1994 | 1995 | 1996 | 1997 | 1998 | 1999 |
|---|---|---|---|---|---|---|---|---|---|---|---|---|
| Orders received US$ (millions) | 17,822 | 21,640 | 29,281 | 29,621 | 31,634 | 29,406 | 31,794 | 36,224 | 36,349 | 34,803 | 31,462 | 25,379 |
| Net income | 386 | 589 | 590 | 609 | 505 | 68 | 760 | 1,315 | 1,233 | 572 | 1,305 | 1,614 |
| Return on equity (%) | 12.5 | 16.8 | 14.5 | 13.9 | 11.8 | 1.8 | 20.2 | 28.4 | 22.2 | 10.3 | 23.2 | 27.9 |
| Employees | 169,459 | 189,493 | 215,154 | 214,399 | 213,407 | 206,490 | 207,557 | 209,637 | 214,894 | 213,057 | 199,232 | 164,154 |
| Total debt[60] US$ (millions) | – | – | – | – | – | – | – | – | – | – | – | 6,344 |

| | 2000 | 2001 | 2002 | 2003 | 2004 | 2005 | 2006 | 2007 | 2008 | 2009 | 2010 | 2011 | 2012 |
|---|---|---|---|---|---|---|---|---|---|---|---|---|---|
| Orders received US$ (millions) | 25,440 | 23,726 | 18,112 | 18,703 | 21,689 | 23,194 | 28,401 | 34,348 | 38,282 | 30,969 | 32,681 | 40,210 | 40,232 |
| Net income | 1,443 | –691 | –783 | –767 | –35 | 735 | 1,390 | 3,757 | 3,118 | 2,901 | 2,561 | 3,168 | 2,704 |
| Return on equity (%) | 30.6 | –19.2 | –52.4 | –38.0 | –1.2 | 21.1 | 24.2 | 34.6 | 28.7 | 21.7 | 17.2 | 20.08 | 15.99 |
| Employees | 160,818 | 156,865 | 139,051 | 116,464 | 102,537 | 104,000 | 108,000 | 112,000 | 120,000 | 116,000 | 116,500 | 133,600 | 146,100 |
| Total debt[60] US$ (millions) | 7,262 | 9,700 | 7,928 | 7,887 | 5,334 | 4,096 | 3,282 | 2,674 | 2,363 | 2,333 | 2,182 | 3,996 | 10,071 |

# Nine Dragons

## Royalty and Recycling
### Angeliki Papachroni and Robert MacIntosh

### Introduction

**Zhang Yin** (or Cheung Yan, according to the Cantonese pronunciation of her name), the founder of Nine Dragons Paper, was the first businesswoman to top China's annual list of richest individuals in 2006 with an estimated fortune of $3.4 billion. In 2010 she was the richest self-made woman in the world, ahead of TV celebrity Oprah Winfrey and Harry Potter author J.K. Rowling.[1] The "waste-paper queen" or the "queen of trash", as the media have called her, earned this nickname by establishing a recycling business to fill a particular niche. Her idea was rather simple: Nine Dragons Paper produces packaging material in China, by recycling cheap wastepaper imported from the US. The company was listed in the Hong Kong Stock Exchange in March 2006 and the same year its share price surged after reports that net profit more than quadrupled to 1.375 billion yuan, or $174 million.[2] One of the factories run by Nine Dragons is now the largest paper mill in the world and over the years, Nine Dragons has evolved into China's largest paper manufacturer.[3] Throughout her career, Cheung Yan has received various awards: she was awarded the "Entrepreneur of the Year in China 2007" by Ernst & Young, was accredited as a "Leader Figure" in "China Cailun Award" by the Chinese Paper Industry's Chamber of Commerce, and was awarded "China Charity Award 2008" by the Ministry of Civil Affairs of the PRC. In May 2009, Ms. Cheung was awarded "Outstanding Entrepreneur in "Pulp and Paper Manufacturing Industry in China" by the Chinese Paper Association.[4]

This case will follow Cheung Yan's impressive journey from an employee in the paper industry to one of the most successful self-made entrepreneurs in the world.

## Building an empire: turning trash into gold

> "I remember what a man in the business told me back then … He said, waste paper is like a forest. Paper recycles itself, generation after generation" Cheung Yan.[5]

The eldest of eight children, and the daughter of an army officer, Yan was born in China's southern Guangdong Province. She started her career working in the textile industry in Guangdong and later at a paper-trading company in Shenzhen,[6] where she built up ties with paper producers. In 1985 she moved to Hong Kong, with $4,000 in savings, to set up her own paper trading business. "At that time people in China didn't have name cards, and I carried around an introduction letter," she recalls.[7] Hong Kong's economy was thriving, generating supply but opportunities for growth were limited by the country's small size. At the same time, China was evolving as an exporter and faced its own limits to growth from a shortage of raw materials.

As China began looking overseas for scrap metal and used paper,[8] Yan decided to move to the US where together with her husband Liu Ming Chung. They founded America Chung Nam in 1990. The US was regarded a valuable source for raw material as most paper was made from wood pulp, contrary to the lower quality paper of China that was usually made from grass, bamboo or rice stalks. Cheung Yan was one of the first to sell scrap paper to China: "The U.S. had rich resources, and if I stayed in Hong Kong I couldn't satisfy demand in China. At the time most of China's paper was imported, and the market potential was vast,"[9] she says recalling her decision to establish a US company to export recycled paper to China. By 2005 America Chung Nam was the largest exporter by volume in the U.S for the fifth consecutive year with ties to recycling yards in New York, Chicago and California, surpassing companies such as DuPont and Procter & Gamble.[10] Looking back, she says getting started in the U.S. wasn't easy because of her limited language skills. But the style of doing business in the U.S., which emphasizes discipline, professional standards and reputation, matched her own. "The U.S. left me with a wonderful impression," she said.[11]

In the meantime, she returned to Hong Kong and founded Nine Dragons Paper in 1995. The first paper making facility was opened in Dongguan, a manufacturing hub in the Pearl River Delta region near Hong Kong. "The domestic paper-and-packaging industry at that time was not developed, and almost everything was imported," she says. Nine Dragons, whose name implies "highest fortune," was founded with a bank loan in 1995. The loan was set against the expectation of rising demand for packaging for exports.[12] On the day that the company went public in Hong Kong in 1996, its share price jumped nearly 40%; half a year later the company's debt-capital ratio was reduced from 187% to 33% adding 24billion to Cheung Yan's fortune making her the richest self-made woman in the world.[13] By 2007 the company had 11 giant papermaking machines, 5300 employees and profits were soaring following the booming growth of Chinese exports.[14]

Nine Dragons was one of the fastest growing paper companies in the world as it capitalized on energy efficiency and lower production costs as opposed to paper makers in the US and Europe which used less efficient machines from the 70s and the 80s burning clean but expensive natural gas.[15] According to Cheung Yan the key to Nine Dragon's success was ensuring long term access to a steady supply of high quality waste paper in large quantities.[16] "Foresight is the key," she said. "While most domestic producers were using machines with a production capacity of less than 50,000 tons, our first machine had a capacity of 200,000 tons. We have higher goals".[17] One more machine was installed in 2000, another in 2002, two more in 2003, another two in 2004, and three in 2005, one of them on a new site outside Shanghai pushing total annual capacity to 5.4m tones.[18]

At the same time, much effort was placed on maintaining a high level of efficiency: "In this Dongguan premise, there are over 5000 people. But for each paper treatment machine, we only need less than 20 people. All the machines are very advanced and automatically controlled. We provide a one-stop service, from resources to products. Everything is controlled automatically. So you may think 5000 staff is a large number, but actually it's not".[19]

Yan's ambition and entrepreneurial thinking was the driving force behind Nine Dragon's success: "I have a passion for the business. I like the paper recycling business. Fortunately, I had the wholehearted support from the bankers because of Nine Dragon's vision of the business and the valuable assets of the company so I was able to get the funding. I believed that, one day, China would be like Europe or the USA. So that's why I started to invest in the first paper machine in Dongguan with an international approach. Meaning that I imported the machines from overseas, components from the USA and Europe and also the scale of the machines were much bigger than my peers at that time".[20] All this is inevitably expensive, but Yan insisted that greater scale creates greater efficiency and reduces the cost per unit of output.[21]

Since the 1990's China's paper making industry has been the fastest growing in the world with an output of 49.5 million tons by 2004. However, recycling levels remained low: only 30% of China's scrap paper was recycled each year, compared with 70% in the US, forcing China to buy foreign scrap. In 2005 china imported 12 million tons of waste paper, nearly half the world's available waste paper.[22] Rebounding from slower sales and profit growth in 2009, due to the global economic crisis, the company reached its peak in 2011 by increasing its production capacity and introducing a series of new products, including whiteboard and recycled printing and writing paper. Following this expansion the following years were focused on operations and profitability.[23] By 2013 the company's total sales volume reached new height at approximately 10.5 million tonnes, bringing approximately 28.7 billion Yuan in sales revenue, a 5.8% increase year-on-year.[24]

Yan's ambition was to make Nine Dragons the leader in containerboards: "My desire has always been to be the leader in an industry,"[25] she said. Sometimes called the Queen of Trash, she doesn't disown the title. But, she said, "Someday, I'd like to be known as the queen of containerboards".[26] According to Yan, Nine Dragon's strategy was based on three success factors: controlled diversification, a flat and agile organizational structure and a strong corporate culture.

> First, we continually diversify our product offering, so that we can maintain our profitability one way or another by evening out the effect of market fluctuations of individual product types. Second, we adopt a management culture that emphasizes "democracy and intelligence" and "flat, simple and fast" operations. These will enable us to respond quickly, efficiently and innovatively to arising business opportunities. Third, it has been our persistent policy that care for our staff carries much weight in our management philosophy. This promotes a cohesive team spirit and helps to build our staff's strong passion and commitment on the industry. As our staff members are determined to excel themselves in the paper business and cherish this as their long-term career, they collaborate to a build an enterprise that is forever becoming bigger, stronger and better.[27]

# Organizational structure & culture

In managerial terms, Nine Dragons is a family firm. Yan overseas all strategic decisions along with her husband, Liu Ming Chung, a Taiwanese-born Brazilian national
who originally trained as a dentist, and now serves as the company's CEO. Liu Ming
Chung focuses on manufacturing technology and international development[28]
Another, five of Zhang's siblings help in the business, but Zhang denies kinship plays
a key part in her management "Out of the whole family, only one brother has entered
the company's management. I chose him for his ability",[29] she said. Her younger
brother, Zhang Chang Fei, is the company's deputy chief executive.[30] "My husband
used to be a doctor, but I discovered his talent and convinced him to do business.
They have proved to do an excellent job".[31] In one of her interviews however Yan is
critical of a strictly family style management: "We're not a company where the family
boss manages every detail. I don't approve of this kind of system, at all. I approve of
how multinational companies are run. Although my company is small, I use this kind
of management".[32] Together with her husband and her brother, both of whom are
senior executives, Cheung Yan owns about 70% of Nine Dragons, which was worth
$6.5 billion in 2007.[33] Criticisms were raised however when Yan appointed her
25-year-old son as a non-executive member of Nine Dragon's board of directors. Yan
herself stood by the choice underlying that Nine Dragons is a family business after
all: "I hope that Nine Dragons can stay in the family for 100 years, too".[34]

The company's headquarters in Dongguan, China, reflects a mixture of Chinese
and international background the Chinese-style buildings have slogans urging hard
work and different flags are displayed (China's flag is in the middle, surrounded by
those of Brazil, Liu's homeland, and the U.S., where Cheung holds a green card and
where their elder son attended graduate school) inside, in a conference room for
guests, a photo of Yan and her husband with former U.S. President George W. Bush
hangs alongside shots of prominent Chinese politicians.[35] Yan describes how this
mixture of cultures forms Nine Dragon's DNA: "In my management, I emphasized
a humanized approach and also an approach that you may say is an amalgamation of
the Chinese and Western management and culture".[36]

The backbone of the company's culture however remains the commitment to green
and low carbon papermaking. "Paper-making can't do without environmental protec-
tion," said Yan. "That's the motto of the Nine Dragons Paper, which puts an average
of two to three percent of each project's investment into preventing pollution and
monitors its waste water discharges 24-hours a day.[37]" This commitment is reflected
in the management philosophy: "No environmental management, No papermaking"
and the company's mission to "use of recovered paper for papermaking to protect
the environment and create a greener and better future for mankind".[38] In order to
achieve this mission the organization is based on the values of integrity and honesty,
fairness and justice, diligence and strong work ethic, unity and pragmatism and
the management principle to respect and care for employees, innovation and long
term prosperity for the organization.[39] Yan further underlines the focus on effective

human resource management: "We like to cultivate our own human resources, with the belief that talents can only be discovered when given opportunity. If not, you cannot retain good people. Such a human resources management philosophy must be supported by an ever-innovating management system. This humanized approach is particularly effective in keeping good management talents, as they are convinced that working in Nine Dragons gives them hope and values for the future".[40] In order to encourage middle managers to become decision makers within their own operations, the company has adopted what they call as the "sub-plant" system, which grants more responsibility for key decisions and urges middle managers to think proactively and innovatively within their area of expertise.

## Leadership characteristics

In my career development, I didn't feel that as a woman I experienced any difficulty because of that. And my belief is in any business transaction, it's not sex that makes the difference. It's actually that you should use your intelligence to win. Whoever has the intelligence will win the game. For the past twenty years, I have been very pleased that I was able to build this success and it was not just because I was a woman", Cheung Yan. [41]

Starting from a modest background, Yan has become one of the most successful entrepreneurs in the world, dominating the paper trade industry. When she was young Cheung Yan's father was jailed during the Cultural Revolution and she ended up working in a textile factory, supporting her seven siblings and mother on a mere 40 yuan ($6) a month; This experience has said to afford her a deep knowledge of business and extraordinarily bold and far-reaching ambitions.[42] Despite her success, she does not seem to focus too much on her individual wealth which she views as a reflection of the value of the company: "my father was a military officer and at that time I did not chase wealth but I did have the ambition to make good achievements in the future. And even today the wealth that is under my name, it's just a reflection of the value of my enterprise. To me personal wealth doesn't mean anything more than if it's sufficient for my daily use – that will be good enough. So I look at the Nine Dragons business as a business with a 100-year foundation. So it's a long-term business for me. And when I was young at that time Chinese society was such that nobody was wealthy anyway so there wasn't such a strong feeling of being rich in contrast to being not as rich.[43]

Over the years, Yan has given few interviews. When she does speak publicly she consults with a group of handlers. Her low profile has helped her remain largely unknown and she is described by acquaintances as a "round-faced, not very tall" woman who "doesn't like dressing up and looks like a person of action".[44] "I'm an entrepreneur. A high profile is unnecessary," Yan told the Shanghai-based China Business News, whose reporter described her speaking as "extremely fast".[45] When Yan was asked about the future of a company which seems to have grown more quickly than the rest of its industry she replied: "the market waits for no one...if I don't develop today, if I wait for a year, or two or three to develop I will have nothing for the market and I will miss the opportunity. And we will just be very ordinary, like any other factory...we only have a certain number of opportunities in our lifetime. Once you miss it, it's gone forever".[46]

Herman Woo, an analyst at BNP Paribas, who helped her paper company list shares in Hong Kong, described her as a "visionary": "She doesn't mind putting a lot of money in at the beginning, to build the company".[47] "Vision and methods", Yan says, "matter more than language." Her early experiences in the U.S. appear to corroborate this view,[48] within five years her firm had become America's largest exporter of waste paper. Ng Weiting, who was her partner in Hong Kong in the 1980s, says Yan was driven and tough and had figured out how to get the best performance out of those who worked for her.[49] "When her employees asked for a pay raise, she would grant it if it was reasonable," he recalled. "But when her employees made mistakes, she would criticize them severely. She made it clear when to reward and when to punish".[50] Analysts described Yan as a great saleswoman and a savvy dealmaker, with a focus on efficiency and a deep faith in the power of production. Yan's sister, Zhang Xiubo said her elder sister cultivated a sense of discipline and rigor: "My sister hates lazy people the most. She is always energetic and more diligent than any other person I know".[51] "We run around the clock. I've never seen a slack period since I worked here," said a company manager.[52]

## Conclusion

This case follows the remarkable journey of Cheung Yan a self-made entrepreneur who, based on a simple idea of turning waste paper into high quality packaging material, managed to grow Nine Dragons Paper into the world's largest recovered paper manufacturer. It has highlighted the ways in which early life experiences and individual values can infuse a much larger organization with a particular ethos. It also highlights the dynamics of family business and demonstrates that bold decisions can sometimes allow a small firm to grow into a market leader.

## Discussion questions

Q1.    The Nine Dragons case describes the emergence of a dominant firm, how would you describe Cheung Yan's strategy style?

Q2.    What was her diagnosis of the challenge facing Nine Dragons in the early years and does this diagnosis change over time?

Q3.    In the case study, can you see any rules of thumb which appear to guide/ explain Nine Dragon's operation?

Q4.    Is there any evidence of positive feedback in the Nine Dragon's case study?

Q5.    How would you describe the narrative that Cheung Yan develops about Nine Dragons?

Q7.    What should Nine Dragons' strategy be for the next 5 to 10 years?

# APPENDICES

Appendix 1: The Strategy Cycle Templates

Appendix 2: Writing a Business Plan

Appendix 3: Writing a Strategy Assignment

# The Strategy Cycle Templates

```
┌─────────────────────────┐
│                         │
│   The **strategy** cycle │
│                       ↑ │
└─────────────────────────┘
```

Throughout Section B, each form of analysis is captured in a template. Cumulatively, these templates form the basis of a comprehensive strategy that runs from diagnosis through to the process of bringing the strategy to life. For ease of use, the individual templates are reproduced here in a single location.

*Diagnostic template (see Chapter 4)*

| | Year 1 | Year 2 | Year 3 | Year 4 | Year 5 |
|---|---|---|---|---|---|
| Measure 1 | | | | | |
| Measure 2 | | | | | |
| Measure n | | | | | |
| Business diagnostic | What do changes in key performance measures over time tell you about competitive positioning for the firm? Are there any product/market/customer issues arising from this? Can you identify any business rules of thumb that underpin the organization's performance? | | | | |
| Cultural rule of thumb 1 | | | | | |
| Cultural rule of thumb 2 | | | | | |
| Cultural rule of thumb n | | | | | |
| Cultural diagnostic | Are there any obvious tensions between the business and cultural rules of thumb within the organization? | | | | |
| Strategic influencer 1 | | | | | |
| Strategic influencer 2 | | | | | |
| Strategic influencer n | | | | | |
| Political diagnostic | By mapping the strategic influencers we get a sense of the political dynamics of the firm's current situation. Ask how strategic influencer will react to the performance measures set out above. Who, if anyone, is generating political pressure for change? | | | | |
| Diagnostic summary | A one-paragraph summary of the organization's current situation and the challenge it needs to overcome. | | | | |

## Strategic intent template (see Chapter 5)

| Characterize your intentions in the following ways: |
| --- |
| **W**... the desired outcome(s) of the strategy<br>**X**... the resources, capabilities or processes<br>**Y**... the external context (hazard or opportunity)<br>**Z**... the time frame which applies |
| Complete the following statement: |
| The challenge we face is [diagnostic statement] and our strategy is to achieve [intent] by [timeframe]. |

## Trends and opportunities template (see Chapter 6)

| From PEST analysis: | Given our strategic intent: |
| --- | --- |
| Trends in the operating environment | Implied strategic moves |
| 1. | 1. |
| 2. | 2. |
| 3. | 3. |

**Specific uncertainties**

A happens — A does not happen

B happens — B does not happen

n happens — n does not happen

**Industry structure**

| | Strength | Trend | Opportunity/threat? | Possible action |
| --- | --- | --- | --- | --- |
| **Customers** | | | | |
| **Suppliers** | | | | |
| **Rivalry** | | | | |
| **Entrants** | | | | |
| **Substitutes** | | | | |

Complete the following statement:

The challenge we face is [diagnostic statement] and our strategy is to achieve [intent] by [timeframe] by exploiting [opportunity].

*Resources and capabilities template (see Chapter 7)*

We have a great reputation □
We have loyal customers □
We have a large customer base □
We have a strong brand □
We have experienced /knowledgeable staff □
We have highly skilled staff □
We are trusted □
We have strong relationships with customers/suppliers □
We have innovators on our team □
We have great products / services □
We have great reliability □
We have good quality □
We have excellent processes □
We have licence(s) □
We hold patents for our products/services/processes □
We have exclusivity (e.g. products/territories/time periods) □
We have prime location(s) □
We own valuable assets □
We have great facilities □
We have financial reserves □
We make good margins □
We achieve efficiencies of scale / scope □

Translate items selected above from "we have" to "It's our ability to _____ "

| Q1. | It's our ability to _____ that means we do _____ very well. |
|---|---|
| Q2. | Is this ability embedded in every part of our business ? |
| Q3. | Is our ability to _____ demonstrably superior to that of our competitors ? |
| Q4. | Does this specific ability result in outcomes which matter to our customers? |
| Q5. | Is our advantage here durable? |
| Q6. | Given our strategic intent, does our ability to _____ remain relevant? |

Complete the statement:

The challenge we face is [diagnostic statement] and our strategy is to achieve [intent] by [timeframe] by using our superior ability to [capability statement] to address [opportunity].

## *Strategic options template (see Chapter 8)*

| Core strategy statement | The challenge we face is [diagnostic statement] and our strategy is to achieve [intent] by [timeframe] by using our superior ability to [capability] to address [opportunity]. We will achieve this by ... | | | |
|---|---|---|---|---|
| Circle one item from each row below: | | | | |
| Aim | Retrenchment | | Consolidation | Growth |
| Tactic | Market penetration | Market development | Product development | Diversification |
| Method | Organic growth | | Acquisition | Partnership |
| Competitive stance | Cost | Differentiation | Premium | Blue Ocean Strategy |
| Strategic group | Within current strategic group | | In new strategic group | |

## *Evaluation template (see Chapter 9)*

| | Use a ✓ or a ✗ to assess each option against each criterion | | | |
|---|---|---|---|---|
| | Appropriate? | Achievable? | Astute? | Sustainable? |
| Strategic option 1 | | | | |
| Strategic option 2 | | | | |
| Strategic option n | | | | |

## *Comprehensive strategy templates (see Chapter 10)*

| **Complete at least one strategy statement from the choices below:** | |
|---|---|
| Minimal robust strategy | The challenge we face is [DIAGNOSTIC STATEMENT]. We will develop and exploit our superior [CAPABILITY] to capitalize on [OPPORTUNITY] and achieve [INTENT] by [TIMEFRAME]. |
| Intermediate strategy | The challenge we face is [DIAGNOSTIC STATEMENT]. Our strategy is therefore one of [AIM] delivered through [METHOD]. We will develop and exploit our superior [CAPABILITY] as the provider of [OFFERING] to [AUDIENCE]. This will allow us to capitalize on [OPPORTUNITY] and achieve [INTENT] by [TIMEFRAME]. |
| Fully specified strategy | The challenge we face is [DIAGNOSTIC STATEMENT]. Our strategy is therefore one of [AIM] delivered through a combination of [TACTIC] and [METHOD] competing on the basis of [STANCE] within [STRATEGIC GROUP]. We will develop and exploit our superior [CAPABILITY] as the provider of [OFFERING] to [AUDIENCE]. This will allow us to capitalize on [OPPORTUNITY] and achieve [INTENT] by [TIMEFRAME]. |

*Strategy cycle template (see Chapter 11)*

| Desired rules of thumb | |
|---|---|
| Business:<br>1.<br>2.<br>n. | Organizational:<br>1.<br>2.<br>n. |
| **Habits to break** | |
| Business: | Organizational: |
| **Turning the soil** | |
| To create conditions for change we will:<br>Change processes ☐<br>Change roles and remits ☐<br>Relocate people / resources ☐<br>Alter measures / incentives ☐<br>Change the structure(s) ☐<br>Change our infrastructure ☐<br>etc. | |
| **Managing feedback** | |
| We'll deliver positive feedback by: | We'll deliver negative feedback by: |

# APPENDIX 2

# Writing a Strategic Plan

Organizations are required to produce strategic plans (and business plans) for a variety of reasons and for many audiences. One of our key messages in this book is that plans do not always come to fruition. Indeed, it has been observed that few plans survive first contact with the enemy (see Moltke, 1993). In organizational settings we have argued that plans often change during the process of implementation. The strategy statements crafted in Chapters 4–11 set out the 12 key components of a robust and coherent strategy. Our recommendation is that to convert these short, focused statements into a strategic plan is simply a question of elaborating these key decision points.

Capturing strategy in written and/or visual form is a related but separate skill from that required to craft a robust strategy statement. The latter rests on an ability to iron out logical inconsistencies and to select appropriate combinations from a variety of analyses. The former rests on your ability to engage an audience. We would suggest that the structure below ensures that your strategic plan is rooted in a comprehensive and inter-locking set of decisions. Such plans can be used to communicate internally with colleagues, especially those not directly involved in crafting the strategy statement. They can be used to convince potential funders, customers or suppliers of the credibility of your endeavours. By taking the outputs from the templates embedded in each chapter of section B and using these as headings, it is possible to produce a document which sets out key decisions and an explanation of the choices underpinning each key term. Adding an executive summary, an introduction, an evaluation, some financial data and an implementation schedule you arrive at the prototypical contents of a strategic plan. The following headings offer a useful guide. Each section would draw on relevant data to present a convincing and cumulative case.

Our suggested outline of a strategic plan is as follows:

1 Executive Summary – The strategy statement (see Chapter 10) plus key evaluation points (see point 12 below) and key implementation issues (see point 13 below). Should be less than 1 page long and should allow the reader to grasp the argument without having to read the remainder of the document. Note, an executive summary is not an abstract.

2 Introduction – A short section setting out the format and structure of the report as well as the rationale behind the timing of the report itself and the period that it covers. Finally, the introduction should set out your diagnosis of the challenge(s)

facing the organization using supporting data to create a compelling sense of the need for action.

3   Strategic Intent... A summary of what the organization needs to achieve with appropriate performance measures and supporting data showing historical performance (as well perhaps as the performance of key competitors) in order to calibrate the reader on the scale of the challenge ahead. There should be a clear and unmissable link between the intent of the organization and the diagnostic material presented in the introduction.

4   Capability... A review of the core skillset, resources and distinctive attributes of the organization. This should set out comparative data for competitors as well as articulating how customers and potential customers value the organization's capabilities. Though this section may feature a SWOT analysis it is important to move beyond claims of particular strengths and set out the generative processes which produce those strengths. It may also be helpful to set out capability gaps if these are implied by the diagnosis and strategic intent set out thus far.

5   Foresight... An overview of key trends in the organization's operating environment and more locally, in the particular industry within which the organization sits. Supporting data is again important as is the sense in which independent features of the environment such as demographic changes and technological changes may interact with each other to create opportunities or threats to the organization.

6   Aim... An elaboration of strategic intent setting out whether the organization plans to consolidate, grow or retrench from its current position. The choice should be linked to the combination of diagnosis and points 3, 4 and 5 above. It may be that the strategy involves more than one aim for example consolidation in one area of activity whilst growth occurs in another area. If so, the logic for the combination as well as details of the timing and sequence need to be provided.

7   Tactic... Here, the plan needs to specify the combination, weighting and timing of efforts across the available choices, which include market penetration, market development, product development and diversification. An assessment of competitor moves in the recent past and near term future should also be offered to show how the competitive landscape is shifting.

8   Method... The choices covered in this section review whether the plan will be delivered by organic growth, acquisition or some form of partnership such as a joint venture or alliance. Whichever choice is being proposed should be supported by historic data as well as a review of the methods used by competitors. If a partnership method is being recommended, potential partners should be specified and criteria used in the eventual choice of partners made clear.

9   Competitive Stance... Here, the plan needs to justify the choice of competitive orientation from the available options of economics, differentiation, premium or Blue Ocean. The rationale should set out clear links to points 4 and 5 above as well as reviewing market data and the competitive stance adopted by competitors. Ideally these data would be presented as a timeline showing trends and changes in recent years.

10  Grouping... In this part of the strategic plan, the purpose is to map the strategic space within which the organization sits. Strategic Group Analysis should be used to identify both who the organization currently competes with, and whether the plan involves a shift to a new strategic group. The use of actual or proxy data is important in corroborating the choice of strategic group. Where a switch from one group to another is suggested, issues such as barriers to switching and the competitive stance within the target group should be set out clearly. Obvious links exist between this section and points 3 and 9 above.

11  Offering... Setting out how the organization creates value and whether this is either a direct or indirectly achieved is important. Identifying how customer perceptions of value may be changing, perhaps by reviewing new business models and the offerings of competitors would be helpful.

12  Audience... The plan should identify customers, markets and segments that the organization wishes to service. There should be data on the shape, size and evolution of the organization's audience with clear links to the external environment as described in point 5 above.

13  Evalution... Here the plan should set out a clear and structured review of the development trajectory envisaged using the following sub headings:

    a)  Appropriateness – response to current challenge(s) as well as the medium to long term implications of your response.

    b)  Achievability – a summary business case covering resourcing, returns/benefits, risks, key partners, measures, control, flexibility, finance, cash-flow, sensitivity analysis, etc.

    c)  Astuteness – predicted stakeholder interests and reactions, engagement strategies for key stakeholders groups, governance issues, ethics, key risks and contingency plans.

    d)  Sustainability – the availability of on-going support, links to organizational culture, a review of the long term viability of the organization and whether this is helped or hindered by the proposed strategy.

14  Implementation Blueprint... Setting out the action plan by which the strategy document will become a reality. This typically incorporates a timeline setting out milestones, deliverables, actions by named individuals or groups, monitoring processes, performance measures, etc.

Populating the 14 points set out above produces a comprehensive strategic plan which could be used for a variety of purposes. Such plans are not works of art. They follow in the rational tradition and should be concise and clear. Whilst the structure set out above runs to more than the few sentences recommended in Section B of this book, brevity remains important. In particular, the executive summary should be written on the basis that all key decision-making information should be included such that reading the full detail of the plan itself is optional. Of course, it is true that such plans can become works of art by engaging professionals to help polish and present the core ideas. The use of professional copy editors and graphic designers is commonplace amongst many larger organizations. A cursory examination of annual reports or strategy documents from larger organizations makes it clear that the eventual glossy document is far removed from the original word processed document. The additional sheen that such efforts introduce can cut both ways. The result can help hone and refine the core message, making it easier to grasp. Equally, the result can appear a triumph of style over substance. No amount of gloss or design can overcome flaws in the basic components of a strategic plan. For this reason we purposely set out a robust strategy statement in one or two paragraphs and work toward a longer articulation rather than approaching the problem in the reverse of this order.

# Writing a Strategy Assignment

Many of those reading this book will be students studying strategy as a part of a business or management course. Often such courses require participants to compose strategy assignments which are then assessed. Indeed, this group may represent the single largest strategy writing community at present. For this reason, we have included some thoughts on the production of strategy assignments.

We have seen many thousands of strategy assignments as both tutors and external examiners in a range of institutions. The best assignments have familiar hallmarks. Like good strategic plans, they are clear and concise with a good summary or abstract. Poorer ones tend to be turgid, repetitive and meandering. Better assignments tend to have an appropriate number of references, they avoid speculative assertions unless specifically asked to do so, and the arguments presented are both well-rehearsed and well-supported. Perhaps most obviously of all, good assignments answer the question set, rather than the one desired. They give the reader the impression that student is confident, has researched the subject and is adept at critical thinking. They know where the limitations of their work lie and they point these out as a means of bounding their findings out without undermining the value of what has been submitted.

A long established gauge of quality in academic work is Benjamin Bloom's taxonomy (1956). Assessment processes often work with this framework either explicitly or implicitly.

**Knowledge** – does the assignment present the right data, models, ideas or stories. Has the appropriate information been recalled?

**Comprehension** – is there evidence that the student fully understands the knowledge which has been recalled? Given the ease of access to other sources via the internet, it is also important to consider whether the student moves beyond recall and repetition to place ideas or concepts in their own words and exemplify their use.

**Analysis** – a typical strategy assignment involves the analysis of a case organization, often from a written case study. In analytical terms, has the issue, situation, case or illustration been broken down into appropriate components for investigation?

**Application** – are the right analytical tools being applied correctly to appropriate aspects of the case, situation or problem?

**Synthesis** – is there evidence of the student's own creative thinking, ideas and opinions to offer a contribution beyond that already embedded in the case?

**Evaluation** – has any contribution been critiqued and its benefits and limitations articulated? For example, are the weaknesses or limitations of any tools, data or concepts considered?

| Weaker assignments | Stronger assignments |
|---|---|
| ➤ Present lists instead of an argument<br>➤ No explanation of findings<br>➤ No specific conclusions<br>➤ Lack cross referencing between types of analysis<br>➤ Contain irrelevant material "because we spent a weekend on it"<br>➤ Lack evidence, data, corroboration<br>➤ Lack diagnosis of the challenge facing the organization<br>➤ Fail to identify potential criticisms or weaknesses<br>➤ Doesn't state key assumptions | ➤ Don't features any of the characteristics of a poor report!<br>➤ Has a strong narrative and a "strategic feel"<br>➤ Draws on multiple forms of self-reinforcing analysis, based on multiple sources of evidence<br>➤ Present a clearly articulated diagnosis of the challenge which the organization faces<br>➤ Present enough information but is succinct<br>➤ Offers limited but convincing conclusions |
| Common phrases used in feedback to such assignments include: | Common phrases used in feedback to such assignments include: |
| Fragmented, compartmentalised, vague, unconvincing, overly assertive, poorly structured, rambling, underwhelming. | Clear, precise, compelling, persuasive, reassuring, snappy, digestible, insightful, readable, integrated, grounded. |

*Figure A3.1* **Characteristics of weaker and stronger strategy assignments**

As a general rule, the elements of Bloom's taxonomy become progressively more demanding in the sequence presented above. Outstanding recall, comprehension and analysis are usually insufficient to achieve outstanding grades in the absence of synthesis and evaluation. These latter two categories are almost always present in highly graded work yet are the two areas most commonly overlooked in assignments and examinations.

Figure A3.1 below is drawn from a content analysis of feedback sheets for many hundreds of strategy assignments where students were asked to present an analysis of the strategy of an organization of their own choosing.

Just as with strategic plans, strategy assignments have clear requirements. Once these requirements have been surfaced, it is a relatively simple task to produce something, which matches those requirements. Taking the time to understand the assignment brief, consider what the assessment process is looking for and building a sufficient evidence base on which to build your argument should ensure good outcomes.

## Who to read?

**Benjamin Bloom** edited the first volume of "Taxonomy of Educational Objectives" in 1956 and since then it has influenced generations of teachers, lecturers and educationalists. His views have invited criticism but this is hardly surprising given how widely his approach has been adopted. We have found it a useful way of structuring a conversation about expectations and outcomes in the context of formal taught programmes.

# Notes

## 1 Introduction

1. Rob Grant presented an analysis of the curricula of strategy classes at a range of leading business schools during the 2012 Strategic Management Society conference in Prague.
2. In 2013 we hosted a Strategic Management Society conference in Glasgow on the theme of "strategy in complex settings".
3. Apple appears as one of the cases featured in Section D of the book.

## 4 Diagnosis

1. A more detailed account of Apple is presented in Part C, Case 1.
2. A snippet is a short extract or fragment drawn from a longer narrative. A snippet from the IBM story might be that the firm dropped the ball when it lost control of the operating system.

## 5 Strategic Intent

1. Source, Amazon.com web-site, 2012.
2. Bovine spongiform encephalopathy (BSE) is more commonly known as mad cow disease. In 1996 the UK government ordered a cull of all potentially infected herds which led to the slaughter of over 4 million animals to try to eradicate the problem. During the crisis, sales of products containing processed meat fell sharply as public confidence in the safety of such products was eroded.
3. See www.ndpaper.com.

## 6 Trends and Opportunities

1. A combined vaccination for measles, mumps and rubella (MMR) was introduced in 1971 but subsequent claims linked the vaccine to autism in children. The research on which these claims were made was declared fraudulent by the British Medical Journal yet participation in the vaccination programme still dropped from 92% to below 80%.
2. Microsoft saw changes in their industry coming. They made strategic moves into both mobile telephony and later, the tablet market. Three years after launch Windows holds around 5% of the global smartphone market. In July 2013, Microsoft wrote off $900M against unsold models of its tablet device (the Surface). This represents more than the firm had earned from sales of the Surface. Seeing change coming is helpful but other aspects of the strategy cycle remain critical to overall success or failure.
3. Case 2 in Section D describes Nokia in more detail and in particular, its decision to partner with Microsoft.

## 7 Resources and Capability

1. Matthew Syed's book "Bounce" offers an excellent review of the original research which is all the more compelling since it draws on his own background as an outstanding table tennis player. Malcolm

Gladwell's book Outliers covers similar territory.

2. The same quote is also attributed to Herbert Simon whose work predates that of van der Heijden.

3. Amazon is rightly praised for the efficiency of its logistics processes and customer service but it has also been criticized for its use of zero hours contracts and its behaviour in relation to taxation.

4. This is reminiscent of the time lag observed in the concept of strategic drift (see Hensmans, Johnson and Yip, 2013).

# 8 Strategic Options

1. Ansoff updated his core ideas in 1988, adding geography as a third dimension in the matrix.

2. Cliff Bowman developed his strategy clock model which has five competitive strategies (No Frills, Low Cost, Hybrid, Differentiation and Focused Differentiation) as well as three uncompetitive strategies. See Faulkner and Bowman (1995).

3. See McGee and Thomas (1986) for a thorough review of strategic group analysis.

4. At the time of writing, the Independent newspaper had a selling price of £1.40.

# 9 Evaluating Strategy

1. Hammond and his colleagues identify further eight decision making traps, including the sunk cost trap (where we persist with efforts to build on prior investments despite counter evidence that this will be fruitless), the overconfidence trap (where we overestimate our ability to achieve a goal) and the recallability trap (where atypical but memorable events hold undue influence).

# 10 Building a Comprehensive Strategy

1. Checkland also uses less flattering examples to illustrate the same point. For example he suggests that it is not credible to call your elbow an idiot. Rather, idiocy resides at the level of the individual as the emergent property of all organs, structures and processes behaving in concert. He terms these systemic collections of components a holon because he is concerned that the word system has fallen into disrepair through overuse.

2. The most detailed strategy statement in Figure 10.2 requires a minimum of 59 words and more typically runs to around 100 words. Nevertheless, the artificial target of 50 words serves a useful purpose in focusing the mind.

# 11 The Strategy Cycle

1. This phrase is often attributed to former heavyweight champion Mike Tyson but appears to be in common usage with some accounts tracing it back to Joe Louis in the 1930s.

2. We came across this statement in a conversation with John Wright, the former Chief Executive of the Clydesdale Bank and now a visiting professor at Heriot-Watt University. It is also attributed to Peter Drucker and was used by Mark Fields, then the President of the Ford Motor Company.

3. Paradoxically, feedback which amplifies behaviours consistent with the new rule could be read as both positive and negative. Positive in the sense that it is amplifying a particular dynamic, yet negative in the sense that it is managing consistency to a known set of rules.

## 12 From Logic to Action

1. Thanks to Campbell Powrie of Heriot-Watt University who introduced us to this phrase.
2. See the Nokia case for an example of an organization attempting to change culture.

## 13 Strategy's History Revisited and Strategic Management Reframed

1. We are adopting a particular perspective within the broader complexity theory literature, namely that of dissipative structures. See MacLean and MacIntosh (2011) for a detailed comparison of this and the other common view which is the so-called edge of chaos perspective.
2. In 1986 Reynolds managed to produce a computer simulation which he called Boids. In the simulation each individual boid follows 3 simple rules: (1) steer to avoid crowding and collision (2) align toward the average line of flight of other local boids and (3) head toward the average positional location of other boids in the flock. Using these three rules a whole flock of boids emulate the flocking behaviour of real birds. An internet search for the term "boids" will identify several on-line versions of the simulation that you can experiment with.
3. Positive feedback here is used to denote any feedback which amplifies the change causing it. In contrast, negative feedback, which is a restoring feedback, suppresses the change causing it.
4. To demonstrate this point, ask a group to collaborate in the creation of a drawing. If you allow each person only to add one line or feature before passing on to the next you can get an insight into the way in which we make sense from multiple potential interpretations. This is especially powerful if you ask each group member to write down what they think is being drawn at each stage in the process.

## Case 1: Apple

1. http://www.forbes.com/sites/petercohan/2013/01/22/with-apple-profit-falling-board-should-replace-tim-cook-with-jony-ive/.
2. http://tech.fortune.cnn.com/2011/11/10/tim-cook-and-jony-ive-are-joined-at-the-hip-says-steve-jobs-biographer/.
3. http://www.wired.co.uk/news/archive/2012-07/30/jonathan-ive-revenue-good-design.
4. Linzmayer, O. W. 2004. Apple Confidential 2.0: The Definitive History of the World's Most Colorful Company. San Francisco: No Starch Press.
5. http://appleinsider.com/articles/14/04/29/apples-smartphone-only-lineup-poised-to-pass-nokia-in-total-mobile-phone-shipments.
6. http://www.businessweek.com/articles/2013-09-19/cook-ive-and-federighi-on-the-new-iphone-and-apples-once-and-future-strategy#p4.
7. http://content.time.com/time/business/article/0,8599,2096251,00.html#ixzz1kxgHRRtE.
8. http://www.economist.com/node/21537946.
9. http://www.economist.com/node/15394190.
10. http://money.cnn.com/galleries/2008/fortune/0803/gallery.jobsqna.fortune/5.html.
11. http://www.wired.com/business/2011/10/column-jobs-obsession-whales/.
12. http://www.usatoday.com/story/tech/2013/09/19/apple-jony-ive-craig-federighi/2834575/.
13. //www.dailymail.co.uk/home/moslive/article-1367481/Apples-Jonathan-Ive-

How-did-British-polytechnic-graduate-design-genius.html#ixzz2j1gH9BDA.

14. www.dailymail.co.uk/home/moslive/article-1367481/Apples-Jonathan-Ive-How-did-British-polytechnic-graduate-design-genius.html#ixzz2j1hUeTxp.

15. www.huffingtonpost.com/2011/08/29/jonathan-ive-apple-designer_n_940115.html.

16. www.businessinsider.com/jony-ive-2012-10#ixzz2jgjXulam.

17. www.businessinsider.com/jony-ive-2012-10#ixzz2jgjfQ7tH.

18. www.businessinsider.com/jony-ive-2012-10#ixzz2jgk1kAr4.

19. www.businessinsider.com/jony-ive-2012-10#ixzz2jgjnMHCc.

20. www.dailymail.co.uk/home/moslive/article-1367481/Apples-Jonathan-Ive-How-did-British-polytechnic-graduate-design-genius.html#ixzz2j1gH9BDA.

21. www.dailymail.co.uk/home/moslive/article-1367481/Apples-Jonathan-Ive-How-did-British-polytechnic-graduate-design-genius.html#ixzz2j1gH9BDA.

22. www.usatoday.com/story/tech/2013/09/19/apple-jony-ive-craig-federighi/2834575/.

23. www.businessweek.com/innovate/next/archives/2009/07/jonathan_ive_th.html.

24. www.wired.co.uk/news/archive/2012-07/30/jonathan-ive-revenue-good-design.

25. www.usatoday.com/story/tech/2013/09/19/apple-jony-ive-craig-federighi/2834575/.

26. www.businessweek.com/printer/articles/155086-apples-jonathan-ive-and-craig-federighi-the-complete-interview.

27. www.businessinsider.com/jony-ive-2012-10#ixzz2jgiuHdAG.

28. www.money.cnn.com/2008/03/02/news/companies/elkind_jobs.fortune/.

29. www.forbes.com/sites/gregsatell/2013/06/04/why-tim-cooks-level-5-leadership-might-not-be-enough-to-secure-apples-future/.

30. http://www.bloomberg.com/news/2012-12-06/cook-says-lives-enriched-matters-more-than-money-made-interview.html.

31. http://online.wsj.com/news/articles/SB116096027141893457.

32. http://www.bloomberg.com/news/2012-12-06/cook-says-lives-enriched-matters-more-than-money-made-interview.html.

33. www.reuters.com/article/2013/08/22/usa-apple-cook-idUS-L1N0G91GF20130822.

34. http://www.bloomberg.com/news/2012-12-06/cook-says-lives-enriched-matters-more-than-money-made-interview.html.

35. www.bloomberg.com/news/2012-12-06/cook-says-lives-enriched-matters-more-than-money-made-interview.html.

36. http://www.businessweek.com/printer/articles/153204-apple-chiefs-discuss-strategy-market-share-and-the-new-iphones.

37. www.theguardian.com/technology/2011/aug/25/tim-cook-apple-staff-email.

38. http://www.businessweek.com/articles/2013-09-20/apple-ceo-tim-cooks-complete-interview-with-bloomberg-businessweek.

39. http://www.businessweek.com/articles/2012-12-06/tim-cooks-freshman-year-the-apple-ceo-speaks#p5.

40. http://www.businessweek.com/articles/2012-12-06/tim-cooks-freshman-year-the-apple-ceo-speaks#p6.

41. http://www.businessinsider.com/tim-cook-explains-his-strategy-for-running-apple-2013-6.

42. http://www.bloomberg.com/news/2013-05-01/apple-s-ive-seen-risking-ios-7-delay-on-software-overhaul-tech.html.

43. http://www.cnbc.com/id/101087596.

44. http://articles.washingtonpost.com/2012-12-27/

business/36015446_1_samsung-products-foxconn-apple-tv.

45. http://www.businessweek.com/articles/2012-12-06/tim-cooks-freshman-year-the-apple-ceo-speaks.

46. www.apple.com/letter-from-tim-cook-on-maps/.

47. http://www.businessweek.com/articles/2013-09-19/cook-ive-and-federighi-on-the-new-iphone-and-apples-once-and-future-strategy.

48. http://www.businessweek.com/articles/2013-09-19/cook-ive-and-federighi-on-the-new-iphone-and-apples-once-and-future-strategy.

49. http://www.businessweek.com/articles/2013-09-19/cook-ive-and-federighi-on-the-new-iphone-and-apples-once-and-future-strategy.

50. www.businessweek.com/printer/articles/153204-apple-chiefs-discuss-strategy-market-share-and-the-new-iphones.

51. *http://9to5mac.com/2013/10/04/tim-cook-reflects-on-second-anniversary-of-steve-jobs-passing-in-letter-to-employees/.*

## Case 2: Nokia

1. http://www.nokia.com/global/about-nokia/about-us/the-nokia-story/.

2. http://articles.economictimes.indiatimes.com/2013-11-20/news/44285333_1_risto-siilasmaa-handset-business-michael-halbherr.

3. http://www.dailymail.co.uk/home/moslive/article-2011778/Nokia-The-end-line.html#ixzz2lmVNxzZj.

4. Interestingly, the term platform has a specific meaning in the technology world and Nokia's Ovi could be interpreted as being the platform to which Elop was referring.

5. http://www.reuters.com/article/2010/09/20/us-nokia-idUSTRE68J1YW20100920.

6. http://www.cnbc.com/id/101040631.

7. http://www.cnbc.com/id/101040631.

8. http://www.cnbc.com/id/101040631.

9. http://news.sky.com/story/793770/nokia-seeks-new-ceo-to-take-on-competition.

10. http://www.channel4.com/news/how-tech-giants-like-nokia-were-dwarfed-by-apple.

11. http://www.reuters.com/article/2010/09/20/us-nokia-idUSTRE68J1YW20100920.

12. http://www.ft.com/cms/s/0/20137ef0-6480-11e0-a69a-00144feab49a.html#axzz2lmK5gU2f.

13. http://www.cnbc.com/id/101040631.

14. http://www.economist.com/node/21560867.

15. http://news.sky.com/story/793770/nokia-seeks-new-ceo-to-take-on-competition.

16. http://www.businessinsider.com/who-should-be-nokias-next-ceo-2010-7.

17. http://www.businessinsider.com/wow-nokia-steals-microsoft-office-boss-stephen-elop-as-new-ceo-2010-9.

18. http://www.nokia.com/global/about-nokia/governance/leadership/nokia-leadership-team.

19. http://www.businessinsider.com/nokia-makes-the-same-mistake-again-hires-a-manager-not-a-product-visionary-2010-9.

20. http://www.reuters.com/article/2010/09/20/us-nokia-idUSTRE68J1YW20100920.

21. http://uk.reuters.com/article/2010/09/20/us-nokia-idUSTRE68J1YW20100920.

22. http://uk.reuters.com/article/2010/09/20/us-nokia-idUSTRE68J1YW20100920.

23. http://www.reuters.com/article/2010/09/20/us-nokia-idUSTRE68J1YW20100920.

24. http://www.reuters.com/article/2010/09/20/us-nokia-idUSTRE68J1YW20100920.

25. http://www.reuters.com/article/2010/09/20/us-nokia-idUSTRE68J1YW20100920.

26. http://www.businessweek.com/magazine/content/11_24/b4232056703101.htm#p4.
27. http://www.ft.com/cms/s/0/20137ef0-6480-11e0-a69a-00144feab49a.html#ixzz2lmOoUca0.
28. http://www.ft.com/cms/s/0/20137ef0-6480-11e0-a69a-00144feab49a.html#ixzz2lmOoUca0.
29. http://www.businessweek.com/magazine/content/11_24/b4232056703101.htm#p4.
30. http://www.ft.com/cms/s/0/20137ef0-6480-11e0-a69a-00144feab49a.html#ixzz2lmQ1Kx2w.
31. http://www.technologyreview.com/news/426379/nokias-stephen-elop-speaks/.
32. http://blogs.wsj.com/tech-europe/2011/02/09/full-text-nokia-ceo-stephen-elops-burning-platform-memo/.
33. http://blogs.wsj.com/tech-europe/2011/02/09/full-text-nokia-ceo-stephen-elops-burning-platform-memo/.
34. http://www.ft.com/cms/s/0/9ec857b6-65f7-11e0-9d40-00144feab49a.html#ixzz2lrSCVaz3.
35. http://www.computerworld.com/s/article/9209039/Update_Nokia_adopts_Microsoft_s_Windows_Phone_7_OS.
36. https://www.microsoft.com/en-us/news/press/2011/feb11/02-11-partnership.aspx.
37. http://www.dailymail.co.uk/home/moslive/article-2011778/Nokia-The-end-line.html#ixzz2lmZdV2SX.
38. http://www.ft.com/cms/s/0/20137ef0-6480-11e0-a69a-00144feab49a.html#ixzz2lmQVXM00.
39. http://www.ft.com/cms/s/0/20137ef0-6480-11e0-a69a-00144feab49a.html#ixzz2lmQVXM00.
40. http://www.networkworld.com/news/2011/021111-microsoft-nokia.html.
41. http://www.networkworld.com/news/2011/021111-microsoft-nokia.html.
42. http://www.businessinsider.com/heres-why-nokia-is-still-doomed-2011-2#ixzz2lf7Du5me.
43. http://www.businessinsider.com/nokia-ceo-elop-we-need-a-challenger-mindset-2011-5#ixzz2lfBgnV57.
44. http://www.technologyreview.com/news/426379/nokias-stephen-elop-speaks/.
45. http://www.ft.com/cms/s/0/9ec857b6-65f7-11e0-9d40-00144feab49a.html#ixzz2lrQaPaVP.
46. http://www.ft.com/cms/s/0/9ec857b6-65f7-11e0-9d40-00144feab49a.html#ixzz2lrR87000.
47. http://www.ft.com/cms/s/0/9ec857b6-65f7-11e0-9d40-00144feab49a.html#ixzz2lrR87000.
48. http://www.ft.com/cms/s/0/9ec857b6-65f7-11e0-9d40-00144feab49a.html#ixzz2lrQaPaVP.
49. http://www.ft.com/cms/s/0/20137ef0-6480-11e0-a69a-00144feab49a.html#ixzz2lmQVXM00.
50. http://www.ft.com/cms/s/0/9ec857b6-65f7-11e0-9d40-00144feab49a.html#ixzz2lrR87000.
51. http://www.ft.com/cms/s/0/9ec857b6-65f7-11e0-9d40-00144feab49a.html#ixzz2lrR87000.
52. http://www.ft.com/cms/s/0/9ec857b6-65f7-11e0-9d40-00144feab49a.html#ixzz2lrR87000.
53. http://www.cnbc.com/id/100494062.
54. http://www.cnbc.com/id/100494062.
55. http://www.cnbc.com/id/100494062.
56. http://www.cnbc.com/id/100494062.
57. http://www.forbes.com/sites/ericsavitz/2012/10/18/nokia-onthe-brink/.
58. http://online.wsj.com/news/articles/SB10000872396390443571904577631961444490258.

59. http://www.forbes.com/sites/ericsavitz/2012/10/18/nokia-onthe-brink/.
60. http://www.forbes.com/sites/ericsavitz/2012/10/18/nokia-onthe-brink/.
61. http://www.businessinsider.com/this-one-stat-tells-us-how-desperate-nokia-was-for-microsoft-to-rescue-it-2013-9.
62. http://www.bbc.com/news/business-23940171.
63. http://www.bbc.com/news/business-23940171.
64. http://www.washingtonpost.com/blogs/the-switch/wp/2013/09/03/heres-why-microsoft-is-buying-nokias-phone-business/.
65. http://www.nokia.com/global/about-nokia/governance/leadership/nokia-leadership-team/.
66. http://www.ft.com/cms/s/0/20137ef0-6480-11e0-a69a-00144feab49a.html#axzz2lmK5gU2f.

## Case 3: ABB (1988–2013)

1. http://new.abb.com/.
2. Pinto, J 2005, 'Tough turnarounds (one down, one to go)', *Process & Control Engineering (PACE)*, 58, 5, p. 12.
3. http://hbr.org/1991/03/the-logic-of-global-business-an-interview-with-abbs-percy-barnevik/ar/1.
4. http://www.economist.com/node/1059157?zid=295&ah=0bca374e65f2354d553956ea65f756e0.
5. http://online.wsj.com/news/articles/SB10432774436921386664.
6. http://hbr.org/1991/03/the-logic-of-global-business-an-interview-with-abbs-percy-barnevik/ar/1.
7. http://hbr.org/1991/03/the-logic-of-global-business-an-interview-with-abbs-percy-barnevik/ar/1.
8. http://online.wsj.com/news/articles/SB10432774436921386664.
9. http://hbr.org/1991/03/the-logic-of-global-business-an-interview-with-abbs-percy-barnevik/ar/1.
10. http://online.wsj.com/news/articles/SB10432774436921386664.
11. http://online.wsj.com/news/articles/SB10432774436921386664.
12. http://www.economist.com/node/1407761.
13. http://www.economist.com/node/1059157.
14. http://hbr.org/1991/03/the-logic-of-global-business-an-interview-with-abbs-percy-barnevik/ar/1.
15. http://hbr.org/1991/03/the-logic-of-global-business-an-interview-with-abbs-percy-barnevik/ar/1.
16. http://hbr.org/1991/03/the-logic-of-global-business-an-interview-with-abbs-percy-barnevik/ar/1.
17. http://hbr.org/1991/03/the-logic-of-global-business-an-interview-with-abbs-percy-barnevik/ar/1
18. http://hbr.org/1991/03/the-logic-of-global-business-an-interview-with-abbs-percy-barnevik/ar/1.
19. http://hbr.org/1991/03/the-logic-of-global-business-an-interview-with-abbs-percy-barnevik/ar/1.
20. http://hbr.org/1991/03/the-logic-of-global-business-an-interview-with-abbs-percy-barnevik/ar/1.
21. http://online.wsj.com/news/articles/SB10432774436921386664.
22. http://hbr.org/1991/03/the-logic-of-global-business-an-interview-with-abbs-percy-barnevik/ar/1.
23. Bilefsky, D, & Raghavan, A 2003, 'How 'Europe's GE' And Its Star CEO Tumbled to Earth. (cover story)', *Wall Street Journal - Eastern Edition*, 23 January.
24. http://www.bain.com/Images/BB_Building_winning_culture.pdf.
25. Bilefsky, D, & Raghavan, A 2003, 'How 'Europe's GE' And Its Star CEO Tumbled to Earth. (cover story)', *Wall Street Journal - Eastern Edition*, 23 January.

26. Bilefsky, D, & Raghavan, A 2003, 'How 'Europe's GE' And Its Star CEO Tumbled to Earth. (cover story)', *Wall Street Journal - Eastern Edition*, 23 January.

27. http://hbr.org/1991/03/the-logic-of-global-business-an-interview-with-abbs-percy-barnevik/ar/1.

28. http://www.economist.com/node/1059157?zid=295&ah=0bca374e65f2354d553956ea65f756e0.

29. http://www.economist.com/node/1011457.

30. http://www.bain.com/Images/BB_Building_winning_culture.pdf.

31. Bilefsky, D, & Raghavan, A 2003, 'How 'Europe's GE' And Its Star CEO Tumbled to Earth. (cover story)', *Wall Street Journal - Eastern Edition*, 23 January.

32. http://online.wsj.com/news/articles/SB1043277443692138664.

33. http://www.bain.com/Images/BB_Building_winning_culture.pdf.

34. Cervenka, A 2005, 'CEO'S STRATEGY: ASBESTOS REMOVAL', *Fortune International (Europe)*, 151, 8, p. 17.

35. Cervenka, A 2005, 'CEO'S STRATEGY: ASBESTOS REMOVAL', *Fortune International (Europe)*, 151, 8, p. 17.

36. Cervenka, A 2005, 'CEO'S STRATEGY: ASBESTOS REMOVAL', *Fortune International (Europe)*, 151, 8, p. 17.

37. ABB evolves for growth' 2005, *Process Engineering*, 86, 10, p. 5.

38. http://www.bain.com/Images/BB_Building_winning_culture.pdf.

39. Cervenka, A 2005, 'CEO'S STRATEGY: ASBESTOS REMOVAL', *Fortune International (Europe)*, 151, 8, p. 17.

40. http://www.forbes.com/2007/09/05/abb-technology-switzerland-markets-equity-cx_vr_0905markets05.html.

41. http://www.independent.co.uk/news/business/news/abb-shares-down-5-on-news-that-restructuring-ceo-kindle-has-quit-782065.html.

42. ttp://www.forbes.com/2008/02/13/abb-fred-kindle-markets-equity-cx_vr_0213markets06.html.

43. http://www.abb.co.uk/cawp/seitp202/11833c3d0f8702e1c12573ee001f539c.aspx.

44. http://www.forbes.com/2008/02/13/abb-fred-kindle-markets-equity-cx_vr_0213markets06.html.

45. http://www.ft.com/cms/s/0/72a70092-51ef-11de-b986-00144feabdc0,dwp_uuid=6cae5056-0734-11de-9294-000077b07658.html#ixzz2pdLnwyuL.

46. http://www.ft.com/cms/s/0/72a70092-51ef-11de-b986-00144feabdc0,dwp_uuid=6cae5056-0734-11de-9294-000077b07658.html#ixzz2pdMcw0XJ.

47. http://www.ft.com/cms/s/0/72a70092-51ef-11de-b986-00144feabdc0,dwp_uuid=6cae5056-0734-11de-9294-000077b07658.html#ixzz2pdMcw0XJ.

48. http://www.ft.com/cms/s/0/72a70092-51ef-11de-b986-00144feabdc0,dwp_uuid=6cae5056-0734-11de-9294-000077b07658.html#ixzz2pdMcw0XJ.

49. http://www.ft.com/cms/s/0/72a70092-51ef-11de-b986-00144feabdc0.html#axzz2qeypMJQv.

50. http://www.ft.com/cms/s/0/72a70092-51ef-11de-b986-00144feabdc0,dwp_uuid=6cae5056-0734-11de-9294-000077b07658.html#ixzz2pdMcw0XJ.

51. http://www.businessweek.com/news/2011-11-07/abb-s-hogan-highlights-m-a-thirst-as-earnings-outlook-pared.html.

52. http://www.bloomberg.com/news/2013-05-10/abb-says-ceo-hogan-to-quit-for-private-reasons-.html.

53. http://www.bloomberg.com/news/2013-05-10/abb-says-ceo-hogan-to-quit-for-private-reasons-.html.

54. http://www.ft.com/cms/s/0/ff2e64a0-b939-11e2-9a9f-00144feabdc0.html#axzz2qOBgbbuG.
55. http://www.businessweek.com/news/2011-11-07/abb-s-hogan-highlights-m-a-thirst-as-earnings-outlook-pared.html.
56. http://www.marketwatch.com/story/abb-to-focus-on-fast-growing-markets-ceo-2013-07-25.
57. http://www.bloomberg.com/news/2013-05-10/abb-says-ceo-hogan-to-quit-for-private-reasons-.html.
58. http://www.bloomberg.com/news/2013-05-10/abb-says-ceo-hogan-to-quit-for-private-reasons-.html.
59. All figures sourced from ABB annual reports. However, from 2006 onwards ABB's annual reports do not specify Return on Equity and these figures from 2006-2010 are taken from the Amadeus database & http://www.stock-analysis-on.net/NYSE/Company/ABB-Ltd/Ratios/Profitability#ROE.
60. Total debt is not specified in ABB's annual reports for the period 1988-1998.

## Case 4: Nine Dragons

1. http://news.bbc.co.uk/2/hi/business/6039296.stm.
2. http://www.nytimes.com/2006/10/10/business/worldbusiness/10iht-chimoney.3103733.html.
3. http://www.newyorker.com/reporting/2009/03/30/090330fa_fact_osnos.
4. http://www.pwc.com/gx/en/ceo-survey/2012/ceo-profiles/cheung-yan.jhtml.
5. http://www.nytimes.com/2007/01/15/business/worldbusiness/15iht-trash.4211783.html?pagewanted=all&_r=0.
6. http://www.forbes.com/lists/2012/13/power-women-asia-12_Cheung-Yan_V8WZ.html
7. http://www.forbes.com/global/2006/1113/060.html.
8. http://www.nytimes.com/2007/01/16/business/16trash.html?pagewanted=all&_r=0.
9. http://www.forbes.com/global/2006/1113/060.html.
10. http://www.newyorker.com/reporting/2009/03/30/090330fa_fact_osnos.
11. http://www.forbes.com/global/2006/1113/060.html.
12. http://www.forbes.com/global/2006/1113/060.html.
13. http://www.chinadaily.com.cn/china/2006-10/20/content_713250_2.htm.
14. http://www.nytimes.com/2007/01/15/business/worldbusiness/15iht-trash.4211783.html?pagewanted=all.
15. http://www.nytimes.com/2007/01/15/business/worldbusiness/15iht-trash.4211783.html?pagewanted=all&_r=0.
16. http://www.chinadaily.com.cn/china/2006-10/20/content_713250_2.htm.
17. http://www.chinadaily.com.cn/china/2006-10/20/content_713250_2.htm.
18. http://www.economist.com/node/9298884.
19. http://edition.cnn.com/2007/WORLD/asiapcf/06/03/talkasia.cheungyan/.
20. http://edition.cnn.com/2007/WORLD/asiapcf/06/03/talkasia.cheungyan/.
21. http://www.economist.com/node/9298884.
22. http://www.chinadaily.com.cn/china/2006-10/20/content_713250_2.htm.
23. http://www.pwc.com/gx/en/ceo-survey/2012/ceo-profiles/cheung-yan.jhtml.
24. http://www.ndpaper.com/eng/media/press/p130926.pdf.

25. http://www.nytimes.com/2007/01/15/business/worldbusiness/15iht-trash.4211783.html?pagewanted=all&_r=0.

26. http://www.nytimes.com/2007/01/15/business/worldbusiness/15iht-trash.4211783.html?pagewanted=all&_r=0.

27. http://www.pwc.com/gx/en/ceo-survey/2012/ceo-profiles/cheung-yan.jhtml.

28. http://www.forbes.com/lists/2012/13/power-women-asia-12_Cheung-Yan_V8WZ.html

29. http://www.chinadaily.com.cn/china/2006-10/20/content_713250.htm.

30. http://www.nytimes.com/2007/01/15/business/worldbusiness/15iht-trash.4211783.html?pagewanted=all&_r=0.

31. http://www.chinadaily.com.cn/china/2006-10/20/content_713250.htm.

32. http://www.forbes.com/global/2006/1113/060.html.

33. http://www.economist.com/node/17248052?fsrc=nwl.

34. http://www.forbes.com/global/2006/1113/060.html.

35. http://www.forbes.com/global/2006/1113/060.html.

36. http://edition.cnn.com/2007/WORLD/asiapcf/06/03/talkasia.cheungyan/.

37. http://www.chinadaily.com.cn/china/2006-10/20/content_713250.htm.

38. http://www.ndpaper.com/eng/aboutnd/profile.htm.

39. http://www.ndpaper.com/eng/.

40. http://www.pwc.com/gx/en/ceo-survey/2012/ceo-profiles/cheung-yan.jhtml.

41. http://edition.cnn.com/2007/WORLD/asiapcf/06/03/talkasia.cheungyan/.

42. http://www.economist.com/node/9298884.

43. http://edition.cnn.com/2007/WORLD/asiapcf/06/03/talkasia.cheungyan/.

44. http://www.chinadaily.com.cn/china/2006-10/20/content_713250.htm.

45. http://www.chinadaily.com.cn/china/2006-10/20/content_713250.htm.

46. http://www.newyorker.com/reporting/2009/03/30/090330fa_fact_osnos.

47. http://www.nytimes.com/2007/01/16/business/16trash.html?pagewanted=all&_r=0.

48. http://www.economist.com/node/9298884.

49. http://www.nytimes.com/2007/01/15/business/worldbusiness/15iht-trash.4211783.html?pagewanted=all&_r=0.

50. http://www.nytimes.com/2007/01/15/business/worldbusiness/15iht-trash.4211783.html?pagewanted=all&_r=0.

51. http://www.chinadaily.com.cn/china/2006-10/20/content_713250.htm.

52. http://www.chinadaily.com.cn/china/2006-10/20/content_713250.htm.

# References

2012. The rise and rise of Amazon.com. *Management Today*, http://www.managementtoday.co.uk/news/1150329/rise-rise-Amazon.com/. [Accessed 2 April 2014].

Aguilar, F. J. 1967. *Scanning the Business Environment*, New York, Macmillan.

Andrews, K. R. 1965. *Business Policy: Text and Cases*, Homewood, Irwin.

Andrews, K. R. 1971. *The Concept of Corporate Strategy*, Homewood Irwin.

Ansoff, I. 1957. Strategies for diversification. *Harvard Business Review*, 35(2), 113–124.

Ansoff, I. 1965. *Corporate Strategy: An Analytical Approach to Business Policy for Growth and Expansion*, New York McGraw-Hill.

Ansoff, I. H. & Mcdonnell, E. J. 1988. *The New Corporate Strategy*, Wiley

Argyris, C. 1977. Organizational learning and management information systems. *Accounting, Organizations & Society*, 2, 113–123.

Argyris, C. 1991. Teaching smart people how to learn. *Harvard Business Review*, 69, 99–109.

Argyris, C. A. and Schön, D. A. 1974. *Theory in Practice: Increasing Professional Effectiveness*, Jossey Bass Publishers: San Francisco.

Baer, M., Dirks, K. T. & Nickerson, J. A. 2013. Microfoundations of strategic problem formulation *Strategic Management Journal*, 34, 197–214.

Barney, J. 1991. Firm resources and sustained competitive advantage. *Journal of Management*, 17, 99.

Barney, J. 1991. Firm resources and sustained competitive advantage. *Journal of Management*, 17, 99.

Barney, J. B., Ketchen, D. J. & Wright, M. 2011. The future of resource-based theory: revitalization or decline? *Journal of Management*, 37, 1299–1315.

Beech, N. & MacIntosh, R. 2012. *Managing Change: Enquiry and Action*, Cambridge, UK, Cambridge University Press.

Beech, N., Burns, H., Caestecker, L. d., MacIntosh, R. and MacLean, D. (2004). Paradox as an invitation to act in problematic change situations, *Human Relations*, 57, 1311–1332.

Berger, P. & Luckman, T. 1967. *The Social Construction of Reality*, New York, Doubleday.

Bloom, B. S., Engelhart, M. D., Furst, E. J., Hill, W. H. & Krathwohl, D. R. 1956. *Taxonomy of Educational Objectives: The Classification of Educational Goals*, New York, David Mackay Company.

Brown, J. S. & Duguid, P. 2001. Knowledge and organization: a social-practice perspective. *Organization Science*, 12, 198–213.

Burns, J. 1978. *Leadership*, New York, Harper & Row.

Burns, R. 1785. *To a Mouse, on Turning Her Up in Her Nest with the Plough. Poems, Chiefly in the Scottish Dialect*. Kilmarnock: John Wilson Publishers.

Carter, C. 2013. The age of strategy: strategy, organizations and society. *Business History*, 55, 1047–1057.

Carter, C., Clegg, S. R. & Kornberger, M. 2008. S-A-P zapping the field. *Strategic Organization*, 6, 107–112.

Chadwick, N. 2002. *The Celts,* London, The Folio Society.

Chandler, A. D. 1962. *Strategy and Structure: Chapters in the History of American Industrial Enterprise,* MIT Press.

Checkland, P. 1990. *Soft Systems Methodology in Action,* Chichester, John Wiley & Sons.

Cherkin, D. C., Deyo, R. A., Wheeler, K. & Ciol, M. A. 1994. Physician variation in diagnostic testing for low back pain. Who you see is what you get. *Arthritis & Rheumatism,* 37, 15–22.

Chia, R. & Holt, R. 2006. Strategy as practical coping: a heideggerian perpective. *Organization Studies (01708406),* 27, 635–655.

Cilliers, P. 1998. *Complexity and Postmodernism,* London, Routledge.

Clausewitz, C. 1830. *On War,* Princeton NJ Princeton University Press.

Cohen, P.S. 1968. *Modern Social Theory.* New York: Basic Books.

Cohen, W. 2006. *The Marketing Plan,* New York, Wiley.

Collins, J. 2001. *Good to Great: Why Some Companies Make the Leap and Others Don't,* Random House Business.

Coulter, M. 2009. *Strategic Management in Action,* Englewood Cliffs, NJ,Prentice Hall.

Coveney, P. & Highfield, R. 1996. *Frontiers of Complexity,* London, Faber and Faber.

Cunliffe, A. L. 2001. Managers as practical authors: reconstructing our understanding of management practice. *Journal of Management Studies,* 38, 351–371.

Cyert, R. M. & March, J. G. 1963. *A Behavioural Theory of the Firm,* Englewood Cliffs, NJ, Prentice Hall.

D'aveni, R. 1994. *Hypercompetition,* New York, Free Press.

Drazin, R. & Sandelands, L. 1992. Autogenesis: a perspective on the process of organizing. *Organization Science,* 3, 230–249.

Drennan, D. 1992. *Transforming Company Culture,* London, McGraw-Hill.

Dutton, J. E. 1993. Interpretations on automatic: a different view of strategic issue diagnosis. *Journal of Management Studies,* 30, 339–357.

Eisenhardt, K. E. and Sull, D. N. 2001. Strategy as simple rules. *Harvard Business Review* 79(1): 107–116.

Faulkner, D. & Bowman, C. 1995. *The Essence of Competitive Strategy,* Prentice Hall.

Fenton, C. & Langley, A. 2011. Strategy as practice and the narrative turn. *Organization Studies* 32, 1171–1196.

Floyd, S. W. & Wooldridge, B. 2000. *Building Strategy from the Middle: Reconceptualising Strategy Process,* London, SAGE.

Foot, C., Naylor, C. & Imison, C. 2010. *The Quality of GP Diagnosis and Referral* London, UK: Kings Fund

Foss, N.J. 2003. Selective Intervention and Internal Hybrids: interpreting and learning from the rise and decline of the Oticon spaghetti organization, *Organization Science,* 14(3), 331–349.

Freedman, L. 2013. *Strategy: A history,* New York, Oxford University Press.

Fu, P. P., Tsui, A. S., Liu, J. & Li, L. 2010. Pursuit of whose happiness? Executive leaders' transformational behaviors and personal values. *Administrative Science Quarterly,* 55, 222–254.

Gladwell, M. 2008. *Outliers: The Story of Success,* New York, Little, Brown and Company

Goldstein, J. 1999. Emergence as a construct: history and issues. *Emergence,* 1, 49.

Golsorkhi, D., Rouleau, L., Seidl, D. & Vaara, E. 2010. *Handbook of Strategy as Practice,* Cambridge, Cambridge University Press.

Goodwin, B. 1999. From control to participation via a science of qualities. *ReVision,* 21, 2–10.

Groopman, J. 2007. *How Doctors Think,* Boston: MA, Houghton Mifflin Company.

Hall, E. T. 1976. *Beyond Culture,* Garden City, NY, Anchor Press.

Hamel, G. & Prahalad, C. K. 1996. *Competing for the Future,* MA, Harvard Business School Press.

Hammond, J. S., Keeney, R. L. & Raiffa, H. 2006. The hidden traps in decision making. *Harvard Business Review,* 84, 118–126.

Heijden, K. V. D. 1997. *Scenarios: The Art of Strategic Conversation,* UK, John Wiley & Sons.

Helfat, C. E., Finkelstein, S., Mitchell, W., Peteraf, M., Singh, H., Teece, D. & Winter, S. G. 2007. *Dynamic Capabilities: Understanding Strategic Change in Organizations,* Malden, Blackwell.

Hensmans, M., Johnson, G. & Yip, G. 2013. *Strategic Transformation: Changing While Winning,* Palgrave MacMillan.

Honey, P. & Mumford, A. 1992. *The Manual of Learning Styles: Revised Version,* Maidenhead, Peter Honey.

Huxham, C. & Vangen, S. 2005. *Managing to Collaborate: The Theory and Practice of Collaborative Advantage,* Abingdon, UK, Routledge.

Javidan, M. 1998. Core competence: what does it mean in practice? *Long Range Planning,* 31, 60–71.

Joas, H. 1996. *The Creativity of Action,* Cambridge, UK, Polity Press.

Johnson, G. 1988. Rethinking incrementalism. *Strategic Management Journal,* 9, 75–91.

Johnson, G., Melin, L. & Whittington, R. 2003. Micro strategy and strategizing: towards an activity-based view. *Journal of Management Studies,* 40, 3–22.

Johnson, G., Melin, L. & Whittington, R. 2003. Micro strategy and strategizing: towards an activity-based view. *Journal of Management Studies,* 40, 3–22.

Johnson, G., Prashantham, S., Floyd, S. W. & Bourque, N. 2010. The ritualization of strategy workshops. *Organization Studies* 31, 1589–1618.

Johnson, G., Whittington, R., Scholes, K., Angwin, D. & Regnér, P. 2013. *Exploring Strategy: Text and Cases,* (10th edition), Pearson: Cambridge.

Kauffman, S. A. 1993. *The Origins of Order: Self organisation and Selection in Evolution,* Oxford, Oxford University Press.

Kay, J. 1993. *The Foundations of Corporate Success,* Oxford Oxford University Press.

Kay, J. 2011. *Obliquity: Why Our Goals are Best Achieved Indirectly,* London, Profile Books.

Kennedy, C. 1991. *Guide to the Management Gurus,* London, Business Books Ltd.

Kim, C. W. & Mauborgne, R. 2005. *Blue Ocean Strategy: How to Create Uncontested Market Space and Make the Competition Irrelevant,* Harvard Business School Publishing Corporation

Kim, D. H. 1993. The link between individual and organizational learning. *Sloan Management Review,* 35, 37–50.

Kolb, D. A., Rubin, I. M. & Mcintyre, J. M. 1971. *Organisational Psychology: An Experiential Approach,* Englewood Cliffs, NJ, Prentice Hall.

Kornberger, M. & Clegg, S. 2011. Strategy as performative practice: the case of Sydney 2030. *Strategic Organization,* 9, 136–162.

Kornberger, M. 2013. Clausewitz: on strategy. *Business History,* 55, 1058–1073.

Küpers, W., Mantere, S. & Statler, M. 2013. Strategy as storytelling: a phenomenological collaboration. *Journal of Management Inquiry,* 22, 83–100.

Lehane, B. 2005. *Early Celtic Christianity,* London, Continuum.

Leonard-Barton, D. 1992. Core capabilities and core rigidities: a paradox in managing new product development. *Strategic Management Journal,* 13, 111–125.

Lewis, M. W. 2000. Exploring paradox: toward a more comprehensive guide. *Academy of Management Review,* 25, 760–776.

Lorenz, E. N. 1963. Deterministic nonperiodic flow. *Journal of the Atmospheric Sciences,* 20, 130–141.

Lyles, M. A. & Mitroff, I. I. 1980. Organizational problem formulation: an empirical study. *Administrative Science Quarterly,* 25, 102–119.

Machiavelli, N. 1961. *The Prince,* Harmondsworth, Penguin.

MacIntosh, R. & Beech, N. 2011. Strategy, strategists and fantasy: a dialogic constructionist perspective. *Accounting,*

*Auditing & Accountability Journal*, 24, 15–37.

MacIntosh, R. & MacLean, D. 1999. Conditioned emergence: a dissipative structures approach to transformation. *Strategic Management Journal*, 20, 297–316.

MacIntosh, R. & MacLean, D. 2001. Conditioned emergence: researching change and changing research. *International Journal of Operations & Production Management*, 21, 1343.

MacIntosh, R., MacLean, D. & Burns, H. 2007. Health in organization: towards a process-based view. *Journal of Management Studies*, 44, 206–221.

MacIntosh, R., MacLean, D. & Seidl, D. 2010. *Unpacking the Effectivity Paradox of Strategy Workshops: Do Strategy Workshops Produce Strategic Change? Cambridge Handbook of Strategy as Practice*, Cambridge University Press.

MacIntosh, R., MacLean, D., Stacey, R. & Griffin, D. 2006. *Complexity and Organization: Readings and Conversations,*, London, Routledge.

MacLean, D. & MacIntosh, R. 2012. Strategic change as creative action. *International Journal of Strategic Change Management*, 4, 80–97.

MacLean, D. and MacIntosh, R. 2011. Organizing at the Edge of Chaos: Insights from Action Research, in S Maguire, B McKelvey and P Allen (eds), *The SAGE Handbook of Complexity and Management*, Chapter 14, 423–458, SAGE: London.

Mailer, N. 2000. *When we Were Kings*. PolyGram Filmed Entertainment Ltd.

Margetta, J. 2012. *Understanding Michael Porter: The Essential Guide to Competition and Strategy*. Boston MA, Harvard Business Press.

Mcgee, J. & Thomas, H. 1986. Strategic groups: theory, research and taxonomy. *Strategic Management Journal*, 7, 141–160.

McIntosh, A. 2004. *Soil and Soul*, London, Aurum Press.

Miller, D. 1990. *The Icarus Paradox: How Exceptional Companies Bring About Their Own Downfall*, New York, Harper Business.

Mintzberg, H. & Waters, J. A. 2006. Of strategies, deliberate and emergent. *Strategic Management Journal*, 6, 257–272.

Mintzberg, H. 1973. *The Nature of Managerial Work*, New York, Harper & Row.

Mintzberg, H. 1994. *The Rise and Fall of Strategic Planning*. Hemel Hempstead, Prentice Hall.

Mintzberg, H., Ahlstrand, B. & Lampel, J. B. 2008. *Strategy Safari: Your Complete Guide to the Wilds of Strategic Management*, London, FT Pearson.

Mitroff, I. I. & Mitroff, D. D. 2012. *Fables and the Art of Leadership: Applying the Wisdom of Mister Rogers to the Workplace*, Palgrave Macmillan.

Mitroff, I. I. & Silvers, A. 2009. *Dirty Rotten Strategies:How We Trick Ourselves and Others into Solving the Wrong Problems Precisely*, Stanford University Press.

Moltke, H Militarische Werke. vol. 2, part 2., Translated in Hughes, D. J. 1993. ed. *Moltke on the Art of War: Selected Writings*. Presido Press: New York.

Orwell, G. 1946. *James Burnham and the Managerial Revolution*, London, Socialist Book Centre.

Penrose, E. 1959. *The Theory of the Growth of the Firm*, New York, John Wiley and Sons.

Peters, T. 1994. *Liberation Management*, Ballantine Books.

Pettigrew, A. 1973. *Politics of Organisational Decision Making*, London, Tavistock.

Pettigrew, A. 1985. *The Awakening Giant: Continuity and Change in Imperial Chemical Industries*, Oxford, Blackwell.

Pettigrew, A. 1992. The character and significance of strategy process research. *Strategic Management Journal*, 13, 5–16.

Plesk, P. & Greenhalgh, T. 2001. The challenge of complexity in healthcare. *British Medical Journal*, 323, 625–628.

Porter, M. E. & Kramer, M. R. 2011. Creating shared value. *Harvard Business Review*, 89, 62–77.

Porter, M. E. 1980. *Competitive Strategy,* New York, Free Press.

Porter, M. E. 1985. *Competitive Advantage: Creating and Sustaining Superior Performance,* New York, Free Press.

Porter, M. E. 1991. Towards a dynamic theory of strategy. *Strategic Management Journal,* 12, 95–117.

Porter, M. E. 2008. The five competitive forces that shape strategy. *Harvard Business Review,* 86, 78–93.

Prahalad, C. K. & Hamel, G. 1990. The core competence of the corporation. *Harvard Business Review,* 68, 79–91.

Priem, R. L. & Butler, J. E. 2001. Is the resource-based "view" a useful perspective for strategic management research? *Academy of Management Review,* 26, 22–40.

Prigogine, I. & Stengers, I. 1984. *Order Out of Chaos: Man's New Dialogue with Nature,* New York, Bantram.

Quinn, J. B. 1980. *Strategies for Change: Logical Incrementalism,* Illinois, R D Irwin.

Rumelt, R. 2007. *Strategy's Strategist: An Interview with Richard Rumelt.* McKinsey Quarterly.

Rumelt, R. 2011. *Good Strategy, Bad Strategy: The Difference and Why it Matters,* London, Profile Books.

Schoemaker, P. J. H. 1995. Scenario planning: a tool for strategic thinking. *Sloan Management Review,* 36, 25–40.

Scruton, R. 1997. *Modern Philosophy,* London, Arrow Books.

Simon, H. 2000. Bounded rationality in social science: today and tomorrow. *Mind & Society,* 1, 25–39.

Sloan, A. 1963. *My Years with General Motors,* Garden City, NY, Doubleday.

Sull, D. N. and Eisenhardt, K. E. 2012. Simple rules for a complex world, *Harvard Business Review,* x(y), p-q.

Sussman, G. J. 1973. *A Computational Model of Skill Acquisition.* Massachusetts Institute of Technology.

Syed, M. 2010. *Bounce: How Champions are Made,* London, Fourth Estate.

Teece, D. J. 2007. Explicating dynamic capabilities: the nature and microfoundations of (sustainable) enterprise performance. *Strategic Management Journal,* 28, 1319–1350.

Tsoukas, H. & Hatch, M. J. 2001. Complex thinking, complex practice: the case for a narrative approach to organizational complexity. *Human Relations,* 54, 979–1013.

Tzu, S. 2009. *The Art of War,* Pax Librorum.

Wack, P. 1985. Scenarios: uncharted waters ahead. *Harvard Business Review,* 63, 73–89.

Weick, K. E. 1995. *Sensemaking in Organizations,* Thousand Oaks: CA, SAGE.

Wernerfelt, B. 1984. A resource-based view of the firm. *Strategic Management Journal,* 5, 171–180.

Whittington, R. 2000. *What is Strategy and Does it Matter?,* Cengage Learning

Winter, S. G. 2003. Understanding dynamic capabilities. *Strategic Management Journal,* 24, 991–995.

# Index